DRAMATISED BIBLE READINGS FOR FESTIVALS

Edited by Michael Perry

BRITISH & FOREIGN
BIBLE
SOCIETY

MarshallPickering
An Imprint of HarperCollins*Publishers*

Marshall Pickering is an imprint of
HarperCollins*Religious*
Part of HarperCollins*Publishers*
77–85 Fulham Palace Road, London W6 8JB

The Dramatised Bible was first published
in 1989 by Marshall Morgan & Scott Publications Ltd.,
part of the Marshall Pickering Holdings Group,
a subsidiary of the Zondervan Corporation,
and Bible Society

Dramatised Bible Readings for Festivals
was first published in Great Britain
in 1991 by Marshall Pickering and the Bible Society

Bible Society
Stonehill Green, Westlea, Swindon SN5 7DG, England

Copyright in *The Dramatised Bible* © 1989 by Michael Perry
Copyright in *Dramatised Bible Readings for Festivals* © 1991 by Michael Perry

The editor asserts the moral right to
be identified as the editor of this work

A catalogue record for this book
is available from the British Library

Text set by Falcon Typographic Art Ltd,
Edinburgh & London
Printed and bound in Great Britain
by HarperCollinsManufacturing Glasgow

DRAMATISED BIBLE READINGS FOR FESTIVALS

Also edited by Michael Perry:

The Dramatised Bible
The Daily Bible
Church Family Worship
Carols for Today
Psalms for Today
Prayers for the People
Bible Praying

CONTENTS

Editor's Preface

The Dramatised Bible created the opportunity for a vivid presentation of Bible narrative and teaching. Generations of ministers and teachers or youth and children's leaders had done it before – turned the Bible text into drama so that worshippers or students could become actively involved in its teaching. But publication was always piecemeal. Episodes were available previously in dramatised form (viz. the events leading up to Easter in various books, and the Christmas story in our *Church Family Worship* and *Carols for Today*) but never, so far as we are aware, all the Bible narrative.

In *Readings for Festivals* we offer an extended selection of readings not just for Easter and Christmas but for other popular church festivals and special events of the year – Pentecost, Harvest, Mothering Sunday, etc. We hope that those who enjoy this book and see its possibilities will want to 'splash out' and buy the full volume eventually. *The Dramatised Bible* is now being used in churches of all denominations, in youth and children's groups, in home groups and in schools and colleges.

There follow some suggestions on how the *Dramatised Bible*, and also *Readings for Festivals*, can best be used.

Realism
In designing *The Dramatised Bible* and *Readings for Festivals* we have tried to be realistic about the pressure upon ministers, teachers and leaders: on the whole they require a book that can be used spontaneously and without great forethought, preparation or rehearsal. We suggest that each organisation using *Readings for Festivals* eventually needs five copies because, on average, there are five characters to a script. Then, at a moment's notice, willing readers can be given a copy each, and invited to fill a character part. All characters are listed at the foot of each 'reading'.

Superfluous 'Moses said' and the like are already excised from the text (with the permission of the copyright-holders). While appropriate in prose, they are intrusive – sometimes even humorous – in drama. Usually in these dramatisations they are left in at the beginning of the piece, in order to establish the character, and then omitted thereafter. Further phrases which for similar reasons might be thought to make performance stilted are enclosed in square brackets [and]. But such phrases/sentences should not be omitted without considering the particular implications. To omit them may well enliven the drama, but it will require the cast to compensate for the omission. This can either be done visually – by turning to one of the other characters – or orally – by a change of voice. The best solution will depend on the local circumstances, the initiative of the leader, and the ability of the participants. Hence, a rule of thumb might be – *only when consultation or rehearsal is possible omit phrases in square brackets.*

Shortening an episode
Square brackets have a different function when they enclose one or more paragraphs: they indicate where the 'reading' may sensibly be shortened. Unless a sermon/ service/talk/discussion requires use of these longer sections they are best left out in the interests of lively presentation and greater impact upon an audience.

Psalms for the congregation or group

Readings for Festivals contains forty psalms prepared for congregational or worship group use. They are marked 'LIT' (Liturgical Version). These (but no other material) may be photo-copied freely in sufficient quantities for use by the whole congregation or local organisation, on condition that any item so used is marked '© The Dramatised Bible'.

Local reproduction

Applications for reproduction of material from *Readings for Festivals* in the world outside North America may be addressed to The Copyright Manager, Jubilate Hymns Ltd, 61 Chessel Avenue, Southampton, SO2 4DY (telephone 0703 630038). Jubilate's Agent in the United States of America is Hope Publishing Company, Carol Stream, Illinois 60188 (call 708–665–3200). For further information see: Legal Information. Permission to reproduce material is also available under the CMPA licence scheme.

Audibility

Use of *The Dramatised Bible* has a very positive effect on the attention that a 'reading' is given by an audience – congregation, class, youth group or study group. It also makes the content of the 'reading' more memorable – not least to those who have participated. Much depends on audibility; so care needs to be taken in larger buildings. In church, or in a school assembly hall, a dais holding a minimum of five people can be used to advantage. Where appropriate, a microphone with a wide field that will pick up all the speakers should be used; or separate microphones might be considered. This sort of preparation will enable the minister/leader to involve people whose voices are less clear and not so strong.

Casting

It is obviously important that a strong voice should be cast for any 'key' character, such as the frequent 'Narrator'. In a church service, this part can most usefully be given to the person who would have taken the scripture reading if it had not been dramatised, thus ensuring that no one feels unsurped by what should be a welcome development in worship. It is worth noting that more male than female characters speak in the Bible. However, when using *The Dramatised Bible* or *Readings for Festivals*, a good balance can still be obtained by employing female voices for narration, for the frequent anonymous '**Persons**', and in the teaching passages which divide into '**Voice 1**', '**Voice 2**', etc. Here it is good to have a contrast between the speakers.

Actions

There will be occasions – both formal and informal – when participants can add *actions* to a presentation from *Readings for Festivals*. Then, prior agreement over what is to be done is a safeguard against unintended humorous accidents! And a rehearsal will be necessary unless the actors are very confident and experienced. At the rehearsal it is sensible to have someone watching who is able to assess the drama's impact on the proposed audience, and for the cast to listen and respond to that person's objective criticism. When actions are used in the context of large gatherings, visibility and audibility (especially when the speaker turns away from the audience) are of utmost importance. In seminar and class work, or in small groups, carefully prepared actions will add a startlingly fresh dynamic.

As editor of *The Dramatised Bible* and of *Readings for Festivals* I gladly acknowledge the skills of the teams of experts who prepared the outstanding and now celebrated *Good News* and *New International* English texts of the Bible. I have appreciated the advice of the Reverend Kathleen Bowe upon the translation of my Liturgical Psalms, of the Reverend Robert Backhouse on all aspects of dramatisation and typesetting, and of Miss Janet Henderson on matters of copyright. I am grateful to the Church Pastoral Aid Society, The Bible Reading Fellowship, The Association of Christian Teachers, The Scripture Union, and to senior figures in the denominations, including the Anglican, Baptist, Roman Catholic, and United Reformed Churches, for their encouragement and commendation.

MICHAEL PERRY
Pentecost, 1991

Legal Information

The Bible text used in this publication is that of:

a) The *Good News Bible* (Today's English Version), British usage edition, published by The Bible Societies and Collins. Old Testament: copyright © American Bible Society 1976; New Testament: copyright © American Bible Society 1966, 1971, 1976. Used by permission.

b) The *New International Version* copyright © 1973, 1978, 1984 by International Bible Society. Used with permission of Hodder and Stoughton and (USA) of the Zondervan Corporation.

c) The *Jubilate Liturgical Psalms* © 1986, 1989, 1991, Michael Perry/ Jubilate Hymns; © 1986, 1989, 1991 Hope Publishing Company, Carol Stream, Illinois 60188.

The version being used in each dramatised reading is specified in the Index to Dramatised Versions in *The Dramatised Bible* (New Testament page 465).

Permission for limited reproduction for local and temporary use of material in this volume may be obtained from the Copyright Manager, Jubilate Hymns, 61 Chessel Avenue, Southampton SO2 4DY (0703 630038). *The Dramatised Bible* is also a listed book under the Christian Music Association licence scheme, Glyndley Manor, Stone Cross, Pevensey, East Sussex BN24 5BS (0323 440440). All reproduction should credit the version from which the text was drawn:

Good News Bible dramatised texts:
'From "The Dramatised Bible" © 1989 Michael Perry
Text © 1966, 1971, 1976 American Bible Society'

Liturgical Psalms
UK and world except USA:
'From "The Dramatised Bible"
Text © 1986, 1989 Michael Perry/Jubilate Hymns"
United States of America
'From "The Dramatised Bible"
Text Michael Perry © 1986, 1989, 1991 Hope Publishing Company'

New International Version dramatised texts:
'From "The Dramatised Bible" © 1989 Michael Perry
Text © 1973, 1978, 1984 by International Bible Society'

ADVENT
AND
CHRISTMAS

The goodness of God
From Psalm 36.5–9 (LIT)

Leader 1	Your love, O Lord, reaches the heavens:
All (group 1)	**your faithfulness extends to the skies.**
Leader 2	Your righteousness is towering like the mountains:
All (group 2)	**your justice is like the great deep.**
Leader 1	How precious is your love, O God:
All (group 1)	**we find shelter beneath your wings!**
Leader 2	We feast on the food you provide:
All (group 2)	**we drink from the river of your goodness:**
Leader 1	For with you is the fountain of life:
All	**in your light we see light.**
All	**Glory to the Father, and to the Son, and to the Holy Spirit: as it was in the beginning, is now, and shall be for ever. Amen.**

Cast: **Leader 1, Leader 2** (can be the same as Leader 1), **All** (group 1—two or more persons/part of congregation), **All** (group 2—two or more persons/part of congregation).

Longing for God's House
Psalm 84.1–12

Worshipper 1　How I love your Temple, Lord Almighty!
How I want to be there!

Worshipper 2　I long to be in the Lord's Temple.
With my whole being I sing for joy
to the living God.

Worshipper 1　Even the sparrows have built a nest,
and the swallows have their own home;
they keep their young near your altars,
Lord Almighty, my king and my God.

Worshipper 2　How happy are those who live in your Temple,
always singing praise to you.

Worshipper 1　How happy are those whose strength comes from you,
who are eager to make the pilgrimage to Mount Zion.
As they pass through the dry valley of Baca,
it becomes a place of springs;
the autumn rain fills it with pools.
They grow stronger as they go;
they will see the God of gods on Zion.

Worshipper 2　Hear my prayer, Lord God Almighty.
Listen, O God of Jacob!
Bless our king, O God,
the king you have chosen.

3

Worshipper 1   One day spent in your Temple
                       is better than a thousand anywhere else.

Worshipper 2   I would rather stand at the gate of the house of my God
                       than live in the homes of the wicked.

Worshipper 1   The Lord is our protector and glorious king,
                       blessing us with kindness and honour.
                       He does not refuse any good thing
                       to those who do what is right.

**Worshippers
  1 and 2**   Almighty Lord, how happy are those who trust in you!

Cast [This is] the word of the Lord. OR   **All Glory to the Father, and to the Son, and to the Holy Spirit:**
All   **Thanks be to God.**   **as it was in the beginning, is now, and shall be for ever. Amen.**

Cast: **Worshipper 1, Worshipper 2.**

God, the ruler of the world
From Psalm 98.1–9 (LIT)

Leader   Sing to the Lord a new song:
All   **for he has done marvellous things.**

Leader   His right hand and his holy arm:
All   **have brought a great triumph to us.**

All (group 1) **He lets his salvation be known:**
All (group 2) **his righteousness shines in the world.**
All (group 1) **To us he continues his love:**
All (group 2) **his glory is witnessed by all.**

Leader   Shout for joy to the Lord, all the earth:
All   **and burst into jubilant song.**

All (group 1) **Make music to God with the harp:**
All (group 2) **with songs and the sound of your praise.**
All (group 1) **With trumpets and blast of the horn:**
All (group 2) **sing praises to God as your king.**

Leader   Let rivers and streams clap their hands:
All   **the mountains together sing praise.**

Leader   The Lord comes to judge the whole earth:
All   **in righteousness God rules the world.**

All   **Glory to the Father, and to the Son, and to the Holy Spirit:**
                   as it was in the beginning, is now, and shall be for ever. Amen.

Cast: **Leader, All** (group 1—two or more persons/part of congregation), **All** (group 2—two or more persons/part of congregation).

In praise of the Lord's goodness
From Psalm 113.1–9 (LIT)

Leaders 1 and 2	Praise the Lord:
All	**praise the Lord!**

Leader 2   You servants of the Lord, praise his name:
All   **let the name of the Lord be praised,
both now and for evermore!**

Leader 1   From the rising of the sun to the place where it sets:
All   **the name of the Lord be praised!**

Leader 2   The Lord is exalted above the earth:
All   **his glory over the heavens.**

Leader 1   Who is like the Lord our God?
All   **He is throned in the heights above**

Leader 2   Yet he bends down:
All   **he stoops to look at our world.**

Leader 1   He raises the poor from the dust:
All   **and lifts the needy from their sorrow.**

Leader 2   He honours the childless wife in her home:
All   **he makes her happy, the mother of children.**

Leaders 1 and 2   Praise the Lord:
All   **Amen.**

All   **Glory to the Father, and to the Son, and to the Holy Spirit:
as it was in the beginning, is now, and shall be for ever. Amen.**

Cast: **Leader 1, Leader 2, All** (two or more persons/congregation).

In praise of the Lord
From Psalm 117.1–2 (LIT)

Leader   Praise the Lord, all you nations:
All (group 1)   **praise him, all you people!**

Leader   Great is his love towards us:
All (group 2)   **his faithfulness shall last for ever.**

Leader   Praise the Lord:
All   **Amen.**

All   **Glory to the Father, and to the Son, and to the Holy Spirit:
as it was in the beginning, is now, and shall be for ever. Amen.**

Cast: **Leader, All** (group 1—two or more persons/part of congregation), **All** (group 2—two or more persons/part of congregation).

5

The sign of Immanuel
Isaiah 7.10–14

Narrator   The Lord spoke to Ahaz, the King of Judah:

The Lord   Ask the Lord your God for a sign, whether in the deepest depths or in the highest heights.

Narrator   But Ahaz said:

Ahaz   I will not ask; I will not put the Lord to the test.

Narrator   Then Isaiah said:

Isaiah   Hear now, you house of David! Is it not enough to try the patience of men? Will you try the patience of my God also? Therefore the Lord himself will give you a sign:
The virgin will be with child
and will give birth to a son,
and will call him Immanuel.

Cast   [This is] the word of the Lord.
All   **Thanks be to God.**

Cast: **Narrator, The Lord, Ahaz, Isaiah.**

The future King
Isaiah 9.2–7

Voice 1   The people who walked in darkness have seen a great light.

Voice 2   They lived in a land of shadows, but now light is shining on them.

Voice 3   You have given them great joy, Lord: you have made them happy.

Voice 1   They rejoice in what you have done, as people rejoice when they harvest their corn—

Voice 2   Or when they divide captured wealth.

Voice 3   For you have broken the yoke that burdened them—

Voice 1   And the rod that beat their shoulders.

Voice 2   You have defeated the nation that oppressed and exploited your people, just as you defeated the army of Midian long ago.

Voice 3   The boots of the invading army and all their bloodstained clothing will be destroyed by fire. (PAUSE)

Voice 1   A child is born to us!

Voice 2   A son is given to us!

Voice 3   And he will be our ruler.

Voice 1   He will be called—

Voice 2	'Wonderful Counsellor'
Voice 3	'Mighty God'
Voice 2	'Eternal Father'
Voice 3	Prince of Peace'.
Voice 1	His royal power will continue to grow.
Voice 2	His kingdom will always be at peace.
Voice 3	He will rule as King David's successor, basing his power on right and justice, from now until the end of time.
Voices 1–3 (with flourish)	The Lord Almighty is determined to do all this!
Cast	[This is] the word of the Lord.
All	**Thanks be to God.**

Cast: **Voice 1, Voice 2, Voice 3.**

The peaceful kingdom
Isaiah 11.1–9

Isaiah	The royal line of David is like a tree that has been cut down; but just as new branches sprout from a stump, so a new king will arise from among David's descendants.
Singer 1	The spirit of the Lord will give him wisdom, and the knowledge and skill to rule his people.
Singer 2	He will know the Lord's will and have reverence for him, and find pleasure in obeying him.
Singer 1	He will not judge by appearance or hearsay.
Singer 2	He will judge the poor fairly and defend the rights of the helpless.
Singer 1	At his command the people will be punished, and evil persons will die.
Singers 1 and **2**	He will rule his people with justice and integrity. (PAUSE)
Singer 1	Wolves and sheep will live together in peace,
Singer 2	And leopards will lie down with young goats.
Singer 1	Calves and lion cubs will feed together, and little children will take care of them.
Singer 2	Cows and bears will eat together, and their calves and cubs will lie down in peace.
Singer 1	Lions will eat straw as cattle do.
Singer 2	Even a baby will not be harmed if it plays near a poisonous snake.
Singer 1	On Zion, God's sacred hill, there will be nothing harmful or evil.

Singers 1 and **2**	The land will be as full of knowledge of the Lord as the seas are full of water.
Cast	[This is] the word of the Lord.
All	**Thanks be to God.**

Cast: **Isaiah, Singer 1, Singer 2.**

The Lord's mercy on Israel
Jeremiah 31.15–22

Jeremiah	The Lord says:
The Lord	A sound is heard in Ramah, the sound of bitter weeping. Rachel is crying for her children; they are gone, and she refuses to be comforted. Stop your crying and wipe away your tears. All that you have done for your children will not go unrewarded; they will return from the enemy's land. There is hope for your future; your children will come back home. I, the Lord, have spoken.
	I hear the people of Israel say in grief:
Person 1	Lord, we were like an untamed animal, but you taught us to obey.
Person 2	Bring us back; we are ready to return to you, the Lord our God.
Person 1	We turned away from you but soon we wanted to return.
Person 2	After you had punished us, we hung our heads in grief.
Person 3	We were ashamed and disgraced, because we sinned when we were young.
The Lord	Israel, you are my dearest son, the child I love best. Whenever I mention your name, I think of you with love. My heart goes out to you; I will be merciful.
(urgently)	Set up signs and mark the road; find again the way by which you left. Come back, people of Israel, come home to the towns you left. How long will you hesitate, faithless people? I have created something new and different, as different as a woman protecting a man.
Cast	[This is] the word of the Lord.
All	**Thanks be to God.**

Cast: **Jeremiah, The Lord, Person 1, Person 2, Person 3** (Persons 1–3 can be the same).

God promises a ruler from Bethlehem
Micah 5.2–5

Micah (with flourish)	The Lord says:
The Lord	Bethlehem Ephrathah, you are one of the smallest towns in Judah,

	but out of you I will bring a ruler for Israel, whose family line goes back to ancient times.
Micah	So the Lord will abandon his people to their enemies until the woman who is to give birth has her son. Then his fellow-countrymen who are in exile will be reunited with their own people. When he comes, he will rule his people with the strength that comes from the Lord and with the majesty of the Lord God himself. His people will live in safety because people all over the earth will acknowledge his greatness (PAUSE) and he will bring peace.
Cast	[This is] the word of the Lord.
All	**Thanks be to God.**

Cast: **Micah, The Lord.**

The birth of John the Baptist
Luke 1.57–80

Narrator	The time came for Elizabeth to have her baby, and she gave birth to a son. Her neighbours and relatives heard how wonderfully good the Lord had been to her, and they all rejoiced with her. (PAUSE)
	When the baby was a week old, they came to circumcise him, and they were going to name him Zechariah, after his father. But his mother said:
Elizabeth	No! His name is to be John.
[Narrator	They said to her:]
Relative	But you have no relatives with that name!
Narrator	Then they made signs to his father, asking him what name he would like the boy to have. Zechariah asked for a writing tablet and wrote:
Zechariah*	His name is John.
Narrator	How surprised they all were! At that moment Zechariah was able to speak again, and he started praising God. The neighbours were all filled with fear, and the news about these things spread through all the hill-country of Judaea. Everyone who heard of it thought about it and asked:
Relative	What is this child going to be?
Narrator	For it was plain that the Lord's power was upon him.
	John's father Zechariah was filled with the Holy Spirit, and he spoke God's message:
Zechariah	Let us praise the Lord, the God of Israel! He has come to the help of his people and has set them free. He has provided for us a mighty Saviour, a descendant of his servant David.

9

He promised through his holy prophets long ago
that he would save us from our enemies,
from the power of all those who hate us.
He said he would show mercy to our ancestors
and remember his sacred covenant.
With a solemn oath to our ancestor Abraham
he promised to rescue us from our enemies
and allow us to serve him without fear,
so that we might be holy and righteous before him
all the days of our life.

You, my child, will be called a prophet of the Most High God.
You will go ahead of the Lord
to prepare his road for him,
to tell his people that they will be saved
by having their sins forgiven.
Our God is merciful and tender.
He will cause the bright dawn of salvation to rise on us
and to shine from heaven on all those who
live in the dark shadow of death,
to guide our steps into the path of peace.

Narrator   The child grew and developed in body and spirit. He lived in the desert until the day when he appeared publicly to the people of Israel.

Cast   [This is] the word of the Lord. OR   This is the Gospel of Christ / *This is the Gospel of the Lord.*
All   **Thanks be to God.**   **Praise to Christ our Lord** / *Praise to you, Lord Jesus Christ.*

Cast: **Narrator, Elizabeth, Relative, Zechariah** (*At this point it is better if Zechariah does not speak, but holds up a previously written placard with the words 'His name is John').

The Word became flesh
John 1.1–14 [15–18]

Voice 1   In the beginning was the Word, and the Word was with God, and the Word was God. He was with God in the beginning.

Voice 2   Through him all things were made; without him nothing was made that has been made.

Voice 1   In him was life, and that life was the light of men. The light shines in the darkness, but the darkness has not understood it.

Voice 3   There came a man who was sent from God; his name was John. He came as a witness to testify concerning that light, so that through him all men might believe.

Voice 4   He himself was not the light; he came only as a witness to the light.

Voice 2   The true light that gives light to every man was coming into the world.

Voice 1	He was in the world, and though the world was made through him, the world did not recognise him.
Voice 2	He came to that which was his own, but his own did not receive him. Yet to all who received him, to those who believed in his name, he gave the right to become children of God—
Voice 4	Children born not of natural descent, nor of human decision or a husband's will, but born of God.
Voice 1	The Word became flesh and made his dwelling among us. We have seen his glory, the glory of the One and Only, who came from the Father, full of grace and truth.
[Voice 3	John testifies concerning him. He cries out, saying:
John the Baptist	This was he of whom I said, 'He who comes after me has surpassed me because he was before me.'
Voice 2	From the fulness of his grace we have all received one blessing after another.
Voice 3	For the law was given through Moses; grace and truth came through Jesus Christ.
Voice 1	No-one has ever seen God, but God the One and Only, who is at the Father's side, has made him known.]

Cast   [This is] the word of the Lord.   OR   This is the Gospel of Christ / *This is the Gospel of the Lord.*
All   **Thanks to be God.**   **Praise to Christ our Lord** / *Praise to you, Lord Jesus Christ.*

Cast: **Voice 1, Voice 2, Voice 3, Voice 4, [John the Baptist].** (See also Appendix: Christmas Readings, page 411.)

Duties towards one another
Romans 13.8–14

Paul	Be under obligation to no one—the only obligation you have is to love one another. Whoever does this has obeyed the Law. The commandments:
Reader	Do not commit adultery; do not commit murder; do not steal; do not desire what belongs to someone else:
Paul	All these, and any others besides, are summed up in the one command:
Reader	Love your neighbour as you love yourself.
Paul	If you love someone, you will never do him wrong; to love, then, is to obey the whole Law. You must do this, because you know that the time has come for you to wake up from your sleep. For the moment when we will be saved is closer now than it was when we first believed. The night is nearly over, day is almost here. Let us stop doing the things that belong to the dark, and let us take up weapons for fighting

in the light. Let us conduct ourselves properly, as people who live in the light of day—no orgies or drunkenness, no immorality or indecency, no fighting or jealousy. But take up the weapons of the Lord Jesus Christ, and stop paying attention to your sinful nature and satisfying its desires.

Cast	[This is] the word of the Lord.
All	**Thanks be to God.**

Cast: **Paul, Reader.**

The supremacy of Christ
Colossians 1.15–20

Voice 1 Christ is the image of the invisible God, the firstborn over all creation.

Voice 2 By him all things were created—

Voice 3 Things in heaven and on earth, visible and invisible, whether thrones or powers or rulers or authorities.

Voice 1 All things were created by him and for him.

Voice 2 He is before all things, and in him all things hold together.

Voice 3 And he is the head of the body, the church.

Voice 1 He is the beginning and the firstborn from among the dead, so that in everything he might have the supremacy.

Voice 2 For God was pleased to have all his fulness dwell in him, and through him to reconcile to himself all things.

Voice 3 Whether things on earth or things in heaven—

Voice 1 By making peace through his blood, shed on the cross.

Cast	[This is] the word of the Lord.
All	**Thanks be to God.**

Cast: **Voice 1, Voice 2, Voice 3.**

The grace of Christ
From Titus 2.11–3.7

Voice 1 The grace of God that brings salvation has appeared to all. It teaches us to say:

Voices 1–3 No!

Voice 1 . . . to ungodliness and worldly passions, and to live self-controlled, upright and godly lives in this present age, while we wait for the blessed hope—

Voice 2 The glorious appearing of our great God and Saviour, Jesus Christ, who gave himself for us to redeem us from all wickedness—

Voice 3	And to purify for himself a people that are his very own, eager to do what is good.
Voice 1	At one time we too were foolish . . .
Voice 2	Disobedient . . .
Voice 3	Deceived and enslaved by all kinds of passions and pleasures.
Voice 1	We lived in malice and envy, being hated and hating one another.
Voice 2	But when the kindness and love of God our Saviour appeared, he saved us—
Voice 3	Not because of righteous things we had done, but because of his mercy.
Voice 2	He saved us through the washing of rebirth and renewal by the Holy Spirit, whom he poured out on us generously through Jesus Christ our Saviour.
Voice 1	So that, having been justified by his grace, we might become heirs having the hope of eternal life.
Cast	[This is] the word of the Lord.
All	**Thanks be to God.**

Cast: **Voice 1, Voice 2, Voice 3.**

God's word through his Son
Hebrews 1.1–14

Narrator	In the past, God spoke to our ancestors many times and in many ways through the prophets, but in these last days he has spoken to us through his Son. He is the one through whom God created the universe, the one whom God has chosen to possess all things at the end. He reflects the brightness of God's glory and is the exact likeness of God's own being, sustaining the universe with his powerful word. After achieving forgiveness for the sins of mankind, he sat down in heaven at the right-hand side of God, the Supreme Power.

The Son was made greater than the angels, just as the name that God gave him is greater than theirs. For God never said to any of his *angels*: |
God	You are my Son; today I have become your Father.
Narrator	Nor did God say about any *angel*:
God	I will be his Father, and he will be my Son.
Narrator	But when God was about to send his first-born *Son* into the world, he said:
God	All God's angels must worship him.

Narrator	But about the *angels* God said:
God	God makes his angels winds, and his servants flames of fire.
Narrator	About the *Son*, however, God said:
God	Your kingdom, O God, will last for ever and ever! You rule over your people with justice. You love what is right and hate what is wrong. That is why God, your God, has chosen you and has given you the joy of an honour far greater than he gave to your companions.
Narrator	He also said:
God	You, Lord, in the beginning created the earth, and with your own hands you made the heavens. They will disappear, but you will remain; they will all wear out like clothes. You will fold them up like a coat, and they will be changed like clothes. But you are always the same. and your life never ends.
Narrator	God never said to any of his *angels*:
God	Sit here on my right until I put your enemies as a footstool under your feet.
Narrator	What *are* the angels, then? They are spirits who serve God, and are sent by him to help those who are to receive salvation.
Cast	[This is] the word of the Lord.
All	**Thanks be to God.**

Cast: **Narrator, God.**

The one who leads us to salvation
Hebrews 2.5–18

Narrator	It is not to angels that God has subjected the world to come, about which we are speaking. But there is a place where someone has testified:
Psalmist	What is man that you are mindful of him, the son of man that you care for him? You made him a little lower than the angels: you crowned him with glory and honour and put everything under his feet.
Narrator	In putting everything under him, God left nothing that is not subject to him. Yet at present we do not see everything subject to him. But we see Jesus, who was made a little lower than the angels, now crowned with glory and honour because he suffered

death, so that by the grace of God he might taste death for everyone. In bringing many sons to glory, it was fitting that God, for whom and through whom everything exists, should make the author of their salvation perfect through suffering. Both the one who makes men holy and those who are made holy are of the same family. So Jesus is not ashamed to call them brothers. [He says:]

Psalmist   I will declare your name to my brothers;
in the presence of the congregation I will sing your praises.

Narrator   And again:

Isaiah   I will put my trust in him.

Narrator   And again he says:

Isaiah   Here am I, and the children God has given me.

Narrator   Since the children have flesh and blood, he too shared in their humanity so that by his death he might destroy him who holds the power of death—that is, the Devil—and free those who all their lives were held in slavery by their fear of death. For surely it is not angels he helps, but Abraham's descendants. For this reason he had to be made like his brothers in every way, in order that he might become a merciful and faithful high priest in service to God, and that he might make atonement for the sins of the people. Because he himself suffered when he was tempted, he is able to help those who are being tempted.

Cast   [This is] the word of the Lord.
All   **Thanks be to God.**

Cast: **Narrator, Psalmist, Isaiah.**

A living hope
1 Peter 1.3–12

Voices 1 and **2**   Let us give thanks to the God and Father of our Lord Jesus Christ!

Voice 1   Because of his great mercy he gave us new life by raising Jesus Christ from death.

Voice 2   This fills us with a living hope, and so we look forward to possessing the rich blessings that God keeps for his people.

Voice 1   He keeps them for you in heaven, where they cannot decay or spoil or fade away.

Voice 2   They are for you, who through faith are kept safe by God's power for the salvation which is ready to be revealed at the end of time.

Voice 3   Be glad about this, even though it may now be necessary for you to be sad for a while because of the many kinds of trials you suffer.

Voice 1   Their purpose is to prove that your faith is genuine. Even gold, which can be destroyed, is tested by fire; and so your faith, which is much more precious than gold, must also be tested, so that it may endure.

Voice 3   Then you will receive praise and glory and honour on the Day when Jesus Christ is revealed.

Voice 1   You love him, although you have not seen him.

Voice 2   And you believe in him, although you do not now see him.

Voice 1   So you rejoice with a great and glorious joy which words cannot express, because you are receiving the salvation of your souls, which is the purpose of your faith in him.

Voice 2   It was concerning this salvation that the prophets made careful search and investigation, and they prophesied about this gift which God would give you.

Voice 3   They tried to find out when the time would be and how it would come. This was the time to which Christ's Spirit in them was pointing, in predicting the sufferings that Christ would have to endure and the glory that would follow.

Voice 2   God revealed to these prophets that their work was not for their own benefit, but for yours; as they spoke about those things which you have now heard from the messengers who announced the Good News by the power of the Holy Spirit sent from heaven.

Voice 1   These are things which even the angels would like to understand.

Cast   [This is] the word of the Lord.
All   **Thanks be to God.**

Cast: **Voice 1, Voice 2, Voice 3** (can be the same as Voice 1).

The Word of life
1 John 1.1–3

Voice 1   The Word of life has existed from the very beginning.

Voice 2   We have heard it, and we have seen it with our eyes.

Voice 1   Yes, we have seen it, and our hands have touched it.

Voice 2   When this life became visible, we saw it; so we speak of it and tell you about the eternal life which was with the Father and was made known to us.

Voice 1   What we have seen and heard we announce to you also, so that you will join with us in the fellowship that we have with the Father and with his Son Jesus Christ.

Cast   [This is] the word of the Lord.
All   **Thanks be to God.**

Cast: **Voice 1, Voice 2.**

CHRISTMAS READINGS

CAST OF READERS
for the dramatised Christmas Readings

Sometimes the dramatised Christmas Readings will be used in public at a crowded service where there is little space for a large cast, or where amplification of the cast is needed but only a single directional microphone is available. In such circumstances it will be as well to keep those participating to a minimum. The cast list below (not in order of appearance) is arranged in groupings to allow each reader to take more than one part in the series, but not in the same reading. This is the minimum configuration which also takes into account a male-female balance of voices. Where such a balance is not possible, please ignore the instructions in brackets.

First Reader (strong female voice)
    Narrator—except in 'Mary visits Elizabeth'
    Narrator 1—in 'The shepherds find the baby'
    Elizabeth

Second Reader (older male voice)
    Commentator
    Shepherd 1
    Teacher 1
    Simeon
    Hebrews

Third Reader (male voice)
    Isaiah
    Prophet
    Chorus
    Magi 1
    Colossians

Fourth Reader (male voice)
    Jeremiah
    Chorus
    Magi 2
    John
    Narrator—in 'Mary visits Elizabeth'
    Narrator 2—in 'The shepherds find the baby'

Fifth Reader (authoritative male voice)
    Micah
    Angel
    Shepherd 2
    Herod
    Philippians

Sixth Reader (female voice)
    Numbers
    Mary
    Chorus
    Teacher 2
    2 Corinthians

Suggested carols to match some of the Christmas readings will be found at the back of our *Carols for Today* (music edition, from Hodder & Stoughton / Hope Publishing Company). Carols to match the Christmas themes will be found indexed at the back of our *Carol Praise* (music edition, from Marshall Pickering Hope Publishing Company). Further dramatised readings are available in our publications *The Dramatised Bible* (Marshall Pickering / Hope Publishing Company).

The prophets promise the saviour
Numbers 24.16–17; Isaiah 7.14; Jeremiah 23. 5–6; Micah 5.2, 4; Isaiah 9.6

Numbers   The oracle of one who hears the words of God, who has knowledge from the Most High: I see him, but not now; I behold him, but not near. A star will come out of Jacob; a sceptre will rise out of Israel.

Isaiah   The Lord himself will give you a sign: The virgin will be with child and will give birth to a son, and will call him Immanuel.

Jeremiah   'The days are coming,' declares the Lord, 'when I will raise up to David a righteous Branch, a King who will reign wisely and do what is just and right in the land. This is the name by which he will be called: The Lord Our Righteousness.'

Micah   Bethlehem Ephrathah, though you are small among the clans of Judah, out of you will come for me one who will be ruler over Israel, whose origins are from of old, from ancient times. He will stand and shepherd his flock in the strength of the Lord, in the majesty of the name of the Lord his God.

Isaiah   To us a child is born, to us a son is given, and the government will be on his shoulders. And he will be called Wonderful Counsellor, Mighty God, Everlasting Father, Prince of Peace.

Cast   [This is] the word of the lord.
All   **Thanks be to God**.

Mary hears the news
From Luke 1. 26–38

Narrator   In the sixth month, God sent the angel Gabriel to Nazareth, a town in Galilee, to a virgin pledged to be married to a man named Joseph, a descendant of David. The virgin's name was Mary. The angel went to her [and said]:

Angel   Greetings, you who are highly favoured! The Lord is with you.

Narrator   Mary was greatly troubled at his words and wondered what kind of greeting this might be. But the angel said to her:

Angel   Do not be afraid, Mary, you have found favour with God. You will be with child and give birth to a son, and you are to give him the name Jesus. He will be great and will be called the Son of the Most High. The Lord God will give him the throne of his father David, and he will reign over the house of Jacob for ever; his kingdom will never end.

[Narrator   Mary asked the angel:]

Mary   How will this be, since I am a virgin?

Angel   The Holy Spirit will come upon you, and the power of the Most High will overshadow you. So the holy one to be born will be called the Son of God.

[Narrator   Mary answered:]

Mary   I am the Lord's servant. May it be to me as you have said.

Narrator   Then the angel left her.

Cast   [This is] the word of the Lord.
All   **Thanks be to God.**

Mary visits Elizabeth*
Luke 1.39–55[56]

Narrator   Mary got ready and hurried off to a town in the hill-country of Judaea. She went into Zechariah's house and greeted Elizabeth. When Elizabeth heard Mary's greeting, the baby moved within her. Elizabeth was filled with the Holy Spirit [and said in a loud voice]:

Elizabeth
(delighted)   You are the most blessed of all women, and blessed is the child you will bear! Why should this great thing happen to me, that my Lord's mother comes to visit me? For as soon as I heard your greeting, the baby within me jumped with gladness. How happy you are to believe that the Lord's message to you will come true!

Narrator   Mary said:

Mary   My heart praises the Lord;
my soul is glad because of God my saviour,
for he has remembered me, his lowly servant!
From now on all people will call me happy,
because of the great things the Mighty God has done for me.
His name is holy;
from one generation to another
he shows mercy to those who honour him.
He has stretched out his mighty arm
and scattered the proud with all their plans.
He has brought down mighty kings from their thrones,
and lifed up the lowly.
He has filled the hungry with good things,
and sent the rich away with empty hands,
He has kept the promise he made to our ancestors,
and has come to the help of his servant Israel.
He has remembered to show mercy to Abraham
and to all his descendants for ever!

[Narrator   Mary stayed about three months with Elizabeth and then went back home.]

Cast   [This is] the word of the Lord.
All   **Thanks be to God.**

Cast: **Narrator, Elizabeth, Mary.** (*This reading can be omitted from the series.)

Joseph learns the truth
Matthew 1.18–25

Narrator	This is how the birth of Jesus Christ came about. His mother Mary was pledged to be married to Joseph, but before they came together, she was found to be with child through the Holy Spirit. Because Joseph her husband was a righteous man and did not want to expose her to public disgrace, he had in mind to divorce her quietly. But after he had considered this, an angel of the Lord appeared to him in a dream [and said]:
Angel	Joseph son of David, do not be afraid to take Mary home as your wife, because what is conceived in her is from the Holy Spirit. She will give birth to a son, and you are to give him the name Jesus, because he will save his people from their sins.
Narrator	All this took place to fulfil what the Lord had said through the prophet:
Prophet	The virgin will be with child and will give birth to a son, and they will call him Immanuel –
Narrator	Which means 'God with us'. (PAUSE) When Joseph woke up, he did what the angel of the Lord had commanded him and took Mary home as his wife. But he had no union with her until she gave birth to a son. And he gave him the name Jesus.
Cast	[This is] the word of the Lord.
All	**Thanks be to God.**

Cast: **Narrator, Angel, Prophet.**

Jesus is born*
Luke 2.1–7

Narrator	The Emperor Augustus ordered a census to be taken throughout the Roman Empire.
Commentator	When this first census took place, Quirinius was the governor of Syria. Everyone, then, went to register himself, each to his own town.
Narrator	Joseph went from the town of Nazareth in Galilee to the town of Bethlehem in Judaea, the birthplace of King David.
Commentator	Joseph went there because he was a descendant of David.
Narrator	He went to register with Mary, who was promised in marriage to him. She was pregnant, and while they were in Bethlehem, the time came for her to have her baby. She gave birth to her first son wrapped him in strips of cloth and laid him in a manger.
Commentator	There was no room for them to stay in the inn.
Cast	[This is] the word of the Lord.
All	**Thanks be to God.**

This reading can be omitted from the series

The angels announce the birth
Luke 2.8–14

Narrator   There were shepherds living out in the fields near Bethlehem, keeping watch over their flocks at night. An angel of the Lord appeared to them, and the glory of the Lord shone around them, and they were terrified. But the angel said to them:

Angel   Do not be afraid. I bring you good news of great joy that will be for all the people. Today in the town of David a Saviour has been born to you; he is Christ the Lord. This will be a sign to you: You will find a baby wrapped in strips of cloth and lying in a manger.

Narrator   Suddenly a great company of the heavenly host appeared with the angel, praising God:

Chorus   Glory to God in the highest and on earth peace to all on whom
(cheerfully)   his favour rests.

Cast   [This is] the word of the Lord.
All   **Thanks be to God**.

The shepherds find the baby
Luke 2.15–20

Narrator 1   When the angels had left them and gone into heaven, the shepherds said to one another:

Shepherds 1 and 2 Let's go to Bethlehem!

Shepherd 1   And see this thing that has happened—

Shepherd 2   Which the Lord has told us about.

Narrator 1   So they hurried off and found Mary and Joseph, and the baby, who was lying in the manger.

Narrator 2   When they had seen him, they spread the word concerning what had been told them about this child, and all who heard it were amazed at what the shepherds said to them.

Narrator 1   But Mary treasured up all these things and pondered them in her heart.

Narrator 2   The shepherds returned, glorifying and praising God for all the things they had heard and seen, which were just as they had been told.

Cast   [This is] the word of the Lord.
All   **Thanks be to God**.

The wise men follow the star
From Matthew 2:1–11

Narrator   After Jesus was born in Bethlehem in Judaea, during the time of King Herod, Magi from the east came to Jerusalem and asked:

21

Magi	Where is the one who has been born king of the Jews? We saw his star in the east and have come to worship him.
Narrator	When King Herod heard this, he was disturbed, and all Jerusalem with him. When he had called together all the people's chief priests and teachers of the law, he asked them:
Herod	Where will the Christ be born?
[Narrator	They replied:]
Teachers 1 and **2**	In Bethlehem in Judaea.
Teacher 2	For this is what the prophet has written:
Prophet	Bethlehem, in the land of Judah, out of you will come a ruler who will be the shepherd of my people Israel.
Narrator	Then Herod called the Magi secretly and found out from them the exact time the star had appeared. He sent them to Bethlehem [and said]:
Herod	Go and make a careful search for the child. As soon as you find him, report to me, so that I too may go and worship him.
Narrator	After they had heard the king, they went on their way, and the star they had seen in the east went ahead of them until it stopped over the place where the child was. When they saw the star, they were overjoyed. On coming to the house, they saw the child with his mother Mary, and they bowed down and worshipped him. Then they opened their treasures and presented him with gifts of gold and of incense and of myrrh.
Cast	[This is] the word of the Lord.
All	**Thanks be to God**.

The child escapes the sword
From Matthew 2.13–18

Narrator	When the Magi had gone, an angel of the Lord appeared to Joseph in a dream:
Angel	Get up. Take the child and his mother and escape to Egypt. Stay there until I tell you, for Herod is going to search for the child to kill him.
Narrator	So Joseph got up, took the child and his mother during the night and left for Egypt, where he stayed until the death of Herod. And so was fulfilled what the Lord had said through the prophet:
Prophet	Out of Egypt I called my son.
Narrator	When Herod realised that he had been outwitted by the Magi, he was furious, and he gave orders to kill all the boys in Bethlehem and its vicinity who were two years old and under, in accordance with the time he had learned from the Magi. Then what was said through the prophet Jeremiah was fulfilled:

22

Jeremiah	A voice is heard in Ramah, weeping and great mourning, Rachel weeping for her children and refusing to be comforted, because they are no more.
Cast	[This is] the word of the Lord.
All	**Thanks be to God.**

The family return from Egypt*
Matthew 2.19–23

Narrator	After Herod died, an angel of the Lord appeared in a dream to Joseph in Egypt:
Angel	Get up, take the child and his mother, and go back to the land of Israel, because those who tried to kill the child are dead.
Narrator	So Joseph got up, took the child and his mother, and went back to Israel. But when Joseph heard that Archelaus had succeeded his father Herod as king of Judaea, he was afraid to go there. He was given more instructions in a dream, so he went to the province of Galilee and made his home in a town named Nazareth. And so what the prophets had said came true:
Prophet	He will be called a Nazarene.
Cast	[This is] the word of the Lord.
All	**Thanks be to God.**

This reading can be omitted from the series

Simeon recognises the Messiah
From Luke 2.25–32

Narrator	There was a man in Jerusalem called Simeon, who was righteous and devout. He was waiting for the consolation of Israel, and the Holy Spirit was upon him. It had been revealed to him by the Holy Spirit that he would not die before he had seen the Lord's Christ. Moved by the Spirit, he went into the temple courts. When the parents brought in the child Jesus to do for him what the custom of the Law required. Simeon took him in his arms and praised God [saying]:
Simeon	Sovereign Lord, as you have promised, you now dismiss your servant in peace. For my eyes have seen your salvation, which you have prepared in the sight of all people, a light for revelation to the Gentiles and for the glory to your people Israel.
Narrator	The child's father and mother marvelled at what was said about him. Then Simeon blessed them and said to Mary, his mother:

Simeon   This child is destined to cause the falling and rising of many in Israel, and to be a sign that will be spoken against, so that the thoughts of many hearts will be revealed. And a sword will pierce your own soul too.

Cast   [This is] the word of the Lord.
All   **Thanks be to God**.

The apostles explain the meaning
John 1.1, 3, 14; Colossians 1.15, 17; Hebrews 1.1–3; 2 Corinthians 4.6; 8.9;
Philippians 2.6–7; John 1.11–12

John   In the beginning was the Word, and the Word was with God, and the Word was God. Through him all things were made. The Word became flesh and lived for a while among us. We have see his glory, the glory of the one and only Son, who came from the Father, full of grace and truth.

Colossians   Christ is the image of the invisible God, the first-born over all creation. He is before all things, and in him all things hold together.

Hebrews   In the past God spoke to our forefathers through the prophets but in these last days he has spoken to us by his Son, who is the radiance of his glory and the exact representation of his being.

2 Corinthians   God, who said, 'Let light shine out of darkness,' made his light shine in our hearts to give us the light of the knowledge of the glory of God in the face of Christ. You know the grace of our Lord Jesus Christ, that though he was rich, yet for your sakes he became poor, so that you through his poverty might become rich.

Philippians   Christ Jesus, being in very nature God, did not consider equality with God something to be grasped, but made himself nothing, taking the very nature of a servant, being made in human likeness.

John   He came to that which was his own, but his own did not receive him. Yet to all who received him, to those who believed in his name, he gave the right to become children of God.

Cast   [This is] the word of the Lord.
All   **Thanks be to God**.

24

MOTHERING SUNDAY/ THE FAMILY

The three visitors
Genesis 18.1–15

Narrator	The Lord appeared to Abraham near the great trees of Mamre while he was sitting at the entrance to his tent in the heat of the day. Abraham looked up and saw three men standing nearby. When he saw them, he hurried from the entrance of his tent to meet them and bowed low to the ground:
Abraham	If I have found favour in your eyes, my lord, do not pass your servant by. Let a little water be brought, and then you may all wash your feet and rest under this tree. Let me get you something to eat, so you can be refreshed and then go on your way—now that you have come to your servant.
[Narrator	They answered:]
Man 1	Very well.
Man 2	Do as you say.
Narrator	So Abraham hurried into the tent to Sarah. [He said:]
Abraham	Quick, get three measures of fine flour and knead it and bake some bread.
Narrator	Then he ran to the herd and selected a choice, tender calf and gave it to a servant, who hurried to prepare it. He then brought some curds and milk and the calf that had been prepared, and set these before them. While they ate, he stood near them under a tree. [They asked him:]
Man 2	Where is your wife Sarah?
Abraham	There, in the tent.
[Narrator	Then the Lord said:]
The Lord	I will surely return to you about this time next year, and Sarah your wife will have a son.
Narrator	Now Sarah was listening at the entrance to the tent, which was behind him. Abraham and Sarah were already old and well advanced in years, and Sarah was past the age of childbearing. So Sarah laughed to herself:
Sarah (laughing)	After I am worn out and my master is old, will I now have this pleasure?
[Narrator	Then the Lord said to Abraham:]
The Lord	Why did Sarah laugh and say, 'Will I really have a child, now that I am old?' Is anything too hard for the Lord? I will return to you at the appointed time next year and Sarah will have a son.
[Narrator	Sarah was afraid, so she lied and said:]
Sarah	I did not laugh.

27

The Lord
(slowly)   Yes . . . you *did* laugh.

Cast   [This is] the word or the Lord.
All   **Thanks be to God.**

Cast: **Narrator, Abraham, Man 1, Man 2, The Lord** (Men 1 and 2 and The Lord can be the same),
Sarah.

Rebecca and Isaac meet
Genesis 24.54–67

Narrator   Abraham's servant and the men with him ate and drank, and
                        spent the night at Laban's house. When they got up in the morn-
                        ing, he said:

Servant   Let me go back to my master.

Narrator   But Rebecca's brother and her mother said:

Mother   Let the girl stay with us a week or ten days.

Brother   Then she may go.

Servant   Don't make us stay. The Lord has made my journey a success; let
                        me go back to my master.

Brother   Let's call the girl and find out what she has to say.

Narrator   So they called Rebecca [and asked]:

Mother   Do you want to go with this man?

[Narrator   She answered:]

Rebecca   Yes.

Narrator   So they let Rebecca and her old family servant go with Abraham's
                        servant and his men. And they gave Rebecca their blessing in
                        these words:

Brother   May you, sister, become the mother of millions!

Mother   May your descendants conquer the cities of their enemies!

Narrator   Then Rebecca and her young women got ready and mounted
                        the camels to go with Abraham's servant, and they all started
                        out. (PAUSE)

                        Isaac had come into the wilderness of 'The Well of the Living One
                        Who Sees Me' and was staying in the southern part of Canaan. He
                        went out in the early evening to take a walk in the fields and saw
                        camels coming. When Rebecca saw Isaac, she got down from her
                        camel and asked Abraham's servant:

Rebecca   Who is that man walking towards us in the field?

Servant   He is my master.

Narrator	So she took her scarf and covered her face. (PAUSE)
	The servant told Isaac everything he had done. Then Isaac brought Rebecca into the tent that his mother Sarah had lived in, and she became his wife. Isaac loved Rebecca, and so he was comforted for the loss of his mother.
Cast	[This is] the word of the Lord.
All	**Thanks be to God.**

Cast: **Narrator, Servant, Mother, Brother, Rebecca.**

Joseph's brothers go to Egypt to buy corn
Genesis 41.46–42.24

Narrator	Joseph was thirty years old when he began to serve the king of Egypt. He left the King's court and travelled all over the land. During the seven years of plenty the land produced abundant crops, all of which Joseph collected and stored in the cities. In each city he stored the food from the fields around it. There was so much corn that Joseph stopped measuring it—it was like the sand of the sea! (PAUSE)
	Before the years of famine came, Joseph had two sons by Asenath. He said:
Joseph	God has made me forget all my sufferings and all my father's family.
Narrator	So he named his first son:
Joseph	Manasseh.
Narrator	He also said:
Joseph	God has given me children in the land of my trouble.
Narrator	So he named his second son:
Joseph	Ephraim.
Narrator	The seven years of plenty that the land of Egypt had enjoyed came to an end, and the seven years of famine began, just as Joseph had said. There was famine in every other country, but there was food throughout Egypt. When the Egyptians began to be hungry, they cried out to the king for food. So he ordered them to go to Joseph and do what he told them. The famine grew worse and spread over the whole country, so Joseph opened all the storehouses and sold corn to the Egyptians. People came to Egypt from all over the world to buy corn from Joseph, because the famine was severe everywhere.
	When Jacob learnt that there was corn in Egypt, he said to his sons:
Jacob	Why don't you do something? I hear that there is corn in Egypt; go there and buy some to keep us from starving to death.

Narrator	So Joseph's ten half-brothers went to buy corn in Egypt, but Jacob did not send Joseph's full-brother Benjamin with them, because he was afraid that something might happen to him.
	The sons of Jacob came with others to buy corn, because there was famine in the land of Canaan. Joseph, as governor of the land of Egypt, was selling corn to people from all over the world. So Joseph's brothers came and bowed down before him with their faces to the ground. When Joseph saw his brothers, he recognized them, but he acted as if he did not know them:
Joseph (harshly)	Where do you come from?
Brother 1	We have come from Canaan—
Brother 2	To buy food.
Narrator	Although Joseph recognized his brothers they did not recognize him. He remembered the dreams he had dreamt about them and said:
Joseph	You are spies; you have come to find out where our country is weak.
Brothers (protesting)	No, sir.
Brother 1	We have come as your slaves, to buy food.
Brother 2	We are all brothers.
Brother 3	We are not spies, sir, we are honest men.
Joseph	No! You have come to find out where our country is weak.
Brother 1	We *were* twelve brothers in all, sir—
Brother 2	Sons of the same man in the land of Canaan.
Brother 3	One brother is dead.
Brother 4	And the youngest is now with our father.
Joseph	It is just as I said. You are spies. This is how you will be tested: I swear by the name of the king that you will never leave unless your youngest brother comes here. One of you must go and get him. The rest of you will be kept under guard until the truth of what you say can be tested. Otherwise, as sure as the king lives, you are spies.
Narrator	Then he put them in prison for three days. On the third day Joseph said to them:
Joseph	I am a God-fearing man, and I will spare your lives on one condition. To prove that you are honest, one of you will stay in the prison where you have been kept; the rest of you may go and take back to your starving families the corn that you have bought. Then you must bring your youngest brother to me. This will prove that you have been telling the truth, and I will not put you to death.

Narrator	They agreed to this and said to one another:
Brother 1	Yes, now we are suffering the consequences of what we did to our brother.
Brother 2	We saw the great trouble he was in when he begged for help, but we would not listen.
Brother 3	That is why we are in this trouble now.
[Narrator	Reuben said:]
Reuben	I told you not to harm the boy, but you wouldn't listen. And now we are being paid back for his death.
Narrator	Joseph understood what they said, but they did not know it, because they had been speaking to him through an interpreter. Joseph left them and began to cry. When he was able to speak again, he came back, picked out Simeon, and had him tied up in front of them.
Cast	[This is] the word of the Lord.
All	**Thanks be to God**.

Cast: **Narrator, Joseph, Jacob, Brother 1, Brother 2, Brother 3, Brother 4, Reuben** (can be the same as Brother 4, or Brothers 1–4 can be the same).

Joseph's brothers return to Canaan
Genesis 42.25–38

Narrator	Joseph gave orders to fill his brothers' packs with corn, to put each man's money back in his sack, and to give them food for the journey. This was done. The brothers loaded their donkeys with the corn they had bought, and then they left. At the place where they spent the night, one of them opened his sack to feed his donkey and found his money at the top of the sack. He called to his brothers:
Brother 1	My money has been returned to me. Here it is in my sack!
Narrator	Their hearts sank, and in fear they asked one another:
Reuben	What has God done to us?
Narrator	When they came to their father Jacob in Canaan, they told him all that had happened to them:
Brother 1	The governor of Egypt spoke harshly to us and accused us of spying against his country.
Brother 2	'We are not spies,' we answered, 'we are honest men. We were twelve brothers in all, sons of the same father. One brother is dead, and the youngest is still in Canaan with our father.'
Brother 3	The man answered, 'This is how I will find out if you are honest men: One of you will stay with me; the rest will take corn for your starving families and leave.'

Brother 2	'Bring your youngest brother to me. Then I will know that you are not spies, but honest men.'
Brother 4	'I will give your brother back to you, and you can stay here and trade.'
Narrator	Then when they emptied out their sacks, every one of them found his bag of money; and when they saw the money, they and their father Jacob were afraid. Their father said to them:
Jacob	Do you want to make me lose *all* my children? Joseph is gone; Simeon is gone; and now you want to take away Benjamin. *I* am the one who suffers!
Narrator	Reuben said to his father:
Reuben	If I do not bring Benjamin back to you, you can kill my two sons. Put him in my care, and I will bring him back.
Jacob	My son cannot go with you; his brother is dead, and he is the only one left. Something might happen to him on the way. I am an old man, and the sorrow you would cause me would kill me.
Cast	[This is] the word of the Lord.
All	**Thanks be to God.**

Cast: **Narrator, Brother 1, Brother 2, Brother 3, Brother 4, Reuben** (can be the same as Brother 4, OR Brothers 1–4 can be the same), **Jacob.**

Joseph's brothers return to Egypt with Benjamin
Genesis 43.1–34

Narrator	The famine in Canaan got worse, and when the family of Jacob had eaten all the corn which had been brought from Egypt, Jacob said to his sons:
Jacob	Go back and buy a little food for us.
Narrator	Judah said to him:
Judah	The man sternly warned us that we would not be admitted to his presence unless we had our brother with us. If you are willing to send our brother with us, we will go and buy food for you. If you are not willing, we will not go, because the man told us we would not be admitted to his presence unless our brother was with us.
Jacob	Why did you cause me so much trouble by telling the man that you had another brother?
Brother 1	The man kept asking about us and our family—
Brother 2	'Is your father still living?' 'Have you got another brother?'
Brother 3	We had to answer his questions.
Brother 4	How could we know that he would tell us to bring our brother with us?

Judah
(to Jacob)

Send the boy with me, and we will leave at once. Then none of us will starve to death. I will pledge my own life, and you can hold me responsible for him. If I do not bring him back to you safe and sound, I will always bear the blame. If we had not waited so long, we could have been there and back twice by now.

Jacob

If that is how it has to be, then take the best products of the land in your packs as a present for the governor: a little resin, a little honey, spices, pistachio nuts, and almonds. Take with you also twice as much money, because you must take back the money that was returned in the top of your sacks. Maybe it was a mistake. Take your brother and return at once. May Almighty God cause the man to have pity on you, so that he will give Benjamin and your other brother back to you. As for me, if I must lose my children, I must lose them. (PAUSE)

Narrator

So the brothers took the gifts and twice as much money, and set out for Egypt with Benjamin. There they presented themselves to Joseph. When Joseph saw Benjamin with them, he said to the servant in charge of his house:

Joseph
(to Servant)

Take these men to my house. They are going to eat with me at noon, so kill an animal and prepare it.

Narrator

The servant did as he was commanded and took the brothers to Joseph's house. As they were being brought to the house, they were afraid and thought:

Brother 1 (to other brothers)

We are being brought here because of the money that was returned in our sacks the first time.

Brother 2

They will suddenly attack us, take our donkeys, and make us his slaves.

Narrator

So at the door of the house, they said to the servant in charge:

Brother 1

If you please, sir, we came here once before to buy food.

Brother 2

When we set up camp on the way home, we opened our sacks, and each man found his money in the top of his sack—every bit of it.

Brother 3

We have brought it back to you.

Brother 4

We have also brought some more money with us to buy more food.

Brother 2

We do not know who put our money back in our sacks.

Narrator

The servant said:

Servant

Don't worry. Don't be afraid. Your God, the God of your father, must have put the money in your sacks for you. I received your payment.

Narrator

Then he brought Simeon to them. (PAUSE)

The servant took the brothers into the house. He gave them water so that they could wash their feet, and he fed their donkeys. They got their gifts ready to present to Joseph when he arrived at noon, because they had been told that they were to eat with him. When Joseph got home, they took the gifts into the house to him and bowed down to the ground before him. He asked about their health and then said:

Joseph   You told me about your old father—how is he? Is he still alive and well?

Brother 1   Your humble servant, our father, is still alive and well.

Narrator   They knelt and bowed down before him. When Joseph saw his brother Benjamin, he said:

Joseph   So this is your youngest brother, the one you told me about. God bless you, my son.

Narrator   Then Joseph left suddenly, because his heart was full of tender feelings for his brother. He was about to break down, so he went to his room and cried. (PAUSE)

After he had washed his face, he came out, and controlling himself, he ordered the meal to be served. Joseph was served at one table and his brothers at another. The Egyptians who were eating there were served separately, because they considered it beneath their dignity to eat with Hebrews. The brothers had been seated at table, facing Joseph, in the order of their age from the eldest to the youngest. When they saw how they had been seated, they looked at one another in amazement. Food was served to them from Joseph's table, and Benjamin was served five times as much as the rest of them. So they ate and drank with Joseph until they were drunk.

Cast   [This is] the word of the Lord.
All   **Thanks be to God**.

Cast: **Narrator, Jacob, Judah, Brother 1** (can be the same as Judah), **Brother 2, Brother 3, Brother 4** (Brothers 1–4 can be the same), **Joseph, Servant**.

The missing cup
Genesis 44.1–45.15, 25–26

Narrator   Joseph commanded the servant in charge of his house:

Joseph   Fill the men's sacks with as much food as they can carry, and put each man's money in the top of his sack. Put my silver cup in the top of the youngest brother's sack, together with the money for his corn.

Narrator   He did as he was told. Early in the morning the brothers were sent on their way with their donkeys. When they had gone only a short distance from the city, Joseph said to the servant in charge of his house:

Joseph   Hurry after those men. When you catch up with them, ask them, 'Why have you paid back evil for good? Why did you steal my master's silver cup? It is the one he drinks from, the one he uses for divination. You have committed a serious crime!'

Narrator When the servant caught up with them, he repeated these words. They answered him:

Brother 1 What do you mean, sir, by talking like this?

Brother 2 We swear that we have done no such thing.

Brother 3 You know that we brought back to you from the land of Canaan the money we found in the top of our sacks. Why then should we steal silver or gold from your master's house?

Brother 4 Sir, if any one of us is found to have it, he will be put to death, and the rest of us will become your slaves.

Servant I agree; but only the one who has taken the cup will become my slave, and the rest of you can go free.

Narrator So they quickly lowered their sacks to the ground, and each man opened his sack. Joseph's servant searched carefully, beginning with the eldest and ending with the youngest, and the cup was found in Benjamin's sack. The brothers tore their clothes in sorrow, loaded their donkeys, and returned to the city. (PAUSE)

When Judah and his brothers came to Joseph's house, he was still there. They bowed down before him, and Joseph said:

Joseph What have you done? Didn't you know that a man in my position could find you out by practising divination?

Narrator Judah answered:

Judah What can we say to you, sir? How can we argue? How can we
(to Joseph) clear ourselves? God has uncovered our guilt. All of us are now your slaves and not just the one with whom the cup was found.

Joseph Oh, no! I would never do that! Only the one who had the cup will be my slave. The rest of you may go back safe and sound to your father.

Narrator Judah went up to Joseph and said:

Judah Please, sir, allow me to speak with you freely. [Don't be angry with me; you are like the king himself. Sir, you asked us, 'Have you got a father or another brother?' We answered, 'We have a father who is old and a younger brother, born to him in his old age. The boy's brother is dead, and he is the only one of his mother's children still alive; his father loves him very much.' Sir, you told us to bring him here, so that you could see him, and we answered that the boy could not leave his father; if he did, his father would die. Then you said, 'You will not be admitted to my presence again unless your youngest brother comes with you.'

When we went back to our father, we told him what you had said. Then he told us to return and buy a little food. We answered, 'We cannot go: we will not be admitted to the man's presence unless our youngest brother is with us. We can go only if our youngest brother goes also'. Our father said to us, 'You know that my wife Rachel bore me only two sons. One of them has already left me. He must have been torn to pieces by wild animals, because I have not seen him since he left. If you take this one from me now and something happens to him, the sorrow you would cause me would kill me, old as I am.'

And now, sir,] if I go back to my father without the boy, as soon as he sees that the boy is not with me, he will die. His life is wrapped up with the life of the boy, and he is so old that the sorrow we would cause him would kill him. What is more. I pledged my life to my father for the boy. I told him that if I did not bring the boy back to him, I would bear the blame all my life. And now, sir, I will stay here as your slave in place of the boy; let him go back with his brothers. How can I go back to my father if the boy is not with me? I cannot bear to see this disaster come upon my father.

Narrator   Joseph was no longer able to control his feelings in front of his servants, so he ordered them all to leave the room. No one else was with him when Joseph told his brothers who he was. He cried with such loud sobs that the Egyptians heard it, and the news was taken to the king's palace. Joseph said to his brothers:

Joseph   I am Joseph. Is my father still alive?

Narrator   But when his brothers heard this, they were so terrified that they could not answer. [Then Joseph said to them:]

Joseph   Please come closer. (PAUSE)

Narrator   They did [and he said:]

Joseph   I am your brother Joseph, whom you sold into Egypt. Now do not be upset or blame yourselves because you sold me here. It was really God who sent me ahead of you to save people's lives. This is only the second year of famine in the land; there will be five more years in which there will be neither ploughing nor reaping. God sent me ahead of you to rescue you in this amazing way and to make sure that you and your descendants survive. So it was not really you who sent me here, but God. He has made me the king's highest official. I am in charge of his whole country; I am the ruler of all Egypt.

Now hurry back to my father and tell him that this is what his son Joseph says: 'God has made me ruler of all Egypt; come to me without delay. You can live in the region of Goshen, where you can be near me—you, your children, your grandchildren, your sheep, your goats, your cattle, and everything else that you have. If you are in Goshen, I can take care of you. There will still be five years of famine; and I do not want you, your family, and your livestock to starve.'

Now all of you, and you too, Benjamin, can see that I am really

	Joseph. Tell my father how powerful I am here in Egypt and tell him about everything that you have seen. Then hurry and bring him here.
Narrator	He threw his arms round his brother Benjamin and began to cry; Benjamin also cried as he hugged him. Then, still weeping, he embraced each of his brothers and kissed them. After that, his brothers began to talk with him. (PAUSE)
	They left Egypt and went back home to their father Jacob in Canaan. They told him:
Brother 1	Joseph is still alive!
Brother 2	He is the ruler of all Egypt!
Cast	[This is] the word of the Lord.
All	**Thanks be to God**.

Cast: **Narrator, Joseph, Brother 1, Brother 2, Brother 3, Brother 4** (Brothers 1–4 can be the same), **Servant, Judah**, (can be the same as Brother 4).

Jacob and his family in Egypt
Genesis 46.31–47.12

Narrator	Joseph said to his brothers and the rest of his father's family:
Joseph	I must go and tell the king that my brothers and all my father's family, who were living in Canaan, have come to me. I will tell him that you are shepherds and take care of livestock and that you have brought your flocks and herds and everything else that belongs to you. When the king calls for you and asks what your occupation is, be sure to tell him that you have taken care of livestock all your lives, just as your ancestors did. In this way he will let you live in the region of Goshen.
Narrator	Joseph said this because Egyptians will have nothing to do with shepherds.
	So Joseph took five of his brothers and went to the king [He said:]
Joseph (to King)	My father and my brothers have come from Canaan with their flocks, their herds, and all that they own. They are now in the region of Goshen.
Narrator	He then presented his brothers to the king. [The king asked them:]
King	What is your occupation?
Brother 1	We are shepherds, sir, just as our ancestors were.
Brother 2	We have come to live in this country, because in the land of Canaan the famine is so severe that there is no pasture for our flocks.
Brother 3	Please give us permission to live in the region of Goshen.

[Narrator	The king said to Joseph:]
King	Now that your father and your brothers have arrived, the land of Egypt is theirs. Let them settle in the region of Goshen, the best part of the land. And if there are any capable men among them, put them in charge of my own livestock.
Narrator	Then Joseph brought his father Jacob and presented him to the king. Jacob gave the king his blessing, [and the king asked him:]
King	How old are you?
Jacob	My life of wandering has lasted a hundred and thirty years. Those years have been few and difficult, unlike the long years of my ancestors in their wanderings.
Narrator	Jacob gave the king a farewell blessing and left. Then Joseph settled his father and his brothers in Egypt, giving them property in the best of the land near the city of Rameses, as the king had commanded. Joseph provided food for his father, his brothers, and all the rest of his father's family, including the very youngest.
Cast	[This is] the word of the Lord.
All	**Thanks be to God**.

Cast: **Narrator, Joseph, King, Brother 1, Brother 2, Brother 3** (can be the same as Brother 1, OR Brothers 1–3 can be the same), **Jacob**.

The birth of Moses
Exodus 2.1–10

Narrator 1	During the time when the king of Egypt had commanded that every new-born Hebrew boy was to be thrown into the Nile, a man from the tribe of Levi married a woman of his own tribe, and she bore him a son. When she saw what a fine baby he was, she hid him for three months. But when she could not hide him any longer, she took a basket made of reeds and covered it with tar to make it watertight. She put the baby in it and then placed it in the tall grass at the edge of the river. The baby's sister stood some distance away to see what would happen to him.
Narrator 2	The king's daughter came down to the river to bathe, while her servants walked along the bank. Suddenly she noticed the basket in the tall grass and sent a slave-girl to get it. The princess opened it and saw a baby boy. He was crying, and she felt sorry for him:
Princess	This is one of the Hebrew babies.
Narrator 1	Then his sister asked her:
Sister	Shall I go and call a Hebrew woman to act as a nurse?
Princess	Please do.
Narrator 2	So the girl went and brought the baby's *own mother*. (PAUSE) The princess told the woman:

Princess	Take this baby and nurse him for me, and I will pay you.
Narrator 1	So she took the baby and nursed him. (PAUSE)
Narrator 2	Later, when the child was old enough, she took him to the king's daughter, who adopted him as her own son. She said to herself:
Princess	I pulled him out of the water, and so I name him Moses.
Cast	[This is] the word of the Lord.
All	**Thanks be to God**.

Cast: **Narrator 1, Narrator 2, Princess, Sister**.

Naomi and Ruth return to Bethlehem
Ruth 1.6–22

Narrator	Naomi heard that the Lord had blessed his people by giving them a good harvest; so she got ready to leave Moab with her daughters-in-law. They started out together to go back to Judah, but on the way she said to them:
Naomi	Go back home and stay with your mothers. May the Lord be as good to you as you have been to me and to those who have died. And may the Lord make it possible for each of you to marry again and have a home.
Narrator	So Naomi kissed them good-bye. But they started crying [and said to her]:
Ruth and **Orpah**	No!
Orpah	We will go with you to your people.
Naomi	You must go back, my daughters. Why do you want to come with me? Do you think I could have sons again for you to marry? Go back home, for I am too old to get married again. Even if I thought there was still hope, and so got married tonight and had sons, would you wait until they had grown up? Would this keep you from marrying someone else? No, my daughters, you know that's impossible. The Lord has turned against me, and I feel very sorry for you.
Narrator	Again they started crying. Then Orpah kissed her mother-in-law good-bye and went back home, but Ruth held on to her. [So Naomi said to her:]
Naomi (to Ruth)	Ruth, your sister-in-law has gone back to her people and to her god. Go back home with her.
[Narrator	But Ruth answered:]
Ruth	Don't ask me to leave you! Let me go with you. Wherever you go, I will go; wherever you live, I will live. Your people will be my people, and your God will be my God. Wherever you die, I will die, and that is where I will be buried. May the Lord's worst punishment come upon me if I let anything but death separate me from you!

Narrator	When Naomi saw that Ruth was determined to go with her, she said nothing more. (PAUSE)
	They went on until they came to Bethlehem. When they arrived, the whole town got excited, and the women there exclaimed:
Women	Is this really Naomi?
Naomi	Don't call me *Naomi*; call me *Marah*, because Almighty God has made my life bitter. When I left here, I had plenty, but the Lord has brought me back without a thing. Why call me Naomi when the Lord Almighty has condemned me and sent me trouble?
Narrator	This, then, was how Naomi came back from Moab with Ruth, her Moabite daughter-in-law. The barley harvest was just beginning when they arrived in Bethlehem.
Cast	[This is] the word of the Lord.
All	**Thanks be to God**.

Cast: **Narrator, Naomi, Ruth, Orpah** (can be the same as Ruth), **Women** (two or more).

Ruth finds a husband
Ruth 3.1–18

Narrator	[Some time later] Naomi said to Ruth:
Naomi	I must find a husband for you, so that you will have a home of your own. Remember that this man Boaz, whose women you have been working with, is our relative. Now listen. This evening he will be threshing the barley. So wash yourself, put on some perfume, and get dressed in your best clothes. Then go where he is threshing, but don't let him know you are there until he has finished eating and drinking. Be sure to notice where he lies down, and after he falls asleep, go and lift the covers and lie down at his feet. He will tell you what to do.
Narrator	Ruth answered:
Ruth	I will do everything you say.
Narrator	So Ruth went to the threshing-place and did just what her mother-in-law had told her. When Boaz had finished eating and drinking, he was in a good mood. He went to the pile of barley and lay down to sleep. Ruth slipped over quietly, lifted the covers and lay down at his feet. During the night he woke up suddenly, turned over, and was surprised to find a woman at his feet.
Boaz	Who are you?
Ruth	It's Ruth, sir. Because you are a close relative, you are responsible for taking care of me. So please marry me.
Boaz	The Lord bless you. You are showing even greater family loyalty in what you are doing now than in what you did for your mother-in-law. You might have gone looking for a young man, either rich

or poor, but you didn't. Now don't worry. Ruth. I will do everything you ask; as everyone in town knows, you are a fine woman. It is true that I am a close relative and am responsible for you, but there is a man who is a closer relative than I am. Stay here the rest of the night, and in the morning we will find out whether or not he will take responsibility for you. If so, well and good; if not, then I swear by the living Lord that I will take the responsibility. Now lie down and stay here till morning.

Narrator   So she lay there at his feet, but she got up before it was light enough for her to be seen, because Boaz did not want anyone to know that she had been there. Boaz said to her:

Boaz   Take off your cloak and spread it out here.

Narrator   She did, and he poured out nearly twenty kilogrammes of barley and helped her to lift it on her shoulder. Then she returned to the town with it. When she arrived home, her mother-in-law asked her:

Naomi   How did you get on, my daughter?

Narrator   Ruth told her everything that Boaz had done for her. [She added:]

Ruth   He told me I must not come back to you empty-handed, so he gave me all this barley.

Narrator   Naomi said to her:

Naomi   Now be patient, Ruth, until you see how this all turns out. Boaz will not rest today until he settles the matter.

Cast   [This is] the word of the Lord.
All   **Thanks be to God.**

Cast: **Narrator, Naomi, Ruth, Boaz.**

The birth of Samuel
From 1 Samuel 1.1–20

Narrator   There was a certain man from the hill-country of Ephraim, whose name was Elkanah. Year after year this man went up from his town to worship and sacrifice to the Lord Almighty at Shiloh. Whenever the day came for Elkanah to sacrifice, he would give his wife Hannah a double portion of the meat because he loved her, and the Lord had closed her womb. But whenever Hannah went up to the house of the Lord she wept and would not eat. Elkanah her husband would say to her:

Elkanah   Hannah, why are you weeping? Why don't you eat? Why are you downhearted? Don't I mean more to you than ten sons?

Narrator   Once when they had finished eating and drinking in Shiloh, Hannah stood up. Now Eli the priest was sitting on a chair by the doorpost of the Lord's temple. In bitterness of soul Hannah wept much and prayed to the Lord. And she made a vow:

41

Hannah	O Lord Almighty, if you will only look upon your servant's misery and remember me, and not forget your servant but give her a son, then I will give him to the Lord for all the days of his life.
Narrator	As she kept on praying to the Lord, Eli observed her mouth. Hannah was praying in her heart, and her lips were moving but her voice was not heard. Eli thought she was drunk [and said to her:]
Eli (severely)	How long will you keep on getting drunk? Get rid of your wine.
Hannah (sadly)	Not so, my lord. I am a woman who is deeply troubled. I have not been drinking wine or beer; I was pouring out my soul to the Lord. Do not take your servant for a wicked woman; I have been praying here out of my great anguish and grief.
Narrator	Eli answered:
Eli (with compassion)	Go in peace, and may the God of Israel grant you what you have asked of him.
Hannah (pleased)	May your servant find favour in your eyes.
Narrator	Then she went her way and ate something, and her face was no longer downcast. Early the next morning they arose and worshipped before the Lord and then went back to their home. Hannah conceived and gave birth to a son. She named him:
Hannah (slowly)	Samuel—
Narrator	[Saying:]
Hannah	Because I asked the Lord for him.
Cast	[This is] the word of the Lord.
All	**Thanks be to God**.

Cast: **Narrator, Elkanah, Hannah, Eli.**

Samuel's dedication
1 Samuel 1.21–2.11

Narrator	The time came again for Elkanah and his family to go to Shiloh and offer to the Lord the yearly sacrifice and the special sacrifice he had promised. But this time Hannah did not go. [She told her husband:]
Hannah (to Elkanah)	As soon as the child is weaned, I will take him to the house of the Lord, where he will stay all his life.
[**Narrator**	Elkanah answered:]
Elkanah	All right, do whatever you think best; stay at home until you have weaned him. And may the Lord make your promise come true.
Narrator	So Hannah stayed at home and nursed her child. (PAUSE)

After she had weaned him, she took him to Shiloh, taking along
a three-year-old bull, ten kilogrammes of flour, and a leather bag
full of wine. She took Samuel, young as he was, to the house of the
Lord at Shiloh. After they had killed the bull, they took the child
to Eli. [Hannah said to him:]

Hannah   Excuse me, sir. Do you remember me? I am the woman you saw
standing here, praying to the Lord. I asked him for this child, and
he gave me what I asked for. So I am dedicating him to the Lord.
As long as he lives, he will belong to the Lord.

Narrator Then they worshipped the Lord there. [Hannah prayed:

Hannah   The Lord has filled my heart with joy;
how happy I am because of what he has done!
I laugh at my enemies;
how joyful I am because God has helped me!

No one is holy like the Lord;
there is none like him,
no protector like our God.

Stop your loud boasting;
silence your proud words.
For the Lord is a God who knows,
and he judges all that people do.

The bows of strong soldiers are broken,
but the weak grow strong.

The people who once were well fed
now hire themselves out to get food,
but the hungry are hungry no more.
The childless wife has borne seven children,
but the mother of many is left with none.

The Lord kills and restores to life;
he sends people to the world of the dead
and brings them back again.
He makes some men poor and others rich;
he humbles some and makes others great.

He lifts the poor from the dust
and raises the needy from their misery.
He makes them companions of princes
and puts them in places of honour.
The foundations of the earth belong to the Lord;
on them he has built the world.

He protects the lives of his faithful people,
but the wicked disappear in darkness;
a man does not triumph by his own strength.

The Lord's enemies will be destroyed;
he will thunder against them from heaven.
The Lord will judge the whole world;
he will give power to his king,

he will make his chosen king victorious.]

Narrator   Elkanah went back home to Ramah, but the boy Samuel stayed in Shiloh and served the Lord under the priest Eli.

Cast   [This is] the word of the Lord.
All   **Thanks be to God**.

Cast: **Narrator, Hannah, Elkanah.**

The sons of Eli
1 Samuel 2.12–26

Narrator   The sons of Eli were scoundrels. They paid no attention to the Lord or to the regulations concerning what the priests could demand from the people. Instead, when a man was offering his sacrifice, the priest's servant would come with a three-pronged fork. While the meat was still cooking, he would stick the fork into the cooking-pot, and whatever the fork brought out belonged to the priest. All the Israelites who came to Shiloh to offer sacrifices were treated like this. In addition, even before the fat was taken off and burnt, the priest's servant would come and say to the man offering the sacrifice:

Servant   Give me some meat for the priest to roast; he won't accept boiled meat from you, only raw meat.

Narrator   If the man answered:

Man   Let us do what is right and burn the fat first; then take what you want—

Narrator   The priest's servant would say:

Servant   No! Give it to me now! If you don't, I will have to take it by force!

Narrator   This sin of the sons of Eli was extremely serious in the Lord's sight, because they treated the offerings to the Lord with such disrespect.

In the meantime the boy Samuel continued to serve the Lord, wearing a sacred linen apron. Each year his mother would make a little robe and take it to him when she accompanied her husband to offer the yearly sacrifice. Then Eli would bless Elkanah and his wife, and say to Elkanah:

Eli   May the Lord give you other children by this woman to take the place of the one you dedicated to him.

Narrator   After that they would go back home. The Lord did bless Hannah, and she had three more sons and two daughters. The boy Samuel grew up in the service of the Lord. Eli was now very old. He kept hearing about everything his sons were doing to the Israelites and that they were even sleeping with the women who worked at the entrance to the Tent of the Lord's presence. So he said to them:

Eli   Why are you doing these things? Everybody tells me about the evil you are doing. Stop it, my sons! This is an awful thing the people of the Lord are talking about! If a man sins against another

	man, God can defend him; but who can defend a man who sins against the Lord?
Narrator	But they would not listen to their father, for the Lord had decided to kill them. The boy Samuel continued to grow and to gain favour both with the Lord and with men.
Cast	[This is] the word of the Lord.
All	**Thanks be to God.**

Cast: **Narrator, Servant, Man, Eli.**

The Lord's message to Eli
1 Samuel 3.11–21

Narrator	The Lord said to Samuel:
The Lord	Some day I am going to do something to the people of Israel that is so terrible that everyone who hears about it will be stunned. On that day I will carry out all my threats against Eli's family, from beginning to end. I have already told him that I am going to punish his family for ever because his sons have spoken evil things against me. Eli knew they were doing this, but he did not stop them. So I solemnly declare to the family of Eli that no sacrifice or offering will ever be able to remove the consequences of this terrible sin.
Narrator	Samuel stayed in bed until morning; then he got up and opened the doors of the house of the Lord. He was afraid to tell Eli about the vision. Eli called him:
Eli	Samuel, my boy!
[Narrator	Samuel answered:]
Samuel	Yes, sir!
Eli	What did the Lord tell you? Don't keep anything from me. God will punish you severely if you don't tell me everything he said.
Narrator	So Samuel told him everything; he did not keep anything back.
Eli (sadly)	He is the Lord; he will do whatever seems best to him.
Narrator	As Samuel grew up, the Lord was with him and made everything that Samuel said come true. So all the people of Israel, from one end of the country to the other, knew that Samuel was indeed a prophet of the Lord. The Lord continued to reveal himself at Shiloh, where he had appeared to Samuel and had spoken to him. And when Samuel spoke, all Israel listened.
Cast	[This is] the word of the Lord.
All	**Thanks be to God.**

Cast: **Narrator, The Lord, Eli, Samuel** (as a boy).

David is told of Absalom's death
2 Samuel 18.19–33

Narrator	Ahimaaz son of Zadok said to Joab:
Ahimaaz	Let me run to the king with the good news that the Lord has saved him from his enemies.
[Narrator	Joab said:]
Joab	No, today you will not take any good news. Some other day you may do so, but not today, for the King's son is dead.
Narrator	Then he said to his Sudanese slave:
Joab	Go and tell the king what you have seen.
Narrator	The slave bowed and ran off.
	[Ahimaaz insisted:]
Ahimaaz	I don't care what happens; please let me take the news also.
Joab	Why do you want to do it, my son? You will get no reward for it.
Ahimaaz	Whatever happens, I want to go.
Joab	Then go.
Narrator	So Ahimaaz ran off down the road through the Jordan Valley, and soon he passed the slave. David was sitting in the space between the inner and outer gates of the city. The watchman went up to the top of the wall and stood on the roof of the gateway; he looked out and saw a man running alone. He called down and told the king, and the king said:
David	If he is alone, he is bringing good news.
Narrator	The runner came nearer and nearer. Then the watchman saw another man running alone, and he called down to the gatekeeper:
Watchman (calling)	Look! There's another man running!
David	This one also is bringing good news.
Watchman (calling)	I can see that the first man runs like Ahimaaz.
David	He's a good man, and he is bringing good news.
Narrator	Ahimaaz called out a greeting to the king, threw himself down to the ground before him [and said:]
Ahimaaz	Praise the Lord your God, who has given you victory over the men who rebelled against Your Majesty!
David (anxiously)	Is the young man Absalom safe?
Ahimaaz	Sir, when your officer Joab sent me, I saw a great commotion, but I couldn't tell what it was.

46

David	Stand over there.
Narrator	He went over and stood there. Then the Sudanese slave arrived and said to the king:
Slave	I have good news for Your Majesty! Today the Lord has given you victory over all who rebelled against you!
David	Is the young man Absalom safe?
Slave	I wish that what has happened to him would happen to all you enemies, sir, and to all who rebel against you.
Narrator	The king was overcome with grief. He went up to the room over the gateway and wept. As he went, he cried:
David	O my son! My son Absalom! Absalom my son! If only I had died in your place my son! Absalom, my son!
Cast	[This is] the word of the Lord.
All	**Thanks be to God.**

Cast: **Narrator, Ahimaaz, Joab, David, Watchman, Slave.**

In praise of the Lord's goodness
From Psalm 113.1–9 (LIT)

Leaders 1 and 2	Praise the Lord:
All	**praise the Lord!**
Leader 2	You servants of the Lord, praise his name:
All	**let the name of the Lord be praised,** **both now and for evermore!**
Leader 1	From the rising of the sun to the place where it sets:
All	**the name of the Lord be praised!**
Leader 2	The Lord is exalted above the earth:
All	**his glory over the heavens.**
Leader 1	Who is like the Lord our God?
All	**He is throned in the heights above—**
Leader 2	Yet he bends down:
All	**he stoops to look at our world.**
Leader 1	He raises the poor from the dust:
All	**and lifts the needy from their sorrow.**
Leader 2	He honours the childless wife in her home:
All	**he makes her happy, the mother of children.**
Leaders 1 and 2	Praise the Lord:
All	**Amen.**
All	**Glory to the Father, and to the Son, and to the Holy Spirit:** **as it was in the beginning, is now, and shall be for ever. Amen.**

Cast: **Leader 1, Leader 2, All** (two or more persons/congregation).

The one true God
Psalm 115.1–18

Psalmist	To you alone, O Lord, to you alone, and not to us, must glory be given because of your constant love and faithfulness. (PAUSE)
Worshipper 1	Why should the nations ask us:
Enquirer	Where is your God?
Worshipper 1	Our God is in heaven; he does whatever he wishes. *Their* gods are made of silver and gold, formed by human hands.
Worshipper 2	They have mouths, but cannot speak, and eyes, but cannot see.
Worshipper 1	They have ears, but cannot hear, and noses, but cannot smell.
Worshipper 2	They have hands, but cannot feel, and feet, but cannot walk; they cannot make a sound.
Psalmist	May all who made them and who trust in them become like the idols they have made. (PAUSE)
	Trust in the Lord, you people of Israel—
Worshippers 1 and **2**	He helps you and protects you.
Psalmist	Trust in the Lord, you priests of God—
Priests 1 and **2**	He helps you and protects you.
Psalmist	Trust in the Lord, all you that worship him—
Worshippers 1 and **2**	He helps you and protects you.
Psalmist	The Lord remembers us and will bless us; he will bless the people of Israel and all the priests of God. He will bless everyone who honours him, the great and the small alike.
Priest 1	May the Lord give you children—you and your descendants!
Priest 2	May you be blessed by the Lord, who made heaven and earth!
Psalmist	Heaven belongs to the Lord alone, but he gave the earth to man. The Lord is not praised by the dead, by any who go down to the land of silence. But we, the living, will give thanks to him now and for ever.
Worshippers and **Priests**	Praise the Lord!

Cast [This is] the word of the Lord. OR **All Glory to the Father, and to the Son, and to the Holy Spirit:**
All Thanks be to God. **as it was in the beginning, is now, and shall be for ever. Amen.**

Cast: **Psalmist, Worshipper 1, Enquirer, Worshipper 2, Priest 1** (can be the same as Enquirer), **Priest 2** (can be the same as Priest 1).

In praise of Jerusalem
From Psalm 122.1–8 (LIT)

Leader	I was glad when they said to me:
All	**let us go to the house of the Lord!**
Leader	Pray for the peace of Jerusalem:
All (group 1)	**may those who love our land be blessed.**
Leader	May there be peace in your homes:
All (group 2)	**and safety for our families.**
Leader	For the sake of those we love we say:
All	**Let there be peace!**
All	**Glory to the Father, and to the Son, and to the Holy Spirit:**
	as it was in the beginning, is now, and shall be for ever. Amen.

Cast: **Leader, All** (group 1, preferably male voices—two or more persons/part of congregation), **All** (group 2, preferably female voices—two or more persons/part of congregation).

The reward of obedience to the Lord
From Psalm 128.1–6 (LIT)

Leader	The pilgrims' song:
All (group 1)	**Blessed are those who fear the Lord,**
All (group 2)	**who walk in his ways.**
Leader	You will eat the fruit of your work; blessings and prosperity will be yours:
All (group 1)	**Blessed are those who fear the Lord,**
All (group 2)	**who walk in his ways.**
Leader	Your wife will be like a fruitful vine within your house; your children will be like young olive trees around your table:
All (group 1)	**Blessed are those who fear the Lord,**
All (group 2)	**who walk in his ways.**
Leader	May the Lord bless you all the days of your life; may you have prosperity; may you live to see your children's children:
All	**Peace be with you.**
All	**Glory to the Father, and to the Son, and to the Holy Spirit:**
	as it was in the beginning, is now, and shall be for ever. Amen.

Cast: **Leader, All** (group 1—two or more persons/part of congregation), **All** (group 2—two or more persons/part of congregation).

The value of Proverbs
Proverbs 1.1.–19

Announcer   The proverbs of Solomon, son of David and king of Israel:

Here are proverbs that will help you to recognize wisdom and good advice, and understand sayings with deep meaning. They can teach you how to live intelligently and how to be honest, just, and fair. They can make an inexperienced person clever and teach young men how to be resourceful. These proverbs can even add to the knowledge of wise men and give guidance to the educated, so that they can understand the hidden meanings of proverbs and the problems that wise men raise. (PAUSE)

Teacher   To have knowledge, you must first have reverence for the Lord. Stupid people have no respect for wisdom and refuse to learn.

Pay attention to what your father and mother tell you, my son. Their teaching will improve your character as a handsome turban or a necklace improves your appearance.

When sinners tempt you, my son, don't give in. Suppose they say:

Sinner 1   Come on; let's find someone to kill!

Sinner 2   Let's attack some innocent people for the fun of it!

Sinner 1   They may be alive and well when we find them, but they'll be dead when we're through with them!

Sinner 2   We'll find all kinds of riches and fill our houses with loot!

Sinner 1   Come and join us, and we'll all share what we steal.

Teacher   Don't go with people like that, my son. Stay away from them. They can't wait to do something bad. They're always ready to kill. It does no good to spread a net when the bird you want to catch is watching, but men like that are setting a trap for themselves, a trap in which they will die. Robbery always claims the life of the robber—this is what happens to anyone who lives by violence.

Cast   [This is] the word of the Lord.
All   **Thanks be God.**

Cast: **Announcer, Teacher, Sinner 1, Sinner 2.**

The people's unfaithfulness to God
From Malachi 2.10–16

Speaker 1	Don't we all have the same father?
Speaker 2	Didn't the same God create us all?
Speaker 1	Then why do we break our promises to one another?
Speaker 2	And why do we despise the covenant that God made with our ancestors?
Speaker 1	You ask why he no longer accepts your offerings.
Speaker 2	It is because he knows you have broken your promise to the wife you married when you were young.
Speaker 1	She was your partner, and you have broken your promise to her, although you promised before God that you would be faithful to her.
Speaker 2	Didn't God make you one body and spirit with her? What was his purpose in this?
Speaker 1	It was that you should have children who are truly God's people. So make sure that none of you breaks his promise to his wife.
Speaker 2	The Lord God of Israel says:
The Lord	I hate divorce. I hate it when one of you does such a cruel thing to his wife. Make sure that you do not break your promise to be faithful to your wife.
Cast	[This is] the word of the Lord.
All	**Thanks be to God.**

Cast: **Speaker 1, Speaker 2, The Lord.**

Jesus' teaching about adultery and divorce
Matthew 5.27–32

Jesus	You have heard that it was said:
Rabbi	Do not commit adultery.
Jesus	But now I tell you: anyone who looks at a woman and wants to possess her is guilty of committing adultery with her in his heart. So if your right eye causes you to sin, take it out and throw it away! It is much better for you to lose a part of your body than to have your whole body thrown into hell. If your right hand causes you to sin, cut it off and throw it away! It is much better for you to lose one of your limbs than for your whole body to go to hell. (PAUSE)
	It was also said:
Rabbi	Anyone who divorces his wife must give her a written notice of divorce.

Jesus   But now I tell you: if a man divorces his wife, for any cause other than her unfaithfulness, then he is guilty of making her commit adultery if she marries again; and the man who marries her commits adultery also.

Cast   [This is] the word of the Lord.   OR   This is the Gospel of Christ / *This the Gospel of the Lord.*
All   **Thanks be to God.**   **Praise to Christ our Lord** / *Praise to you, Lord Jesus Christ.*

Cast: **Jesus, Rabbi.**

Jesus' parable of the two house-builders
Matthew 7.24–29

Voice 1   Anyone who hears these words of mine and obeys them is like a wise man who built his house on rock.

Voice 2   The rain poured down, the rivers overflowed, and the wind blew hard against that house. But it did not fall, because it was built on rock.

Voice 1   But anyone who hears these words of mine and does not obey them is like a foolish man who built his house on sand.

Voice 2   The rain poured down, the rivers overflowed, the wind blew hard against that house, and it fell. And what a terrible fall that was!

Narrator   When Jesus finished saying these things, the crowd was amazed at the way he taught. He wasn't like the teachers of the Law; instead, he taught with authority.

Cast   [This is] the word of the Lord.   OR   This is the Gospel of Christ / *This is the Gospel of the Lord.*
All   **Thanks be to God.**   **Praise to Christ our Lord** / *Praise to you, Lord Jesus Christ.*

Cast: **Voice 1, Voice 2, Narrator.**

Jesus blesses little children
Matthew 19.13–15

Narrator   Some people brought children to Jesus for him to place his hands on them and to pray for them, but the disciples scolded the people. Jesus said:

Jesus   Let the children come to me and do not stop them, because the Kingdom of heaven belongs to such as these. (PAUSE)

Narrator   He placed his hands on them and then went away.

Cast   [This is] the word of the Lord.   OR   This is the Gospel of Christ / *This is the Gospel of the Lord.*
All   **Thanks be to God.**   **Praise to Christ our Lord** / *Praise to you, Lord Jesus Christ.*

Cast: **Narrator, Jesus.**

Jesus warns against the teachers of the Law and the Pharisees
Matthew 23.[1], 13–22

[Narrator   Jesus spoke to the crowds and to his disciples:]

Jesus   How terrible for you, teachers of the Law and Pharisees! You hypocrites! You lock the door to the Kingdom of heaven in people's faces, and you yourselves don't go in, nor do you allow in those who are trying to enter! How terrible for you, teachers of the Law and Pharisees! You hypocrites! You sail the seas and cross whole countries to win one convert; and when you succeed, you make him twice as deserving of going to hell as you yourselves are! How terrible for you, blind guides! (PAUSE)

[You teach:]

Lawyer   If someone swears by the Temple, he isn't bound by his vow.

Pharisee   But if he swears by the gold in the Temple, he is bound.

Jesus   Blind fools! Which is more important, the gold or the Temple which makes the gold holy? (PAUSE)

[You also teach:]

Lawyer   If someone swears by the altar, he isn't bound by his vow.

Pharisee   But if he swears by the gift on the altar, he is bound.

Jesus   How blind you are! Which is the more important, the gift or the altar which makes the gift holy? So then, when a person swears by the altar, he is swearing by it and by all the gifts on it; and when he swears by the Temple, he is swearing by it and by God, who lives there; and when someone swears by heaven, he is swearing by God's throne and by him who sits on it.

Cast [This is] the word of the Lord. OR This is the Gospel of Christ / *This is the Gospel of the Lord.*
All **Thanks be to God.**   **Praise to Christ our Lord** / *Praise to you, Lord Jesus Christ.*

Cast: **[Narrator]** (should be omitted when this reading continues from the previous one), **Jesus, Lawyer, Pharisee.**

Who is the greatest?
Mark 9.33–37

Narrator   They came to Capernaum, and after going indoors Jesus asked his disciples:

Jesus   What were you arguing about on the road?

Narrator   But they would not answer him, because on the road they had been arguing among themselves about who was the greatest. Jesus sat down and called the twelve disciples:

Jesus   Whoever wants to be first must place himself last of all and be the servant of all.

Narrator   Then he took a child and made him stand in front of them. He put his arms round him.

Jesus   Whoever welcomes in my name one of the children, welcomes me; and whoever welcomes me, welcomes not only me but also the one who sent me. ·

Cast [This is] the word of the Lord.   OR   This is the Gospel of Christ / *This is the Gospel of the Lord.*
All   **Thanks be to God.**   **Praise to Christ our Lord** / *Praise to you, Lord Jesus Christ.*

Cast: **Narrator, Jesus, John.**

Jesus teaches about divorce
Mark 10.1–12

Narrator   Jesus went to the province of Judaea, and crossed the River Jordan. Crowds came flocking to him again, and he taught them, as he always did.

Some Pharisees came to him and tried to trap him:

Pharisee   Tell us, does our Law allow a man to divorce his wife?

Narrator   Jesus answered with a question:

Jesus   What law did Moses give you?

Pharisee   Moses gave permission for a man to write a divorce notice and send his wife away.

Jesus   Moses wrote this law for you because you are so hard to teach. But in the beginning, at the time of creation, 'God made them male and female,' as the scripture says. 'And for this reason a man will leave his father and mother and unite with his wife, and the two will become one.' So they are no longer two, but one. Man must not separate, then, what God has joined together.

Narrator   When they went back into the house, the disciples asked Jesus about this matter. He said to them:

Jesus   A man who divorces his wife and marries another woman commits adultery against his wife. In the same way, a woman who divorces her husband and marries another man commits adultery.

Cast [This is] the word of the Lord.   OR   This is the Gospel of Christ / *This is the Gospel of the Lord.*
All   **Thanks be to God.**   **Praise to Christ our Lord** / *Praise to you, Lord Jesus Christ.*

Cast: **Narrator, Pharisee, Jesus.**

Jesus blesses little children
Mark 10.[1], 13–16

Narrator   Jesus crossed the river Jordan. Crowds came flocking to him again, and he taught them, as he always did.

Some people brought children to Jesus for him to place his hands on them, but the disciples scolded the people. When Jesus noticed this, he was angry and said to his disciples:

Jesus   Let the children come to me, and do not stop them, because the Kingdom of God belongs to such as these. I assure you that whoever does not receive the Kingdom of God like a child will never enter it.

Narrator   Then he took the children in his arms, placed his hands on each of them, and blessed them.

Cast   [This is] the word of the Lord.   OR   This is the Gospel of Christ / *This is the Gospel of the Lord.*
All   **Thanks be to God.**   **Praise to Christ our Lord** / *Praise to you, Lord Jesus Christ.*

Cast: **Narrator, Jesus.**

Mary visits Elizabeth
Luke 1.39–56

Narrator   Mary got ready and hurried off to a town in the hill-country of Judaea. She went into Zechariah's house and greeted Elizabeth. When Elizabeth heard Mary's greeting, the baby moved within her. Elizabeth was filled with the Holy Spirit [and said in a loud voice]:

Elizabeth   You are the most blessed of all women, and blessed is the child
(delighted)   you will bear! Why should this great thing happen to me, that my Lord's mother comes to visit me? For as soon as I heard your greeting, the baby within me jumped with gladness. How happy you are to believe that the Lord's message to you will come true!

Narrator   Mary said:

Mary   My heart praises the Lord;
my soul is glad because of God my Saviour,
for he has remembered me, his lowly servant!
From now on all people will call me happy,
because of the great things the Mighty God has done for me.
His name is holy;
from one generation to another
he shows mercy to those who honour him.
He has stretched out his mighty arm
and scattered the proud with all their plans.
He has brought down mighty kings from their thrones,
and lifted up the lowly.
He has filled the hungry with good things,
and sent the rich away with empty hands.

He has kept the promise he made to our ancestors,
and has come to the help of his servant Israel.
He has remembered to show mercy to Abraham
and to all his descendants for ever!

[Narrator   Mary stayed about three months with Elizabeth and then went
back home.]

1**Cast** [This is] the word of the Lord.   OR   This is the Gospel of Christ / *This is the Gospel of the Lord.*
All   Thanks be to God.   **Praise to Christ our Lord** / *Praise to you, Lord Jesus Christ.*

Cast: **Narrator, Elizabeth, Mary**.

Jesus as a boy
From Luke 2.39–52

Narrator   When Joseph and Mary had finished doing all that was required by
the law of the Lord, they returned to their home town of Nazareth
in Galilee. The child Jesus grew and became strong; he was full of
wisdom, and God's blessings were upon him. (PAUSE)

Every year the parents of Jesus went to Jerusalem for the Passover
Festival. When Jesus was twelve years old, they went to the festival
as usual. When the festival was over, they started back home, but
the boy Jesus stayed in Jerusalem. His parents did not know this;
they thought that he was with the group, so they travelled a whole
day and then started looking for him among their relatives and
friends. They did not find him, so they went back to Jerusalem
looking for him. On the third day they found him in the Temple,
sitting with the Jewish teachers, listening to them and asking
questions. All who heard him were amazed at his intelligent
answers. His parents were astonished when they saw him, and
his mother said to him:

Mary   My son, why have you done this to us? Your father and I have
been terribly worried trying to find you.

[Narrator   He answered them:]

Jesus   Why did you have to look for me? Didn't you know that I had to
be in my Father's house?

Narrator   But they did not understand his answer. So Jesus went back with
them to Nazareth, where he was obedient to them. His mother
treasured all these things in her heart. Jesus grew both in body
and in wisdom, gaining favour with God and men.

Cast [This is] the word of the Lord.   OR   This is the Gospel of Christ / *This is the Gospel of the Lord.*
All   Thanks be to God.   **Praise to Christ our Lord** / *Praise to you, Lord Jesus Christ.*

Cast: **Narrator, Mary, Jesus** (as a boy).

The two house-builders
Luke 6.46–49

Narrator 1   Jesus said: Why do you call me:

Narrators 1 & 2   Lord, Lord,

Narrator 1   And yet don't do what I tell you? Anyone who comes to me and listens to my words and obeys them—I will show you what he is like. He is like a man who, in building his house, dug deep and laid the foundation on rock. The river overflowed and hit that house but could not shake it, because it was well built.

Narrator 2   But anyone who hears my words and does not obey them is like a man who built his house without laying a foundation; when the flood hit that house it fell at once—and what a terrible crash that was!

Cast   [This is] the word of the Lord.   OR   This is the Gospel of Christ / *This is the Gospel of the Lord.*
All   **Thanks be to God.**   **Praise to Christ our Lord** / *Praise to you, Lord Jesus Christ.*

Cast: **Narrator 1, Narrator 2.**

Jesus visits Martha and Mary
Luke 10.38–42

Narrator   As Jesus and his disciples went on their way, he came to a village where a woman named Martha welcomed him in her home. She had a sister named Mary, who sat down at the feet of the Lord and listened to his teaching. Martha was upset over all the work she had to do, so she came and said:

Martha   Lord, don't you care that my sister has left me to do all the work by myself? Tell her to come and help me!

[Narrator   The Lord answered her:]

Jesus   Martha, Martha! You are worried and troubled over so many things, but just one is needed. Mary has chosen the right thing, and it will not be taken away from her.

Cast   [This is] the word of the Lord.   OR   This is the Gospel of Christ / *This is the Gospel of the Lord.*
All   **Thanks be to God.**   **Praise to Christ our Lord** / *Praise to you, Lord Jesus Christ.*

Cast: **Narrator, Martha, Jesus**.

Jesus the resurrection and the life
From John 11.1–44

Narrator   A man named Lazarus, who lived in Bethany, was ill. Bethany was the town where Mary and her sister Martha lived. This Mary was the one who poured the perfume on the Lord's feet and wiped them with her hair; it was her brother Lazarus who was ill. The sisters sent Jesus a message:

Mary	Lord, your dear friend is ill.
Narrator	When Jesus heard it, he said:
Jesus	The final result of this illness will not be the death of Lazarus; this has happened in order to bring glory to God, and it will be the means by which the Son of God will receive glory.
Narrator	Jesus loved Martha and her sister and Lazarus. Yet when he received the news that Lazarus was ill, he stayed where he was for two more days. Then he said to the disciples:
Jesus	Let us go back to Judaea. Our friend Lazarus has fallen asleep, but I will go and wake him up.(PAUSE)
Narrator	When Jesus arrived, he found that Lazarus had been buried four days before. When Martha heard that Jesus was coming, she went out to meet him, but Mary stayed in the house. Martha said to Jesus:
Martha	If you had been here, Lord, my brother would not have died! But I know that even now God will give you whatever you ask him for.
Jesus	Your brother will rise to life.
Martha	I know that he will rise to life on the last day.
Jesus	I am the resurrection and the life. Whoever believes in me will live, even though he dies; and whoever lives and believes in me will never die. Do you believe this?
Martha	Yes, Lord! I do believe that you are the Messiah, the Son of God, who was to come into the world.
Narrator	After Martha said this, she went back and called her sister Mary privately:
Martha	The Teacher is here, and is asking for you.
Narrator	When Mary heard this, she got up and hurried out to meet him. The people who were in the house with Mary, comforting her, followed her when they saw her get up and hurry out. They thought that she was going to the grave to weep there.(PAUSE)
	Mary arrived where Jesus was, and as soon as she saw him, she fell at his feet and said:
Mary	Lord, if you had been here, my brother would not have died!
Narrator	Jesus saw her weeping, and he saw how the people who were with her were weeping also; his heart was touched, and he was deeply moved.
Jesus	Where have you buried him?
Mary & Martha	Come and see, Lord.
Narrator (slowly)	Jesus wept.
	The people said:

Person 1	See how much he loved him!
Narrator	But some of them said:
Person 2	He gave sight to the blind man, didn't he? Could he not have kept Lazarus from dying?
Narrator	Deeply moved once more, Jesus went to the tomb, which was a cave with a stone placed at the entrance. [Jesus ordered:]
Jesus	Take the stone away!
Martha	There will be a bad smell, Lord. He has been buried four days!
Jesus	Didn't I tell you that you would see God's glory if you believed?
Narrator	They took the stone away. Jesus looked up and said:
Jesus	I thank you, Father, that you listen to me. I know that you always listen to me, but I say this for the sake of the people here, so that they will believe that you sent me.(PAUSE)
(loudly)	Lazarus, come out!
Narrator	He came out, his hands and feet wrapped in grave clothes, and with a cloth round his face. Jesus told them:
Jesus	Untie him, and let him go.

Cast [This is] the word of the Lord. OR This is the Gospel of Christ / *This is the Gospel of the Lord.*
All   **Thanks be to God.**   **Praise to Christ our Lord** / *Praise to you, Lord Jesus Christ.*

Cast: **Narrator, Mary, Jesus, Martha, Person 1, Person 2.**

Jesus is crucified
John 19.17–30

Narrator	Jesus went out, carrying his cross, and came to 'The Place of the Skull', as it is called. In Hebrew it is called 'Golgotha'. There they crucified him; and they also crucified two other men, one on each side, with Jesus between them. Pilate wrote a notice and had it put on the cross.
Pilate	Jesus of Nazareth, the King of the Jews.
Narrator	Many people read it, because the place where Jesus was crucified was not far from the city. The notice was written in Hebrew, Latin, and Greek. The chief priests said to Pilate:
Priest	Do not write 'The King of the Jews', but rather, 'This man said, I am the King of the Jews.'
Pilate	What I have written stays written.
Narrator	After the soldiers had crucified Jesus, they took his clothes and divided them into four parts, one part for each soldier. They also took the robe, which was made of one piece of woven cloth without any seams in it. [The soldiers said to one another:]

Soldier 1
(to Soldier 2)   Let's not tear it.

Soldier 2
(to Soldier 1)   Let's throw dice to see who will get it.

Narrator   This happened in order to make the scripture come true:

Psalmist   They divided my clothes among themselves and gambled for my robe.

Narrator   And this is what the soldiers did.(PAUSE)

Standing close to Jesus' cross were his mother, his mother's sister, Mary the wife of Clopas, and Mary Magdalene. Jesus saw his mother and the disciple he loved standing there; so he said to his mother:

Jesus   He is your son.

Narrator   Then he said to the disciple:

Jesus   She is your mother.

Narrator   From that time the disciple took her to live in his home. (PAUSE)

Jesus knew that by now everything had been completed; and in order to make the scripture come true, he said:

Jesus   I am thirsty.

Narrator   A bowl was there, full of cheap wine; so a sponge was soaked in the wine, put on a stalk of hyssop, and lifted up to his lips. Jesus drank the wine and said:

Jesus   It is finished! (PAUSE)

Narrator   Then he bowed his head and died.

Cast [This is] the word of the Lord. OR This is the Gospel of Christ / *This is the Gospel of the Lord.*
All **Thanks be to God.**   **Praise to Christ our Lord** / *Praise to you, Lord Jesus Christ.*

Cast: **Narrator, Pilate, Priest, Soldier 1, Soldier 2, Psalmist** (can be the same as Priest), **Jesus**.

The Christian family
From Ephesians 5.1–6.12

**Minister
/Leader**   Be imitators of God, therefore, as dearly loved children and live a life of love, just as Christ loved us and gave himself up for us as a fragrant offering and sacrifice to God. Speak to one another with psalms, hymns and spiritual songs. Sing and make music in your heart to the Lord, always giving thanks to God the Father for everything, in the name of our Lord Jesus Christ. Submit to one another out of reverence for Christ.

Wife   Wives, submit to your husbands as to the Lord. For the husband is the head of the wife as Christ is the head of the church, his body, of which he is the Saviour. Now as the church submits to Christ, so also wives should submit to their husbands in everything.

Husband	Husbands, love your wives, just as Christ loved the church and gave himself up for her to make her holy, cleansing her by the washing with water through the word, and to present her to himself as a radiant church, without stain or wrinkle or any other blemish, but holy and blameless. In this same way, husbands ought to love their wives as their own bodies. He who loves his wife loves himself. After all, no-one ever hated his own body, but he feeds and cares for it, just as Christ does the church.
Minister /Leader	For this reason a man will leave his father and mother and be united to his wife, and the two will become one flesh. This is a profound mystery—but I am talking about Christ and the church. However, each one of you also must love his wife as he loves himself, and the wife must respect her husband.
Child	Children, obey your parents in the Lord, for this is right. 'Honour your father and mother'—which is the first commandment with a promise—'that it may go well with you and that you may enjoy long life on the earth.'
Father	Fathers, do not exasperate your children; instead, bring them up in the training and instruction of the Lord.
Minister /Leader	Finally, be strong in the Lord and in his mighty power. Put on the full armour of God so that you can take your stand against the Devil's schemes. For our struggle is not against flesh and blood, but against the rulers, against the authorities, against the powers of this dark world and against the spiritual forces of evil in the heavenly realms.
Cast	[This is] the word of the Lord.
All	**Thanks be to God.**

Cast: **Minister/Leader, Wife, Husband, Child, Father.**

Christian do's and don'ts
From Ephesians 5.3–20

Don't	Since you are God's people, it is not right that any matters of sexual immorality or indecency or greed should even be mentioned among you. Nor is it fitting for you to use language which is obscene, profane, or vulgar.
Do	Rather you should give thanks to God.
Don't	You may be sure that no one who is immoral, indecent, or greedy—for greed is a form of idolatry—will ever receive a share in the Kingdom of Christ and of God. (PAUSE)
	Do not let anyone deceive you with foolish words; it is because of these very things that God's anger will come upon those who do not obey him. So have nothing at all to do with such people.
Do	You yourselves used to be in the darkness, but since you have become the Lord's people, you are in the light. So you must live

like people who belong to the light, for it is the light that brings a rich harvest of every kind of goodness, righteousness, and truth. Try to learn what pleases the Lord.

Don't   Have nothing to do with the worthless things that people do, things that belong to the darkness.

Do   Instead, bring them out to the light. And when all things are brought out to the light, then their true nature is clearly revealed; for anything that is clearly revealed becomes light.

Don't   Don't live like ignorant people, but like wise people.

Do   Make good use of every opportunity you have, because these are evil days.

Don't   Don't be fools, then.

Do   But try to find out what the Lord wants you to do.

Don't   Do not get drunk with wine, which will only ruin you.

Do   Instead, be filled with the Spirit. (PAUSE) Speak to one another with the words of psalms, hymns, and sacred songs; sing hymns and psalms to the Lord with praise in your hearts. In the name of our Lord Jesus Christ, always give thanks for everything to God the Father.

Cast   [This is] the word of the Lord.
All   **Thanks be to God.**

Cast: **Don't** (a negative voice), **Do** (a positive voice).

God's chosen people
Colossians 3.12–17 [3.18–4.1]

Voice 1   As God's chosen people, holy and dearly loved, clothe yourselves with compassion, kindness, humility, gentleness and patience.

Voice 2   Bear with each other and forgive whatever grievances you may have against one another—

Voice 1   Forgive as the Lord forgave you.

Voice 2   And over all these virtues put on love, which binds them all together in perfect unity.

Voice 1   Let the peace of Christ rule in your hearts, since as members of one body you were called to peace.

Voices 1 and **2**
(slowly)   And be thankful. (PAUSE)

Voice 1   Let the word of Christ dwell in you richly as you teach and admonish one another with all wisdom, and as you sing psalms, hymns and spiritual songs with gratitude in your hearts to God.

Voice 2   And whatever you do, whether in word or deed, do it all in the name of the Lord Jesus, giving thanks to God the Father through him.

[Voice 3	Wives, submit to your husbands, as is fitting in the Lord.
Voice 1	Husbands, love your wives and do not be harsh with them.
Voice 2	Children, obey your parents in everything, for this pleases the Lord.
Voice 3	Fathers, do not embitter your children, or they will become discouraged.
Voice 1	Slaves, obey your earthly masters in everything; and do it, not only when their eye is on you and to win their favour, but with sincerity of heart and reverence for the Lord.
Voice 2	Whatever you do, work at it with all your heart, as working for the Lord, not for men, since you know that you will receive an inheritance from the Lord as a reward. It is the Lord Christ you are serving.
Voice 1	Anyone who does wrong will be repaid for his wrong, and there is no favouritism.
Voice 3	Masters, provide your slaves with what is right and fair, because you know that you also have a Master in heaven.]**
Cast	[This is] the word of the Lord.
All	**Thanks be to God.**

Cast: **Voice 1, Voice 2 [Voice 3** (preferably female)].

PASSIONTIDE/
GOOD FRIDAY/
EASTER EVE

The first Passover
Exodus 12.21–36

Narrator Moses called for all the leaders of Israel [and said to them]:

Moses Each of you is to choose a lamb or a young goat and kill it, so that your families can celebrate Passover. Take a sprig of hyssop, dip it in the bowl containing the animal's blood, and wipe the blood on the door-posts and the beam above the door of your house. Not one of you is to leave the house until morning. When the Lord goes through Egypt to kill the Egyptians, he will see the blood on the beams and the door-posts and will not let the Angel of Death enter your houses and kill you. You and your children must obey these rules for ever. When you enter the land that the Lord has promised to give you, you must perform this ritual. When your children ask you, 'What does this ritual mean?' you will answer, 'It is the sacrifice of Passover to honour the Lord, because he passed over the houses of the Israelites in Egypt. He killed the Egyptians, but spared us.'

Narrator The Israelites knelt down and worshipped. Then they went and did what the Lord had commanded Moses and Aaron. (PAUSE)

At midnight the Lord killed all the first-born sons in Egypt, from the king's son, who was heir to the throne, to the son of the prisoner in the dungeon; all the first-born of the animals were also killed. That night, the king, his officials, and all the other Egyptians were awakened. There was loud crying throughout Egypt, because there was not one home in which there was not a dead son. That same night the king sent for Moses and Aaron [and said]:

King Get out, you and your Israelites! Leave my country; go and worship the Lord, as you asked. Take your sheep, goats and cattle, and leave. Also pray for a blessing on me.

Narrator The Egyptians urged the people to hurry and leave the country:

Egyptian We will all be dead if you don't leave.

Narrator So the people filled their baking-pans with unleavened dough, wrapped them in clothing, and carried them on their shoulders. The Israelites had done as Moses had said, and had asked the Egyptians for gold and silver jewellery and for clothing. The Lord made the Egyptians respect the people and give them what they asked for. In this way the Israelites carried away the wealth of the Egyptians.

Cast [This is] the word of the Lord.
All **Thanks be to God.**

Cast: **Narrator, Moses, King, Egyptian**.

Aaron offers sacrifices
From Leviticus 9.2–24

Narrator   Moses spoke to Aaron:

Moses   Take a young bull and a ram without any defects and offer them to the Lord, the bull for a sin-offering and the ram for a burnt-offering. Then tell the people of Israel to take a male goat for a sin-offering, a one-year-old calf, and a one-year-old lamb without any defects for a burnt-offering, and a bull and a ram for a fellowship-offering. They are to sacrifice them to the Lord with the grain-offering mixed with oil. They must do this because the Lord will appear to them today.

Narrator   They brought to the front of the Tent everything that Moses had commanded, and the whole community assembled there to worship the Lord. [Moses said:]

Moses (to audience)   The Lord has commanded you to do all this, so that the dazzling light of his presence can appear to you.

Narrator   Then he said to Aaron:

Moses   Go to the altar and offer the sin-offering and the burnt-offering to take away your sins and the sins of the people. Present this offering to take away the sins of the people, just as the Lord commanded.

Narrator   Aaron went to the altar and killed the young bull which was for his own sin-offering. His sons brought him the blood, and he dipped his finger in it, put some of it on the projections at the corners of the altar, and poured out the rest of it at the base of the altar.

When Aaron had finished all the sacrifices, he raised his hands over the people and blessed them, and then stepped down. Moses and Aaron went into the Tent of the Lord's presence, and when they came out, they blessed the people, and the dazzling light of the Lord's presence appeared to all the people. Suddenly the Lord sent a fire, and it consumed the burnt-offering and the fat parts on the altar. When the people saw it, they all shouted and bowed down with their faces to the ground.

Cast   [This is] the word of the Lord.
All   **Thanks be to God.**

Cast: **Narrator, Moses.**

The snake made of bronze
Numbers 21.4–9

Narrator   The Israelites left Mount Hor by the road that leads to the Gulf of Aqaba, in order to go round the territory of Edom. But on the way the people lost their patience and spoke against God and Moses. They complained:

Israelite 1   Why did you bring us out of Egypt to die in this desert, where there is no food or water?

Israelite 2	We can't stand any more of this miserable food!
Narrator	Then the Lord sent poisonous snakes among the people, and many Israelites were bitten and died. The people came to Moses and said:
Israelite 2	We sinned when we spoke against the Lord and against you.
Israelite 1	Now pray to the Lord to take these snakes away.
Narrator	So Moses prayed for the people. Then the Lord told Moses to make a metal snake and put it on a pole, so that anyone who was bitten could look at it and be healed. So Moses made a bronze snake and put it on a pole. Anyone who had been bitten would look at the bronze snake and be healed.
Cast	[This is] the word of the Lord.
All	**Thanks be to God.**

Cast: **Narrator, Israelite 1, Israelite 2** (can be the same as Israelite 1).

David flees from Jerusalem
2 Samuel 15.23–37

Narrator	The king crossed the brook of Kidron, followed by his men, and together they went out towards the wilderness.
	Zadok the priest was there, and with him were the Levites, carrying the sacred Covenant Box. They set it down and didn't pick it up again until all the people had left the city. The priest Abiathar was there too. Then the king said to Zadok:
David	Take the Covenant Box back to the city. If the Lord is pleased with me, some day he will let me come back to see it and the place where it stays. But if he isn't pleased with me—well, then, let him do to me what he wishes.
[Narrator	And he went on to say to Zadok:]
David	Look, take your son Ahimaaz and Abiathar's son Jonathan and go back to the city in peace. Meanwhile, I will wait at the river crossings in the wilderness until I receive news from you.
Narrator	So Zadok and Abiathar took the Covenant Box back into Jerusalem and stayed there. David went on up the Mount of Olives weeping; he was barefoot and had his head covered as a sign of grief. All who followed him covered their heads and wept also. When David was told that Ahithophel had joined Absalom's rebellion, he prayed:
David	Please, Lord, turn Ahithophel's advice into nonsense!
Narrator	When David reached the top of the hill, where there was a place of worship, his trusted friend Hushai the Archite met him with his clothes torn and with earth on his head. David said to him:
David	You will be of no help to me if you come with me, but you can help me by returning to the city and telling Absalom that you will

now serve him as faithfully as you served his father. And do all you can to oppose any advice that Ahithophel gives. The priests Zadok and Abiathar will be there; tell them everything you hear in the king's palace. They have their sons Ahimaaz and Jonathan with them, and you can send them to me with all the information you gather.

Narrator   So Hushai, David's friend, returned to the city just as Absalom was arriving.

Cast   [This is] the word of the Lord.
All   **Thanks be to God.**

Cast: **Narrator, David.**

The great king
Psalm 24.1–10 (LIT)

Leader   The earth is the Lord's, and everything in it:
All   **the world, and all who live here.**

Leader   He founded it upon the seas:
All   **and established it upon the waters.**

Enquirer   Who has the right to go up the Lord's hill; who may enter his holy temple?
All   **Those who have clean hands and a pure heart, who do not worship idols or swear by what is false.**

Leader   They receive blessing continually from the Lord:
All   **and righteousness from the God of their salvation.**

Leader   Such are the people who seek for God:
All   **who enter the presence of the God of Jacob.**

Director   Fling wide the gates, open the ancient doors:
All   **that the king of glory may come in.**

Enquirer   Who is the king of glory?
All   **The Lord, strong and mighty, the Lord mighty in battle.**

Director   Fling wide the gates, open the ancient doors:
All   **that the king of glory may come in.**

Enquirer   Who is he, this king of glory?
All   **The Lord almighty, he is the king of glory.**

All   **Glory to the Father, and to the Son, and to the Holy Spirit:**
as it was in the beginning, is now, and shall be for ever. Amen.

Cast: **Leader, All** (two or more persons/congregation), **Enquirer, Director.**

A cry of anguish and a song of praise
Psalm 22.1–31

Lonely person

My God, my God, why have you abandoned me?
I have cried desperately for help,
but still it does not come.
During the day I call to you, my God,
but you do not answer;
I call at night,
but get no rest.

Singer

You are enthroned as the Holy One,
the one whom Israel praises.
Our ancestors put their trust in you;
they trusted you, and you saved them.
They called to you and escaped from danger;
they trusted you and were not disappointed.

Despised person

But I am no longer a man; I am a worm,
despised and scorned by everyone!
All who see me jeer at me;
they stick out their tongues and shake their heads.
They say:

Accuser 1

You relied on the Lord.
Why doesn't he save you?

Accuser 2

If the Lord likes you,
why doesn't he help you?

Lonely person

It was you who brought me safely through birth,
and when I was a baby, you kept me safe.
I have relied on you since the day I was born,
and you have always been my God.
Do not stay away from me!
Trouble is near,
and there is no one to help.

Despised person

Many enemies surround me like bulls;
they are all round me,
like fierce bulls from the land of Bashan.
They open their mouths like lions,
roaring and tearing at me.

Lonely person

My strength is gone,
gone like water spilt on the ground.
All my bones are out of joint;
my heart is like melted wax.
My throat is as dry as dust,
and my tongue sticks to the roof of my mouth.
You have left me for dead in the dust.

Despised person

A gang of evil men is round me;
like a pack of dogs they close in on me;
they tear at my hands and feet.

All my bones can be seen.
My enemies look at me and stare.
They gamble for my clothes
and divide them among themselves.

O Lord, don't stay away from me!
Come quickly to my rescue!
Save me from the sword;
save my life from these dogs.
Rescue me from these lions;
I am helpless before these wild bulls.

Lonely person   I will tell my people what you have done;
I will praise you in their assembly:

Singer   Praise him, you servants of the Lord!
Honour him, you descendants of Jacob!
Worship him, you people of Israel!
He does not neglect the poor or ignore their suffering;
he does not turn away from them,
but answers when they call for help.

Lonely person   In the full assembly I will praise you for what you have done;
in the presence of those who worship you
I will offer the sacrifices I promised.

Despised person   The poor will eat as much as they want;
those who come to the Lord will praise him.
May they prosper for ever!

Lonely person   All nations will remember the Lord.
From every part of the world they will turn to him;
all races will worship him.
The Lord is king,
and he rules the nations.

Despised person   All proud men will bow down to him;
all mortal men will bow down before him.

Lonely person   Future generations will serve him;
men will speak of the Lord to the coming generation.
People not yet born will be told:

Cast   The Lord saved his people.

Cast [This is] the word of the Lord.   OR   **All Glory to the Father, and to the Son, and to the Holy Spirit:**
All   **Thanks be to God.**   **as it was in the beginning, is now, and shall be for ever. Amen.**

Cast: **Lonely person, Singer, Despised person, Accuser 1, Accuser** 2 (can be the same as Accuser 1).

The suffering servant
Isaiah 52.13–53.12

Isaiah   The Lord says:

The Lord   My servant will succeed in his task; he will be highly honoured. Many people were shocked when they saw him; he was so disfigured that he hardly looked human. But now many nations will marvel at him, and kings will be speechless with amazement. They will see and understand something they had never known.

Isaiah   The people reply:

Person 1   Who would have believed what we now report?

Person 2   Who could have seen the Lord's hand in this?

Person 1   It was the will of the Lord that his servant should grow like a plant taking root in dry ground.

Person 2   He had no dignity or beauty to make us take notice of him.

Person 1   There was nothing attractive about him—

Person 2   Nothing that would draw us to him.

Person 1   We despised him and rejected him.

Person 2   He endured suffering and pain.

Person 1   No one would even look at him—

Person 2   We ignored him as if he were nothing.

Person 3   But he endured the suffering that should have been ours—

Person 1   The pain that we should have borne.

Person 2   All the while we thought that his suffering was punishment sent by God.

Person 3   But because of our sins he was wounded—

Person 2   Beaten because of the evil we did.

Person 3   We are healed by the punishment he suffered—

Person 1   Made whole by the blows he received.

Persons 1–3   All of us were like sheep that were lost—

Person 2   Each of us going his own way.

Person 3   But the Lord made the punishment fall on him—

Persons 1 and 2 The punishment all of us deserved.

Person 1   He was treated harshly, but endured it humbly—

Person 3   He never said a word.

Person 1   Like a lamb about to be slaughtered—

Person 2   Like a sheep about to be sheared—

Person 3	He never said a word.
Person 1	He was arrested and sentenced and led off to die—
Person 2	And no one cared about his fate.
Person 3 (slowly)	He was put to death for the sins of our people.
Person 1	He was placed in a grave with evil men.
Person 2	He was buried with the rich—
Person 1	Even though he had never committed a crime—
Person 3	Or ever told a lie.
Isaiah	The Lord says:
The Lord	It was my will that he should suffer; his death was a sacrifice to bring forgiveness. And so he will see his descendants; he will live a long life, and through him my purpose will succeed. After a life of suffering, he will again have joy; he will know that he did not suffer in vain. My devoted servant, with whom I am pleased, will bear the punishment of many and for his sake I will forgive them. And so I will give him a place of honour, a place among great and powerful men. He willingly gave his life and shared the fate of evil men. He took the place of many sinners and prayed that they might be forgiven.
Cast	[This is] the word of the Lord.
All	**Thanks be to God.**

Cast: **Isaiah, The Lord, Person 1, Person 2, Person 3** (Persons 1–3 can be the same).

Jesus speaks a third time about his death
Matthew 20.17–19

Narrator	As Jesus was going up to Jerusalem, he took the twelve disciples aside and spoke to them privately, as they walked along. He told them:
Jesus	Listen, we are going up to Jerusalem, where the Son of Man will be handed over to the chief priests and the teachers of the Law.

They will condemn him to death and then hand him over to the Gentiles, who will mock him, whip him, and crucify him; but three days later he will be raised to life.

Cast [This is] the word of the Lord. OR This is Gospel of Christ / *This is the Gospel of the Lord.*
All **Thanks be to God**.   **Praise to Christ our Lord** / *Praise to you, Lord Jesus Christ.*

Cast: **Narrator, Jesus.**

PASSION READINGS

FROM MARK'S GOSPEL

CAST OF READERS
for the dramatised Passion Readings

Narrator 1, Narrator 2 (strong experienced voice), Voice 1
Jesus
Pilate (authoritative voice)
Priest, Soldier, Young Man, Person 1, Bystander
High Priest, Lawyer 1
Disciple, Peter
Judas, Lawyer 2, Commentator
Girl, Person 2
Voice 2 (to contrast with Voice 1)
Crowd

The cast are best disposed about the building. For instance: 'Jesus' in the pulpit, 'Narrator' at the lectern (if different), 'Pilate' (accompanied by 'Jesus') in a gallery or other place remote from the 'Crowd'. The Crowd, if well-rehearsed and co-ordinated, can be placed about the congregation. Otherwise they are best in a position opposite where 'Pilate' and 'Jesus' will be. It is most effective if they rise from their seats to play their part.

Jesus speaks about his death
Mark 10.32–34

Narrator   Jesus and his disciples were now on the road going up to Jerusalem. Jesus was going ahead of the disciples, who were filled with alarm; the people who followed behind were afraid. Once again Jesus took the twelve disciples aside and spoke of the things that were going to happen to him:

Jesus   Listen, we are going up to Jerusalem where the Son of Man will be handed over to the chief priests and the teachers of the Law. They will condemn him to death and then hand him over to the Gentiles, who will mock him, spit on him, whip him, and kill him; but three days later he will rise to life.

Narrator   [This is] the word of the Lord.
All   **Thanks be to God.**

HYMN: e.g. All glory, laud/praise and honour'

Jesus enters Jerusalem and the Temple
From Mark 11

Narrator   As they approached Jerusalem, near the towns of Bethphage and Bethany, they came to the Mount of Olives. Jesus sent two of his disciples on ahead with these instructions:

Jesus   Go to the village there ahead of you. As soon as you get there, you will find a colt tied up that has never been ridden. Untie it and bring it here. And if someone asks you why you are doing that, tell him that the Master needs it and will send it back at once.

Narrator   So they went and found a colt out in the street, tied to the door of a house. As they were untying it, some of the bystanders asked them:

Person 1   What are you doing—untying that colt?

Narrator   They answered just as Jesus had told them, and the men let them go. They brought the colt to Jesus, threw their cloaks over the animal, and Jesus got on. Many people spread their cloaks on the road, while others cut branches in the fields and spread them on the road. The people who were in front and those who followed behind began to shout:

Persons 1 and **2**   Praise God!

Person 1   God bless him who comes in the name of the Lord!

Person 2   God bless the coming kingdom of King David, our father!

Persons 1 and **2**   Praise God!

Narrator   When they arrived in Jerusalem, Jesus went to the Temple and began to drive out all those who were buying and selling. He overturned the tables of the money-changers and the stools of those who sold pigeons, and he would not let anyone carry anything through the temple courtyards. He then taught the people:

Jesus   It is written in the Scriptures that God said, 'My Temple will be called a house of prayer for the people of all nations.' But you have turned it into a hideout for thieves!

Narrator   The chief priests and the teachers of the Law heard of this, so they began looking for some way to kill Jesus. They were afraid of him, because the whole crowd was amazed at his teaching.

                     When evening came, Jesus and his disciples left the city. (PAUSE)

Narrator   [This is] the word of the Lord.
All   **Thanks be to God**.

HYMN: e.g. 'Ride on, ride on in majesty'

The plot and the passover
From Mark 14.1–21

Narrator   It was now two days before the Festival of Passover and Unleavened Bread. The chief priests and the teachers of the Law were looking for a way to arrest Jesus secretly and put him to death:

Priest   We must not do it during the festival.

Lawyer 1   The people might riot.

Narrator   Then Judas Iscariot, one of the twelve disciples, went off to the chief priests in order to betray Jesus to them. They were pleased to hear what he had to say, and promised to give him money. So Judas started looking for a good chance to hand Jesus over to them.

                     On the first day of the Festival of Unleavened Bread, the day the lambs for the Passover meal were killed, Jesus' disciples asked him:

Disciple   Where do you want us to go and get the Passover meal ready for you?

Narrator   Then Jesus sent two of them with these instructions:

Jesus   Go into the city, and a man carrying a jar of water will meet you. Follow him to the house he enters, and say to the owner of the house: 'The Teacher says, Where is the room where my disciples and I will eat the Passover meal?' Then he will show you a large upstairs room, prepared and furnished, where you will get everything ready for us.

Narrator   The disciples left, went to the city, and found everything just as Jesus had told them; and they prepared the Passover meal. (PAUSE)

                     When it was evening, Jesus came with the twelve disciples. While they were at the table eating, Jesus said:

Jesus   I tell you that one of you will betray me—one who is eating with me.

Narrator	The disciples were upset and began to ask him, one after the other:
Disciple	Surely you don't mean me, do you?
Jesus	It will be one of you twelve, one who dips his bread in the dish with me. The Son of Man will die as the Scriptures say he will; but how terrible for that man who betrays the Son of Man! It would have been better for that man if he had never been born!
Narrator **All**	[This is] the word of the Lord. **Thanks be to God**.

HYMN: e.g. 'No weight of gold or silver'—Passion Chorale

The Lord's Supper
Mark 14.22–26

Narrator	While they were eating, Jesus took a piece of bread, gave a prayer of thanks, broke it, and gave it to his disciples. [He said:]
Jesus	Take it, this is my body.
Narrator	Then he took a cup, gave thanks to God, and handed it to them; and they all drank from it.
Jesus	This is my blood which is poured out for many, my blood which seals God's covenant. I tell you, I will never again drink this wine until the day I drink the new wine in the Kingdom of God.
Narrator	Then they sang a hymn and went out to the Mount of Olives.
Narrator **All**	[This is] the word of the Lord. **Thanks be to God**.

PSALM VERSION: eg Psalm 22

Jesus is deserted and arrested
Mark 14.27–52

Narrator	Jesus said to them:
Jesus	All of you will run away and leave me, for the scripture says, 'God will kill the shepherd, and the sheep will all be scattered.' But after I am raised to life, I will go to Galilee ahead of you.
Narrator	Peter answered:
Peter	I will never leave you, even though all the rest do!
Jesus (to Peter)	I tell you that before the cock crows twice tonight, you will say three times that you do not know me.
Peter (insistently)	I will never say that, even if I have to die with you!
Narrator	And all the other disciples said the same thing.
	They came to a place called Gethsemane, and Jesus said to his disciples:

Jesus	Sit here while I pray.
Narrator	He took Peter, James, and John with him. Distress and anguish came over him:
Jesus	The sorrow in my heart is so great that it almost crushes me. Stay here and keep watch.
Narrator	He went a little farther on, threw himself on the ground, and prayed that, if possible, he might not have to go through that time of suffering:
Jesus	Father, my Father! All things are possible for you. Take this cup of suffering away from me. (PAUSE) Yet not what I want, but what you want.
Narrator	Then he returned and found the three disciples asleep. He said to Peter:
Jesus	Simon, are you asleep? Weren't you able to stay awake even for one hour?
Jesus (looking round)	Keep watch, and pray that you will not fall into temptation. The spirit is willing, but the flesh is weak.
Narrator	He went away once more and prayed, saying the same words.
	(PAUSE) Then he came back to the disciples and found them asleep: they could not keep their eyes open. And they did not know what to say to him. (PAUSE) He came back the third time . . .
Jesus	Are you still sleeping and resting? Enough! The hour has come! Look, the Son of Man is now being handed over to the power of sinful men. Get up, let us go. Look, here is the man who is betraying me!
Narrator	Jesus was still speaking when Judas, one of the twelve disciples, arrived. With him was a crowd armed with swords and clubs, and sent by the chief priests, the teachers of the Law, and the elders. The traitor had given the crowd a signal:
Judas	The man I kiss is the one you want. Arrest him and take him away under guard.
Narrator	As soon as Judas arrived, he went up to Jesus . . .
Judas	Teacher!
Narrator	. . . and kissed him. So they arrested Jesus and held him tight. But one of those standing there drew his sword and struck at the High Priest's slave, cutting off his ear. Then Jesus spoke up:
Jesus	Did you have to come with swords and clubs to capture me, as though I were an outlaw? Day after day I was with you teaching in the Temple, and you did not arrest me. But the Scriptures must come true.
Narrator	Then all the disciples left him and ran away. (PAUSE)
	A certain young man, dressed only in a linen cloth, was following

Jesus. They tried to arrest him, but he ran away naked, leaving the cloth behind.

Narrator   [This is] the word of the Lord.
All   **Thanks be to God**.

HYMN: e.g. 'It is a thing most wonderful'

Jesus before the High Priest
Mark 14. 53–72

Narrator   Jesus was taken to the High Priest's house, where all the chief priests, the elders, and the teachers of the Law were gathering. Peter followed from a distance and went into the courtyard of the High Priest's house. There he sat down with the guards, keeping himself warm by the fire. The chief priests and the whole Council tried to find some evidence against Jesus in order to put him to death, but they could not find any. Many witnesses told lies against Jesus, but their stories did not agree.

Then some men stood up and told this lie against Jesus:

Man   We heard him say, 'I will tear down this Temple which men have made, and after three days I will build one that is not made by men.'

Narrator   Not even they, however, could make their stories agree.

The High Priest stood up in front of them all and questioned Jesus:

High Priest   Have you no answer to the accusation they bring against you?

Narrator   But Jesus kept quiet and would not say a word. Again the High Priest questioned him:

High Priest   Are you the Messiah, the Son of the Blessed God?

Jesus   I am, and you will all see the Son of Man seated on the right of the Almighty and coming with the clouds of heaven!

Narrator   The High Priest tore his robes:

High Priest   We don't need any more witnesses! You heard his blasphemy. What is your decision?

Narrator   They all voted against him: he was guilty and should be put to death.

Some of them began to spit on Jesus, and they blindfolded him and hit him:

Man   Guess who hit you!

Narrator   And the guards took him and slapped him.

Peter was still down in the courtyard when one of the High Priest's servant-girls came by. When she saw Peter warming himself, she looked straight at him:

Girl	You, too, were with Jesus of Nazareth.
Peter (denying)	I don't know . . . I don't understand what you are talking about.
Narrator	And he went out into the passage. Just then a cock crowed. (PAUSE) The servant-girl saw him there and began to repeat to the by-standers:
Girl	He is one of them!
Narrator	But Peter denied it again. (PAUSE) A little while later the bystanders accused Peter again:
Bystander	You can't deny that you are one of them, because you, too, are from Galilee.
Peter	I swear that I am telling the truth! May God punish me if I am not! I do not know the man you are talking about.
Narrator	Just then a cock crowed a second time, and Peter remembered how Jesus had said to him, 'Before the cock crows twice, you will say three times that you do not know me.' And he broke down and cried.
Narrator **All**	[This is] the word of the Lord. **Thanks be to God.**

HYMN: e.g. 'He stood before the court'

Jesus before Pilate
Mark 15. 1–15

Narrator	Early in the morning the chief priests met hurriedly with the elders, the teachers of the Law, and the whole Council, and made their plans. They put Jesus in chains, led him away, and handed him over to Pilate. Pilate questioned him:
Pilate	Are you the king of the Jews?
Jesus	So you say.
Narrator	The chief priests were accusing Jesus of many things, so Pilate questioned him again:
Pilate	Aren't you going to answer? Listen to all their accusations!
Narrator	Again Jesus refused to say a word and Pilate was amazed. (PAUSE) At every Passover Festival Pilate was in the habit of setting free any one prisoner the people asked for. At that time a man named Barabbas was in prison with the rebels who had committed murder in the riot. When the crowd gathered and began to ask Pilate for the usual favour, he asked them:
Pilate (calling)	Do you want me to set free for you the king of the Jews?

Narrator	He knew very well that the chief priests had handed Jesus over to him because they were jealous.
	But the chief priests stirred up the crowd to ask, instead, for Pilate to set Barabbas free for them. Pilate spoke again to the crowd:
Pilate	What, then, do you want me to do with the one you call the king of the Jews?
Crowd	Crucify him!
Pilate	But what crime has he committed?
Crowd (louder)	Crucify him!
Narrator	Pilate wanted to please the crowd, so he set Barabbas free for them. Then he had Jesus whipped and handed him over to be crucified.
Narrator	[This is] the word of the Lord.
All	**Thanks be to God**.

HYMN: e.g. 'There is a green hill'

Jesus is crucified
Mark 15. 16–32

Narrator	The soldiers took Jesus inside to the courtyard of the governor's palace and called together the rest of the company. They put a purple robe on Jesus, made a crown out of thorny branches, and put it on his head. Then they began to salute him:
Soldier(s)	Long live the King of the Jews!
Narrator	They beat him over the head with a stick, spat on him, fell on their knees, and bowed down to him. When they had finished mocking him, they took off the purple robe and put his own clothes back on him. Then they led him out to crucify him. (PAUSE)
	On the way they met a man named Simon, who was coming into the city from the country, and the soldiers forced him to carry Jesus' cross.
Commentator	(Simon was from Cyrene and was the father of Alexander and Rufus.)
Narrator	They took Jesus to a place called Golgotha, which means 'The Place of the Skull'. There they tried to give him wine mixed with a drug called myrrh, but Jesus would not drink it. Then they crucified him and divided his clothes among themselves, throwing dice to see who would get which piece of clothing. It was nine o'clock in the morning when they crucified him. The notice of the accusation against him said:
Voice of Pilate (slowly)	The King of the Jews.
Narrator	They also crucified two bandits with Jesus, one on his right and the other on his left.
	People passing by shook their heads and hurled insults at Jesus:

Persons 1 and **2**	Aha!
Person 1	You were going to tear down the Temple and build it up again in three days!
Person 2	Now come down from the cross and save yourself!
Narrator	In the same way the chief priests and the teachers of the Law jeered at Jesus, saying to each other:
Lawyer 1	He saved others, but he cannot save himself!
Lawyer 2	Let us see the Messiah, the King of Israel, come down from the cross now, and we will believe in him!
Narrator	And the two who were crucified with Jesus insulted him also.
Narrator **All**	[This is] the word of the Lord. **Thanks be to God**.

CHORALE: e.g. 'A purple robe'; 'Were you there'

The death of Jesus
Mark 15.33–39.

Narrator	At noon the whole country was covered with darkness, which lasted for three hours. At three o'clock Jesus cried out with a loud shout:
Jesus	Eloi, Eloi. lema sabachthani?
Narrator	Which means: My God, my God, why did you abandon me? Some of the people there heard him:
Person 1	Listen, he is calling for Elijah!
Narrator	One of them ran up with a sponge, soaked it in cheap wine, and put it on the end of a stick. Then he held it up to Jesus' lips:
Person 2	Wait! Let us see if Elijah is coming to bring him down from the cross! (PAUSE)
Narrator	With a loud cry Jesus died. (PAUSE)
	The curtain hanging in the Temple was torn in two, from top to bottom. The army officer who was standing there in front of the cross saw how Jesus had died:
Soldier	This man was really the **Son of God**!
Narrator **All**	[This is] the word of the Lord. **Thanks be to God**.

PRAYER – Reflecting on the Passion story in response to Prayer—

SONG: e.g. 'Jesus, name above all names'

Christ and us
1 Peter 2. 21–24

Voice 1   Christ himself suffered for you and left you an example, so that you would follow in his steps.

Voice 2   He committed no sin, and no one has ever heard a lie come from his lips.

Voice 1   When he was insulted, he did not answer back with an insult:

Voice 2   When he suffered, he did not threaten, but placed his hopes in God, the righteous Judge.

Voice 1 and **2**   Christ himself carried our sins in his body to the cross, so that we might die to sin and live for righteousness.

Voice 2   It is by his wounds that you have been healed.

Narrator   [This is] the word of the Lord.
All   **Thanks be to God**.

HYMN: e.g. 'When I survey the wondrous cross'

EASTER

The Lord defeats the Egyptians

From Exodus 14.10–29

Narrator

When the Israelites saw the king and his army marching against them, they were terrified and cried out to the Lord for help. They said to Moses:

Israelite 1

Weren't there any graves in Egypt? Did you have to bring us out here in the desert to die?

Israelite 2

Look what you have done by bringing us out of Egypt! Didn't we tell you before we left that this would happen?

Israelite 3

We told you to leave us alone and let us go on being slaves of the Egyptians. It would be better to be slaves there than to die here in the desert.

[Narrator

Moses answered:]

Moses
(firmly)

Don't be afraid! Stand your ground, and you will see what the Lord will do to save you today; you will never see these Egyptians again. The Lord will fight for you, and there is no need for you to do anything.

Narrator

The Lord said to Moses:

The Lord

Why are you crying out for help? Tell the people to move forward. Lift up your stick and hold it out over the sea. The water will divide, and the Israelites will be able to walk through the sea on dry ground. I will make the Egyptians so stubborn that they will go in after them, and I will gain honour by my victory over the king, his army, his chariots, and his drivers. When I defeat them, the Egyptians will know that I am the Lord.

Narrator

Moses held out his hand over the sea, and the Lord drove the sea back with a strong east wind. It blew all night and turned the sea into dry land. The water was divided, and the Israelites went through the sea on dry ground, with walls of water on both sides. The Egyptians pursued them and went after them into the sea with all their horses, chariots, and drivers. Just before dawn the Lord looked down from the pillar of fire and cloud at the Egyptian army and threw them into a panic. He made the wheels of their chariots get stuck, so that they moved with great difficulty. The Egyptians said:

Egyptian 1

The Lord is fighting for the Israelites against us.

Egyptian 2

Let's get out of here!

Narrator

The Lord said to Moses:

The Lord

Hold out your hand over the sea, and the water will come back over the Egyptians and their chariots and drivers.

Narrator

So Moses held out his hand over the sea, and at daybreak the water returned to its normal level. The Egyptians tried to escape from the water, but the Lord threw them into the sea. The water returned and covered the chariots, the drivers, and all the Egyptian army that had followed the Israelites into the sea; not one of them was left. But the Israelites walked through the sea on dry ground, with walls of water on both sides.

Cast	[This is] the word of the Lord.
All	**Thanks be to God.**

Cast: **Narrator, Israelite 1, Israelite 2, Israelite 3** (Israelites 1–3 can be the same), **Moses, The Lord, Egyptian 1, Egyptian 2** (can be the same as Egyptian 1).

The love of God
From Psalm 103.1–22 (LIT)

Leader	Praise the Lord, my soul:
All	**all my being, praise his holy name!**
Leader	Praise the Lord, my soul:
All	**and do not forget how generous he is.**
All (group 1)	**He forgives all my sins:**
All (group 2)	**and heals all my diseases.**
All (group 1)	**He keeps me from the grave:**
All (group 2)	**and blesses me with love and mercy.**
Leader	The Lord is gracious and compassionate:
All (group 1)	**slow to become angry,**
All (group 2)	**and full of constant love.**
All (group 1)	**He does not keep on rebuking:**
All (group 2)	**he is not angry for ever.**
All (group 1)	**He does not punish us as we deserve:**
All (group 2)	**or repay us for our wrongs.**
All (group 1)	**As far as the east is from the west:**
All (group 2)	**so far does he remove our sins from us.**
Leader	As kind as a Father to his children:
All (group 1)	**so kind is the Lord to those who honour him.**
Leader	Praise the Lord, all his creation:
All	**praise the Lord, my soul!**
All	**Glory to the Father, and to the Son, and to the Holy Spirit: as it was in the beginning, is now, and shall be for ever. Amen.**

Cast: **Leader, All** (group 1—two or more persons/part of congregation), **All** (group 2—two or more persons/part of congregation).

God and his people
From Psalm 105.1–45 (LIT)

Leader 1	Give thanks to the Lord, praise his name:
All (group 1)	**tell the nations what he has done.**
Leader 2	Sing to him, sing praise to him:
All (group 2)	**tell of all his wonderful deeds.**

Leader 1	Glory in his holy name:
All (group 1)	**let all who worship him rejoice.**
Leader 2	Go to the Lord for help:
All (group 2)	**and worship him for ever.**
Leader 1	Remember the wonders he does:
All (group 1)	**the miracles he performs.**
Leader 2	He is the Lord our God:
All (group 2)	**he judges the whole wide earth.**
Leader 1	He keeps his word and covenant:
All (group 1)	**for a thousand generations.**
Leader 2	The covenant he made with Abraham:
All (group 2)	**the oath he swore to Israel.**
Leader 1	He brought them out of Egypt:
All (group 1)	**and none of them was lost.**
Leader 2	He gave a cloud for covering:
All (group 2)	**a pillar of fire by night.**
Leader 1	He gave them bread from heaven:
All (group 1)	**and water from the rock.**
Leader 2	He brought his people out rejoicing:
All (group 2)	**his chosen ones with shouts of joy.**
All	**Praise the Lord!**
All	**Glory to the Father, and to the Son, and to the Holy Spirit: as it was in the beginning, is now, and shall be for ever. Amen.**

Cast: **Leader 1, All** (group 1—two or more persons/part of congregation), **Leader 2, All** (group 2—two or more persons/part of congregation).

A testimony of salvation
Psalm 116.1–19

Psalmist I love the Lord, because he hears me;
he listens to my prayers.
He listens to me
every time I call to him.
The danger of death was all round me;
the horrors of the grave closed in on me;
I was filled with fear and anxiety.
Then I called to the Lord,

Young Psalmist I beg you, Lord, save me!

Psalmist The Lord is merciful and good;
our God is compassionate.
The Lord protects the helpless;
when I was in danger, he saved me.

91

Be confident, my heart,
because the Lord has been good to me.

The Lord saved me from death;
he stopped my tears
and kept me from defeat.
And so I walk in the presence of the Lord
in the world of the living.
I kept on believing, even when I said:

Young Psalmist   I am completely crushed.

Psalmist   Even when I was afraid and said:

Young Psalmist
(bitterly)   No one can be trusted. (PAUSE)

Psalmist   What can I offer the Lord
for all his goodness to me?
I will bring a wine-offering to the Lord,
to thank him for saving me.
In the assembly of all his people
I will give him what I have promised. (PAUSE)

How painful it is to the Lord
when one of his people dies!
I am your servant, Lord;
I serve you, just as my mother did.

You have saved me from death.
I will give you a sacrifice of thanksgiving
and offer my prayer to you.
In the assembly of all your people,
in the sanctuary of your Temple in Jerusalem,
I will give you what I have promised.

Psalmist and
  Young
  Psalmist   Praise the Lord!

Cast [This is] the word of the Lord. OR **All Glory to the Father, and to the Son, and to the Holy Spirit:**
All   **Thanks be to God.**   **as it was in the beginning, is now, and shall be for ever. Amen.**

Cast: **Psalmist, Young Psalmist.**

Praising God, who saves from death
From Psalm 116.1–19 (LIT)

Leader   I love the Lord because he heard my voice:
All (group 1)   **the Lord in mercy listened to my prayers.**

Leader   Because the Lord has turned his ear to me:
All (group 2)   **I'll call on him as long as I shall live.**

Leader   The cords of death entangled me around:

All (group 3)	**the horrors of the grave came over me.**
Leader	But then I called upon the Lord my God:
All (group 1)	**I said to him: 'O Lord, I beg you, save!'**
Leader	The Lord our God is merciful and good:
All (group 2)	**the Lord protects the simple-hearted ones.**
Leader	The Lord saved me from death and stopped my tears:
All (group 3)	**he saved me from defeat and picked me up.**
Leader	And so I walk before him all my days:
All (group 1)	**and live to love and praise his holy name.**
Leader	What shall I give the Lord for all his grace?
All (group 2)	**I'll take his saving cup, and pay my vows.**
Leader	Within the congregation of his saints:
All (group 3)	**I'll offer him my sacrifice of praise.**
Leader	Praise the Lord:
All	**Amen, amen!**
All	**Glory to the Father, and to the Son, and to the Holy Spirit: as it was in the beginning, is now, and shall be for ever. Amen.**

Cast: **Leader, All** (group 1—two or more persons/part of congregation), **All,** (group 2—two or more persons/part of congregation), **All** (group 3—two or more persons/part of congregation).

A prayer for deliverance
From Psalm 126.1–6 (LIT)

Leader	When the Lord brought us back from slavery:
All (group 1)	**we were like those who dream.**
Leader	Our mouths were filled with laughter:
All (group 2)	**our tongues with songs of joy.**
Leader	Then those around us said, 'The Lord has done great things for them':
All (group 1)	**The Lord has done great things for us, and we are filled with joy.**
Leader	Those who sow in tears
All (group 2)	**shall reap with songs of joy.**
All	**Glory to the Father, and to the Son, and to the Holy Spirit: as it was in the beginning, is now, and shall be forever. Amen.**

Cast: **Leader, All** (group 1—two or more persons/part of congregation). **All** (group 2—two or more persons/part of congregation).

A hymn of thanksgiving
From Psalm 136.1–26 (LIT)

Leader 1	Give thanks to God, for he is good:
All (group 1)	**his love shall last for ever!**

Leader 2	Give thanks to him, the God of gods:
All (group 2)	**his love shall last for ever!**

Leader 3	Give thanks to him, the Lord of lords:
All (group 3)	**his love shall last for ever!**

Leader 1	For God alone works miracles:
All (group 1)	**his love shall last for ever!**

Leader 2	The skies were made at his command:
All (group 2)	**his love shall last for ever!**

Leader 3	He spread the seas upon the earth:
All (group 3)	**his love shall last for ever!**

Leader 1	He made the stars to shine at night:
All (group 1)	**his love shall last for ever!**

Leader 2	He made the sun to shine by day:
All (group 2)	**his love shall last for ever!**

Leader 3	He brought us out from slavery:
All (group 3)	**his love shall last for ever!**

Leader 1	He leads us onward by his grace:
All (group 1)	**his love shall last for ever!**

Leader 2	He saves us from our enemies:
All (group 2)	**his love shall last for ever!**

Leader 3	Give thanks to God, for he is good:
All	**his love shall last for ever!**

All	**Glory to the Father, and to the Son, and to the Holy Spirit:** **as it was in the beginning, is now, and shall be for ever. Amen.**

Cast: **Leader 1, Leader 2, Leader 3, All** (group 1—two or more persons/part of congregation), **All** (group 2—two or more persons/part of congregation), **All** (group 3—two or more persons/part of congregation). (This reading should not be used with a congregation unless it is divided into three parts.)

A hymn of praise
Psalm 149.1–9 (LIT)

Leader	Praise the Lord:
All	**praise the Lord!**

Leader	Sing a new song to the Lord:
All	**let the people shout his name!**

Leader	Praise your maker, Israel:
All (group 1)	**hail, your king, Jerusalem.**

Leader	Sing and dance to honour him:
All (group 2)	**praise him with the strings and drums.**

Leader	God takes pleasure in his saints:
All (group 1)	**crowns the meek with victory.**

Leader	Rise, you saints, in triumph now:
All (group 2)	**sing the joyful night away!**
Leader	Shout aloud and praise your God!
All (group 1)	**Hold aloft the two-edged sword!**
Leader	Let the judgement now begin:
All (group 2)	**kings shall fail and tyrants die.**
Leader	Through his people, by his word:
All	**God shall have the victory!**
Leader	Praise the Lord!
All	**Praise the Lord!**
All	**Glory to the Father, and to the Son, and to the Holy Spirit:**
	as it was in the beginning, is now, and shall be for ever. Amen.

Cast: **Leader, All** (group 1—two or more persons/part of congregation), **All** (group 2—two or more persons/part of congregation).

A hymn of thanksgiving
Isaiah 12.1–6

Isaiah	A day is coming when people will sing:
Singer 1	I praise you, Lord! You were angry with me,
	but now you comfort me and are angry no longer.
Singer 2	God is my saviour;
	I will trust him and not be afraid.
Singer 3	The Lord gives me power and strength;
	he is my saviour.
Singers 1–3	As fresh water brings joy to the thirsty,
	so God's people rejoice when he saves them. (PAUSE)
Isaiah	A day is coming when people will sing:
Singer 1	Give thanks to the Lord! Call for him to help you!
Singer 2	Tell all the nations what he has done!
Singer 3	Tell them how great he is!
Singer 1	Sing to the Lord because of the great things he has done.
Singer 2	Let the whole world hear the news.
Singer 3	Let everyone who lives in Zion shout and sing!
Singers 1–3	Israel's holy God is great,
	and he lives among his people.
Cast	[This is] the word of the Lord.
All	**Thanks be to God.**

Cast: **Isaiah, Singer 1, Singer 2, Singer 3.**

The valley of dry bones
From Ezekiel 37.1–14

Ezekiel   I felt the powerful presence of the Lord, and his spirit took me and set me down in a valley where the ground was covered with bones. He led me all round the valley, and I could see that there were very many bones and that they were very dry. [He said to me:]

The Lord   Mortal man, can these bones come back to life?

Ezekiel   [I replied:] Sovereign Lord, only you can answer that! [He said:]

The Lord   Prophesy to the bones. Tell these dry bones to listen to the word of the Lord. Tell them that I, the Sovereign Lord, am saying to them, 'I am going to put breath into you and bring you back to life. I will give you sinews and muscles, and cover you with skin. I will put breath into you and bring you back to life. Then you will know that I am the Lord.'

Ezekiel   So I prophesied as I had been told. While I was speaking, I heard a rattling noise, and the bones began to join together. While I watched, the bones were covered with sinews and muscles, and then with skin. But there was no breath in the bodies.

God said to me:

The Lord   Mortal man, prophesy to the wind. Tell the wind that the Sovereign Lord commands it to come from every direction, to breathe into these dead bodies, and to bring them back to life.

Ezekiel   So I prophesied as I had been told. Breath entered the bodies, and they came to life and stood up. There were enough of them to form an army.

God said to me:

The Lord   Mortal man, the people of Israel are like these bones. They say that they are dried up, without any hope and with no future. So prophesy to my people Israel and tell them that I, the Sovereign Lord, am going to open their graves. I am going to take them out and bring them back to the land of Israel. When I open the graves where my people are buried and bring them out, they will know that I am the Lord. I will put my breath in them, bring them back to life, and let them live in their own land. Then they will know that I am the Lord.

(deliberately)   I have promised that I would do this—and I will. (PAUSE) I, the Lord, have spoken!

Cast   [This is] the word of the Lord.
All   **Thanks be to God.**

Cast: **Ezekiel, The Lord.**

The question about rising from death
Matthew 22.23–33

Narrator   Some Sadducees came to Jesus and claimed that people will not rise from death.

Sadducee 1   Teacher, Moses said that if a man who has no children dies, his brother must marry the widow so that they can have children who will be considered the dead man's children.

Sadducee 2   Now, there were seven brothers who used to live here. The eldest got married and died without having children, so he left his widow to his brother.

Sadducee 1   The same thing happened to the second brother, to the third, and finally to all seven.

Sadducee 2   Last of all, the woman died.

Sadducee 1   Now, on the day when the dead rise to life, whose wife will she be?

Sadducee 2   All of them had married her.

[Narrator   Jesus answered them:]

Jesus   How wrong you are! It is because you don't know the Scriptures or God's power. For when the dead rise to life, they will be like the angels in heaven and will not marry. Now, as for the dead rising to life: haven't you ever read what God has told you? [He said:]

Voice   I am the God of Abraham, the God of Isaac, and the God of Jacob.

Jesus   He is the God of the living, not of the dead.

Narrator   When the crowds heard this, they were amazed at his teaching.

Cast [This is] the word of the Lord. OR This is the Gospel of Christ / *This is the Gospel of the Lord.*
All   **Thanks be to God.**   **Praise to Christ our Lord** / *Praise to you, Lord Jesus Christ.*

Cast: **Narrator, Sadducee 1, Sadducee 2, Jesus, Voice** (can be the same as Jesus).

The Resurrection
Matthew 28.1–10

Narrator   After the Sabbath, as Sunday morning was dawning, Mary Magdalene and the other Mary went to look at the tomb. Suddenly there was a violent earthquake; an angel of the Lord came down from heaven, rolled the stone away, and sat on it. His appearance was like lightning, and his clothes were white as snow. The guards were so afraid that they trembled and became like dead men. The angel spoke to the women:

Angel   You must not be afraid. I know you are looking for Jesus, who was crucified. He is not here; he has been raised, just as he said. Come here and see the place where he was lying.

Go quickly now, and tell his disciples, 'He has been raised from death, and now he is going to Galilee ahead of you; there you will see him!' Remember what I have told you.

Narrator   So they left the tomb in a hurry, afraid and yet filled with joy, and ran to tell his disciples. Suddenly Jesus met them:

Jesus   Peace be with you.

Narrator   They came up to him, took hold of his feet, and worshipped him.

Jesus   Do not be afraid. Go and tell my brothers to go to Galilee, and there they will see me.

Cast   [This is] the word of the Lord.   OR   This is the Gospel of Christ / *This is the Gospel of the Lord.*
All   **Thanks be to God.**   **Praise to Christ our Lord** / *Praise to you, Lord Jesus Christ.*

Cast: **Narrator, Angel, Jesus.**

The report of the guard
Matthew 28.11–15

Narrator   While the women went on their way, some of the soldiers guarding the tomb went back to the city and told the chief priests everything that had happened. The chief priests met with the elders and made their plan: they gave a large sum of money to the soldiers and said:

Priest   You are to say that his disciples came during the night and stole his body while you were asleep. And if the Governor should hear of this, we will convince him that you are innocent, and you will have nothing to worry about.

Narrator   The guards took the money and did what they were told to do. And so that is the report spread round by the Jews to this very day.

Cast   [This is] the word of the Lord.   OR   This is the Gospel of Christ / *This is the Gospel of the Lord.*
All   **Thanks be to God.**   **Praise to Christ our Lord** / *Praise to you, Lord Jesus Christ.*

Cast: **Narrator, Priest.** (This reading is short and preferably linked with the preceding one).

The question about rising from death
Mark 12.18–27

Narrator   Some Sadducees, who say that people will not rise from death, came to Jesus:

Sadducee 1   Teacher, Moses wrote this law for us:

Sadducee 2   If a man dies and leaves a wife but no children, that man's brother must marry the widow so that they can have children who will be considered the dead man's children.

Sadducee 1   Once there were seven brothers; the eldest got married and died without having children.

Sadducee 2	Then the second one married the woman, and he also died without having children.
Sadducee 1	The same thing happened to the third brother, and then to the rest.
Sadducee 2	All seven brothers married the woman and died without having children.
Sadducee 1	Last of all, the woman died.
Sadducee 2	Now, when all the dead rise to life on the day of resurrection, whose wife will she be? All seven of them had married her.
Narrator	Jesus answered them:
Jesus	How wrong you are! And do you know why? It is because you don't know the Scriptures or God's power. For when the dead rise to life, they will be like the angels in heaven and will not marry. Now, as for the dead being raised: haven't you ever read in the Book of Moses the passage about the burning bush? There it is written that God said to Moses, 'I am the God of Abraham, the God of Isaac, and the God of Jacob.' He is the God of the living, not of the dead. You are completely wrong!

Cast [This is] the word of the Lord.   OR   This is the Gospel of Christ / *This is the Gospel of the Lord.*
All   **Thanks be to God.**   **Praise to Christ our Lord** / *Praise to you, Lord Jesus Christ.*

Cast: **Narrator, Sadducee 1, Sadducee 2** (can be the same as Sadducee 1), **Jesus.**

Jesus appears to his disciples and is taken up to heaven
Mark 16.9–20

Narrator 1	After Jesus rose from death early on Sunday, he appeared first to Mary Magdalene, from whom he had driven out seven demons. She went and told his companions. They were mourning and crying; and when they heard her say that Jesus was alive and that she had seen him, they did not believe her.
Narrator 2	After this, Jesus appeared in a different manner to two of them while they were on their way to the country. They returned and told the others, but they would not believe it.
Narrator 1	Last of all, Jesus appeared to the eleven disciples as they were eating. He scolded them, because they did not have faith and because they were too stubborn to believe those who had seen him alive. He said to them:
Jesus	Go throughout the whole world and preach the gospel to all mankind. Whoever believes and is baptized will be saved; whoever does not believe will be condemned. Believers will be given the power to perform miracles: they will drive out demons in my name; they will speak in strange tongues; if they pick up snakes or drink any poison, they will not be harmed; they will place their hands on sick people, who will get well.

Narrator 2   After the Lord Jesus had talked with them, he was taken up to heaven and sat at the right side of God. The disciples went and preached everywhere, and the Lord worked with them and proved that their preaching was true by the miracles that were performed.

Cast   [This is] the word of the Lord.   OR   This is the Gospel of Christ / *This is the Gospel of the Lord.*
All   **Thanks be to God.**   **Praise to Christ our Lord** / *Praise to you, Lord Jesus Christ.*

Cast: **Narrator 1, Narrator 2, Jesus.**

Jesus raises a widow's son
Luke 7.11–17

Narrator   Jesus went to a town called Nain, accompanied by his disciples and a large crowd. Just as he arrived at the gate of the town, a funeral procession was coming out. The dead man was the only son of a woman who was a widow, and a large crowd from the town was with her. When the Lord saw her, his heart was filled with pity for her [and he said to her]:

Jesus   Don't cry.

Narrator   Then he walked over and touched the coffin, and the men carrying it stopped. [Jesus said:]

Jesus   Young man! Get up, I tell you!

Narrator   The dead man sat up and began to talk, and Jesus gave him back to his mother. They all were filled with fear and praised God:

Person 1   A great prophet has appeared among us!

Person 2   God has come to save his people!

Narrator   This news about Jesus went out through all the country and the surrounding territory.

Cast   [This is] the word of the Lord.   OR   This is the Gospel of Christ / *This is the Gospel of the Lord.*
All   **Thanks be to God.**   **Praise to Christ our Lord** / *Praise to you, Lord Jesus Christ.*

Cast: **Narrator, Jesus, Person 1, Person 2.**

The question about rising from death
Luke 20.27–40 [40–47]

Narrator   Some Sadducees, who say that people will not rise from death, came to Jesus and said:

Sadducee 1   Teacher, Moses wrote this law for us:

[Moses]   If a man dies and leaves a wife but no children, that man's brother must marry the widow so that they can have children who will be considered the dead man's children.

Sadducee 1	Once there were seven brothers; the eldest got married and died without having children.
Sadducee 2	Then the second one married the woman.
Sadducee 1	And then the third.
Sadducee 2	The same thing happened to all seven—they died without having children.
Sadducee 1	Last of all, the woman died.
Sadducee 2	Now, on the day when the dead rise to life, whose wife will she be?
Sadducee 1	All seven of them had married her.
[Narrator	Jesus answered them:]
Jesus	The men and women of this age marry, but the men and women who are worthy to rise from death and live in the age to come will not then marry. They will be like angels and cannot die. They are the sons of God, because they have risen from death. And Moses clearly proves that the dead are raised to life. In the passage about the burning bush he speaks of the Lord as:
[Moses]	The God of Abraham, the God of Isaac, and the God of Jacob.
Jesus	He is the God of the living, not of the dead, for to him all are alive.
Narrator	Some of the teachers of the Law spoke up:
Lawyer	A good answer, Teacher!
Narrator	For they did not dare ask him any more questions. (PAUSE)
[Jesus	How can it be said that the Messiah will be the descendant of David? For David himself says in the book of Psalms:
Psalmist	The Lord said to my Lord: Sit here on my right until I put your enemies as a footstool under your feet.
Jesus	David called him 'Lord'; how, then, can the Messiah be David's descendant?
Narrator	As all the people listened to him, Jesus said to his disciples:
Jesus	Be on your guard against the teachers of the Law, who like to walk about in their long robes and love to be greeted with respect in the market-place; who choose the reserved seats in the synagogues and the best places at feasts; who take advantage of widows and rob them of their homes, and then make a show of saying long prayers! Their punishment will be all the worse!]

Cast [This is] the word of the Lord.   OR   This is the Gospel of Christ / *This is the Gospel of the Lord.*
All   **Thanks be to God.**   **Praise to Christ our Lord** / *Praise to you, Lord Jesus Christ.*

Cast: Narrator, Sadducee 1, [Moses], Sadducee 2 (can be the same as Sadducee 1), Jesus, Lawyer (can be the same as Moses), **Psalmist** (can be the same as Sadducee).

The Resurrection
Luke 24.1–12

Narrator   Very early on Sunday morning the women went to the tomb, carrying the spices they had prepared. They found the stone rolled away from the entrance to the tomb, so they went in; but they did not find the body of the Lord Jesus. They stood there puzzled about this, when suddenly two men in bright shining clothes stood by them. Full of fear, the women bowed down to the ground, as the men said to them:

Man 1   Why are you looking among the dead for one who is alive?

Man 2   He is not here; he has been raised.

Man 1   Remember what he said to you while he was in Galilee:

Man 2   'The Son of Man must be handed over to sinful men, and be crucified.'

Man 1   'And three days later rise to life.'

Narrator   Then the women remembered his words, returned from the tomb, and told all these things to the eleven disciples and all the rest. The women were Mary Magdalene, Joanna, and Mary the mother of James; they and the other women with them told these things to the apostles. But the apostles thought that what the women said was nonsense, and they did not believe them. But Peter got up and ran to the tomb; he bent down and saw the linen wrappings but nothing else. Then he went back home amazed at what had happened.

Cast   [This is] the word of the Lord.   OR   This is the Gospel of Christ / *This is the Gospel of the Lord.*
All   **Thanks be to God.**   **Praise to Christ our Lord** / *Praise to you, Lord Jesus Christ.*

Cast: **Narrator, Man 1, Man 2.**

On the road to Emmaus
Luke 24.13–35

Narrator   Now that same day two of them were going to a village called Emmaus, about seven miles from Jerusalem. They were talking with each other about everything that had happened. As they talked and discussed these things with each other, Jesus himself came up and walked along with them; but they were kept from recognising him. He asked them:

Jesus   What are you discussing together as you walk along?

Narrator   They stood still, their faces downcast. One of them, named Cleopas, asked him:

Cleopas	Are you only a visitor to Jerusalem and do not know the things that have happened there in these days?
Jesus	What things?
Cleopas	About Jesus of Nazareth.
Companion	He was a prophet, powerful in word and deed before God and all the people.
Cleopas	The chief priests and our rulers handed him over to be sentenced to death, and they crucified him.
Companion	But we had hoped that he was the one who was going to redeem Israel.
Cleopas	And what is more, it is the third day since all this took place.
Companion	In addition, some of our women amazed us. They went to the tomb early this morning but didn't find his body.
Cleopas	They came and told us that they had seen a vision of angels, who said he was alive.
Companion	Then some of our companions went to the tomb and found it just as the women had said.
Cleopas	But him they did not see.
Jesus	How foolish you are, and how slow of heart to believe all that the prophets have spoken! Did not the Christ have to suffer these things and then enter his glory?
Narrator	And beginning with Moses and all the Prophets, he explained to them what was said in all the Scriptures concerning himself. (PAUSE) As they approached the village to which they were going, Jesus acted as if he were going further. But they urged him strongly:
Companion	Stay with us, for it is nearly evening.
Cleopas	The day is almost over.
Narrator	So he went in to stay with them. (PAUSE) When he was at the table with them, he took bread, gave thanks, broke it and began to give it to them. Then their eyes were opened and they recognised him, and he disappeared from their sight. (PAUSE) They asked each other:
Cleopas	Were not our hearts burning within us while he talked with us on the road . . .
Companion	. . . and opened the Scriptures to us?
Narrator	They got up and returned at once to Jerusalem. There they found the Eleven and those with them, assembled together and saying:
Disciple 1	It is true!
Disciple 2	The Lord has risen.
Disciple 1	And has appeared to Simon.

| Narrator | Then the two told what had happened on the way, and how Jesus was recognised by them when he broke the bread. |

Cast [This is] the word of the Lord. OR This is the Gospel of Christ / *This is the Gospel of the Lord.*
All   **Thanks be to God.**   **Praise to Christ our Lord** / *Praise to you, Lord Jesus Christ.*

Cast: **Narrator, Jesus, Cleopas, Companion, Disciple 1, Disciple 2.**

Jesus appears to his disciples and is taken up to heaven
Luke 24.36–53

Narrator	Suddenly the Lord himself stood among his disciples [and said to them]:
Jesus	Peace be with you.
Narrator	They were terrified, thinking that they were seeing a ghost.
Jesus	Why are you alarmed? Why are these doubts coming up in your minds? Look at my hands and my feet, and see that it is I myself. Feel me, and you will know, for a ghost doesn't have flesh and bones, as you can see I have.
Narrator	He said this and showed them his hands and his feet. They still could not believe, they were so full of joy and wonder; so he asked them:
Jesus	Have you anything here to eat?
Narrator	They gave him a piece of cooked fish, which he took and ate in their presence. (PAUSE)
Jesus	These are the very things I told you about while I was still with you: everything written about me in the Law of Moses, the writings of the prophets, and the Psalms had to come true.
Narrator	Then he opened their minds to understand the Scriptures:
Jesus	This is what is written: the Messiah must suffer and must rise from death three days later, and in his name the message about repentance and the forgiveness of sins must be preached to all nations, beginning in Jerusalem. You are witnesses of these things. And I myself will send upon you what my Father has promised. But you must wait in the city until the power from above comes down upon you.
Narrator	Then he led them out of the city as far as Bethany, where he raised his hands and blessed them. As he was blessing them, he departed from them and was taken up into heaven. They worshipped him and went back into Jerusalem, filled with great joy, and spent all their time in the Temple giving thanks to God.

Cast [This is] the word of the Lord. OR This is the Gospel of Christ / *This is the Gospel of the Lord.*
All   **Thanks be to God.**   **Praise to Christ our Lord** / *Praise to you, Lord Jesus Christ.*

Cast: **Narrator, Jesus.**

Jesus the resurrection and the life
From John 11.1–44

Narrator   A man named Lazarus, who lived in Bethany, was ill. Bethany was the town where Mary and her sister Martha lived. This Mary was the one who poured the perfume on the Lord's feet and wiped them with her hair; it was her brother Lazarus who was ill. The sisters sent Jesus a message:

Mary   Lord, your dear friend is ill.

Narrator   When Jesus heard it, he said:

Jesus   The final result of this illness will not be the death of Lazarus; this has happened in order to bring glory to God, and it will be the means by which the Son of God will receive glory.

Narrator   Jesus loved Martha and her sister and Lazarus. Yet when he received the news that Lazarus was ill, he stayed where he was for two more days. Then he said to the disciples:

Jesus   Let us go back to Judaea. Our friend Lazarus has fallen asleep, but I will go and wake him up.(PAUSE)

Narrator   When Jesus arrived, he found that Lazarus had been buried four days before. When Martha heard that Jesus was coming, she went out to meet him, but Mary stayed in the house. Martha said to Jesus:

Martha   If you had been here, Lord, my brother would not have died! But I know that even now God will give you whatever you ask him for.

Jesus   Your brother will rise to life.

Martha   I know that he will rise to life on the last day.

Jesus   I am the resurrection and the life. Whoever believes in me will live, even though he dies; and whoever lives and believes in me will never die. Do you believe this?

Martha   Yes, Lord! I do believe that you are the Messiah, the Son of God, who was to come into the world.

Narrator   After Martha said this, she went back and called her sister Mary privately:

Martha   The Teacher is here, and is asking for you.

Narrator   When Mary heard this, she got up and hurried out to meet him. The people who were in the house with Mary, comforting her, followed her when they saw her get up and hurry out. They thought that she was going to the grave to weep there. (PAUSE)

Mary arrived where Jesus was, and as soon as she saw him, she fell at his feet and said:

Mary   Lord, if you had been here, my brother would not have died!

Narrator   Jesus saw her weeping, and he saw how the people who were with her were weeping also; his heart was touched, and he was deeply moved.

105

Jesus	Where have you buried him?
Mary & Martha	Come and see, Lord.
Narrator (slowly)	Jesus wept. The people said:
Person 1	See how much he loved him!
Narrator	But some of them said:
Person 2	He gave sight to the blind man, didn't he? Could he not have kept Lazarus from dying?
Narrator	Deeply moved once more, Jesus went to the tomb, which was a cave with a stone placed at the entrance. [Jesus ordered:]
Jesus	Take the stone away!
Martha	There will be a bad smell, Lord. He has been buried four days!
Jesus	Didn't I tell you that you would see God's glory if you believed?
Narrator	They took the stone away. Jesus looked up and said:
Jesus	I thank you, Father, that you listen to me. I know that you always listen to me, but I say this for the sake of the people here, so that they will believe that you sent me. (PAUSE)
(loudly)	Lazarus, come out!
Narrator	He came out, his hands and feet wrapped in grave clothes, and with a cloth round his face. Jesus told them:
Jesus	Untie him, and let him go.

Cast [This is] the word of the Lord. OR This is the Gospel of Christ / *This is the Gospel of the Lord.*
All **Thanks be to God.**   **Praise to Christ our Lord** / *Praise to you, Lord Jesus Christ.*

Cast: **Narrator, Mary, Jesus, Martha, Person 1, Person 2.**

The empty tomb
John 20.1–18

Narrator	Early on Sunday morning, while it was still dark, Mary Magdalene went to the tomb and saw that the stone had been taken away from the entrance. She went running to Simon Peter and the other disciple, whom Jesus loved.
Mary	They have taken the Lord from the tomb, and we don't know where they have put him!
Narrator	Then Peter and the other disciple went to the tomb. The two of them were running, but the other disciple ran faster than Peter and reached the tomb first. He bent over and saw the linen wrappings, but he did not go in. Behind him came Simon Peter, and he went straight into the tomb. He saw the linen wrappings lying there and

the cloth which had been round Jesus' head. It was not lying with the linen wrappings but was rolled up by itself. Then the other disciple, who had reached the tomb first, also went in; he saw and believed. They still did not understand the scripture which said that he must rise from death. Then the disciples went back home. (PAUSE)

Mary stood crying outside the tomb. While she was still crying, she bent over and looked in the tomb and saw two angels there dressed in white, sitting where the body of Jesus had been, one at the head and the other at the feet. [They asked her]:

Angel(s)   Woman, why are you crying?

Mary   They have taken my Lord away, and I do not know where they have put him!

Narrator   Then she turned round and saw Jesus standing there; but she did not know that it was Jesus.

Jesus   Woman, why are you crying? Who is it that you are looking for?

Narrator   She thought he was the gardener.

Mary   If you took him away, sir, tell me where you have put him, and I will go and get him.

Jesus   Mary!

Mary   Rabboni! Teacher!

Jesus   Do not hold on to me, because I have not yet gone back up to the Father. But go to my brothers and tell them that I am returning to him who is my Father and their Father, my God and their God.

Narrator   So Mary Magdalene went and told the disciples that she had seen the Lord and related to them what he had told her.

Cast [This is] the word of the Lord.   OR   This is the Gospel of Christ / *This is the Gospel of the Lord.*
All   **Thanks be to God.**   **Praise to Christ our Lord** / *Praise to you, Lord Jesus Christ.*

Cast: **Narrator, Mary, Angel(s), Jesus**.

Jesus appears to his disciples
John 20.19–23

Narrator   It was late that Sunday evening, and the disciples were gathered together behind locked doors, because they were afraid of the Jewish authorities. Then Jesus came and stood among them. [He said:]

Jesus   Peace be with you.

Narrator   After saying this, he showed them his hands and his side. The disciples were filled with joy at seeing the Lord. [Jesus said to them again:]

Jesus   Peace be with you. As the Father sent me, so I send you.

Narrator	Then he breathed on them [and said]:
Jesus	Receive the Holy Spirit. If you forgive people's sins, they are forgiven; if you do not forgive them, they are not forgiven.

Cast [This is] the word of the Lord. OR This is the Gospel of Christ / *This is the Gospel of the Lord.*
All **Thanks be to God.**   **Praise to Christ our Lord** / *Praise to you, Lord Jesus Christ.*

Cast: **Narrator, Jesus.**

Jesus and Thomas
John 20.24–29

Narrator	One of the twelve disciples, Thomas (called the Twin), was not with them when Jesus came. So the other disciples told him:
Disciple(s)	We have seen the Lord!
[Narrator	Thomas said to them:]
Thomas	Unless I see the scars of the nails in his hands and put my finger on those scars and my hand in his side, I will not believe.
Narrator	A week later the disciples were together again indoors, and Thomas was with them. The doors were locked, but Jesus came and stood among them [and said]:
Jesus	Peace be with you.
[Narrator	Then he said to Thomas:]
Jesus (to Thomas)	Put your finger here, and look at my hands; then stretch out your hand and put it in my side. Stop your doubting, and believe!
Thomas	My Lord and my God!
Jesus	Do you believe because you see me? How happy are those who believe without seeing me!

Cast [This is] the word of the Lord. OR This is the Gospel of Christ / *This is the Gospel of the Lord.*
All **Thanks be to God.**   **Praise to Christ our Lord** / *Praise to you, Lord Jesus Christ.*

Cast: **Narrator, Disciple(s), Thomas, Jesus.**

Jesus appears to seven disciples
John 21.1–14

Narrator	Jesus appeared once more to his disciples at Lake Tiberias. This is how it happened. Simon Peter, Thomas—called the Twin, Nathanael—the one from Cana in Galilee, the sons of Zebedee, and two other disciples of Jesus were all together. Simon Peter said to the others:
Peter	I am going fishing.
Disciple	We will come with you.

Narrator	So they went out in a boat, but all that night they did not catch a thing. As the sun was rising, Jesus stood at the water's edge, but the disciples did not know that it was Jesus. [Then he asked them:]
Jesus (calling)	Young men, haven't you caught anything?
Disciple	Not a thing.
Jesus (calling)	Throw your net out on the right side of the boat, and you will catch some.
Narrator	So they threw the net out and could not pull it back in, because they had caught so many fish. The disciple whom Jesus loved said to Peter:
John	It is the Lord!
Narrator	When Peter heard that it was the Lord, he wrapped his outer garment round him—for he had taken his clothes off—and jumped into the water. The other disciples came to shore in the boat, pulling the net full of fish. They were not very far from land, about a hundred metres away. When they stepped ashore, they saw a charcoal fire there with fish on it and some bread. [Then Jesus said to them:]
Jesus	Bring some of the fish you have just caught.
Narrator	Simon Peter went aboard and dragged the net ashore full of big fish, a hundred and fifty-three in all; even though there were so many, still the net did not tear. [Jesus said to them:]
Jesus	Come and eat.
Narrator	None of the disciples dared ask him, 'Who are you?' because they knew it was the Lord. So Jesus went over, took the bread, and gave it to them; he did the same with the fish.
	This, then, was the third time Jesus appeared to the disciples after he was raised from death.

Cast [This is] the word of the Lord. OR This is the Gospel of Christ / *This is the Gospel of the Lord.*
All **Thanks be to God.** **Praise to Christ our Lord** / *Praise to you, Lord Jesus Christ.*

Cast: **Narrator, Peter, Disciple, Jesus, John** (can be the same as Disciple).

Jesus and Peter
John 21.15–22

Narrator	After they had eaten, Jesus said to Simon Peter:
Jesus	Simon son of John, do you love me more than these others do?
Peter	Yes, Lord, you know that I love you.
Jesus	Take care of my lambs. (PAUSE) Simon son of John, do you love me?
Peter	Yes, Lord, you know that I love you.

Jesus	Take care of my sheep. (PAUSE) Simon son of John, do you love me?
Narrator	Peter was sad because Jesus asked him the third time, 'Do you love me?'
Peter	Lord, you know everything; you know that I love you!
Jesus	Take care of my sheep. (PAUSE)
	I am telling you the truth: when you were young, you used to get ready and go anywhere you wanted to; but when you are old, you will stretch out your hands and someone else will bind you and take you where you don't want to go.
Narrator	In saying this, Jesus was indicating the way in which Peter would die and bring glory to God. (PAUSE) Then Jesus said to him:
Jesus	Follow me!
Narrator	Peter turned round and saw behind him that other disciple, whom Jesus loved—the one who had leaned close to Jesus at the meal and had asked, 'Lord, who is going to betray you?' When Peter saw him, he asked Jesus:
Peter	Lord, what about this man?
Jesus	If I want him to live until I come, what is that to you? Follow me!

Cast [This is] the word of the Lord. OR This is the Gospel of Christ / *This is the Gospel of the Lord.*
All   **Thanks to be God.**   **Praise to Christ our Lord** / *Praise to you, Lord Jesus Christ.*

Cast: **Narrator, Jesus, Peter.**

Peter speaks of Christ the Son of David
Acts 2.22–35

Peter	Listen to these words, fellow-Israelites! Jesus of Nazareth was a man whose divine authority was clearly proven to you by all the miracles and wonders which God performed through him. You yourselves know this, for it happened here among you. In accordance with his own plan God had already decided that Jesus would be handed over to you; and you killed him by letting sinful men crucify him. But God raised him from death, setting him free from its power, because it was impossible that death should hold him prisoner. For David said about him:
David	I saw the Lord before me at all times; he is near me, and I will not be troubled. And so I am filled with gladness. and my words are full of joy. And I, mortal though I am, will rest assured in hope, because you will not abandon me in the world of the dead; you will not allow your faithful servant to rot in the grave.

	You have shown me the paths that lead to life, and your presence will fill me with joy.
Peter	My brothers, I must speak to you plainly about our famous ancestor King David. He died and was buried, and his grave is here with us to this very day. He was a prophet, and he knew what God had promised him: God had made a vow that he would make one of David's descendants a king, just as David was. David saw what God was going to do in the future, and so he spoke about the resurrection of the Messiah [when he said]:
David	He was not abandoned in the world of the dead; his body did not rot in the grave.
Peter	God has raised this very Jesus from death, and we are all witnesses to this fact. He has been raised to the right-hand side of God, his Father, and has received from him the Holy Spirit, as he had promised. What you now see and hear is his gift that he has poured out on us. For it was not David who went up into heaven; rather he said:
David	The Lord said to *my Lord*: Sit here at my right until I put your enemies as a footstool under your feet.
Cast	[This is] the word of the Lord.
All	**Thanks be to God.**

Cast: **Peter, David.**

Paul preaches in Antioch
Acts 13.29–52

Paul	After the people who live in Jerusalem and their leaders had done everything that the Scriptures say about Jesus, they took him down from the cross and placed him in a tomb. But God raised him from death, and for many days he appeared to those who had travelled with him from Galilee to Jerusalem. They are now witnesses for him to the people of Israel. And we are here to bring the Good News to you: what God promised our ancestors he would do, he has now done for us, who are their descendants, by raising Jesus to life. As it is written in the second Psalm:
Voice	You are my Son; today I have become your Father.
Paul	And this is what God said about raising him from death, never to rot away in the grave:
Voice	I will give you the sacred and sure blessings that I promised to David.
Paul	As indeed he says in another passage:
Voice	You will not allow your devoted servant to rot in the grave.

Paul	For David served God's purposes in his own time, and then he died, was buried with his ancestors, and his body rotted in the grave. But this did not happen to the one whom God raised from death. We want you to know, my fellow-Israelites, that it is through Jesus that the message about forgiveness of sins is preached to you; and that everyone who believes in him is set free from all the sins from which the Law of Moses could not set you free. Take care, then, so that what the prophets said may not happen to you:
Voice	Look, you scoffers! Be astonished and die! For what I am doing today is something that you will not believe, even when someone explains it to you!
Narrator	As Paul and Barnabas were leaving the synagogue, the people invited them to come back the next Sabbath and tell them more about these things. After the people had left the meeting, Paul and Barnabas were followed by many Jews and by many Gentiles who had been converted to Judaism. The apostles spoke to them and encouraged them to keep on living in the grace of God. (PAUSE)
	The next Sabbath nearly everyone in the town came to hear the word of the Lord. When the Jews saw the crowds, they were filled with jealousy; they disputed what Paul was saying and insulted him. But Paul and Barnabas spoke out even more boldly:
Paul	It was necessary that the word of God should be spoken first to you. But since you reject it and do not consider yourselves worthy of eternal life, we will leave you and go to the Gentiles. For this is the commandment that the Lord has given us:
Voice	I have made you a light for the Gentiles, so that all the world may be saved.
Narrator	When the Gentiles heard this, they were glad and praised the Lord's message; and those who had been chosen for eternal life became believers. (PAUSE)
	The word of the Lord spread everywhere in that region. But the Jews stirred up the leading men of the city and the Gentile women of high social standing who worshipped God. They started a persecution against Paul and Barnabas and threw them out of their region. The apostles shook the dust off their feet in protest against them and went on to Iconium. The believers in Antioch were full of joy and the Holy Spirit.
Cast	[This is] the word of the Lord.
All	**Thanks be to God.**

Cast: **Paul, Voice, Narrator.**

The Resurrection of Christ
1 Corinthians 15.1–11

Paul   Now I want to remind you, my brothers, of the Good News which I preached to you, which you received, and on which your faith stands firm. That is the gospel, the message that I preached to you. You are saved by the gospel if you hold firmly to it—unless it was for nothing that you believed.

I passed on to you what I received, which is of the greatest importance – that:

Young Paul   Christ died for our sins, as written in the Scriptures; that he was buried and that he was raised to life three days later, as written in the Scriptures; that he appeared to Peter and then to all twelve apostles. Then he appeared to more than five hundred of his followers at once, most of whom are still alive, although some have died. Then he appeared to James, and afterwards to all the apostles.

Paul   Last of all he appeared also to me—even though I am like someone whose birth was abnormal. For I am the least of all the apostles—I do not even deserve to be called an apostle, because I persecuted God's church. But by God's grace I am what I am, and the grace that he gave me was not without effect. On the contrary, I have worked harder than any of the other apostles, although it was not really my own doing, but God's grace working with me. So then, whether it came from me or from them, this is what we all preach, and this is what you believe.

Cast   [This is] the word of the Lord.
All   **Thanks be to God.**

Cast: **Paul, Young Paul** (or, perhaps, Peter—see Galatians 1.18).

The resurrection body
From 1 Corinthians 15.35–57

Paul   Someone will ask:

Person   How can the dead be raised to life? What kind of body will they have?

Paul   When you sow a seed in the ground, it does not sprout to life unless it dies. And what you sow is a bare seed, perhaps a grain of wheat or some other grain, not the full-bodied plant that will later grow up. God provides that seed with the body he wishes; he gives each its own proper body. There is, of course, a physical body, so there has to be a spiritual body. For the scripture says:

Scripture   The first man, Adam, was created a living being.

Paul   But the last Adam is the life-giving Spirit. It is not the spiritual that comes first, but the physical, and then the spiritual. The first Adam, made of earth, came from the earth; the second Adam came from heaven. Those who belong to the earth are like the one who was made of earth; those who are of heaven are like the one who came from heaven. Just as we wear the likeness of the man made of earth, so we will wear the likeness of the Man from heaven.

What I mean, brothers, is that what is made of flesh and blood cannot share in God's Kingdom, and what is mortal cannot possess immortality.

Listen to this secret truth: we shall not all die, but when the last trumpet sounds, we shall all be changed in an instant, as quickly as the blinking of an eye. For when the trumpet sounds, the dead will be raised, never to die again, and we shall all be changed. For what is mortal must be changed into what is immortal; what will die must be changed into what cannot die. So when this takes place, and the mortal has been changed into the immortal, then the scripture will come true:

Scripture   Death is destroyed; victory is complete!
Where, Death, is your victory?
Where, Death, is your power to hurt?

Paul   Death gets its power to hurt from sin, and sin gets its power from the Law. But thanks be to God who gives us the victory through our Lord Jesus Christ!

Cast   [This is] the word of the Lord.
All   **Thanks be to God.**

Cast: **Paul, Person, Scripture.**

God's power and the church
Ephesians 1.19–23; 3.20–21

Voice 1   The power working in us is the same as the mighty strength which he used when he raised Christ from death and seated him at his right side in the heavenly world.

Voice 2   Christ rules there above all heavenly rulers, authorities, powers, and lords; he has a title superior to all titles of authority in this world and in the next.

Voice 3   God put all things under Christ's feet and gave him to the church as supreme Lord over all things.

Voice 1   The church is Christ's body, the completion of him who himself completes all things everywhere.

Voice 2   To him who by means of his power working in us is able to do so much more than we can ever ask for, or even think of:

Voice 3   To God be the glory in the church and in Christ Jesus for all time, for ever and ever!

Voices 1–3   Amen.

Cast   [This is] the word of the Lord.
All   **Thanks be to God.**

Cast: **Voice 1, Voice 2, Voice 3.**

The Lord's coming
1 Thessalonians 4.13–18

Voice 1   We want you to know the truth about those who have died, so that you will not be sad, as are those who have no hope.

Voice 2   We believe that Jesus died and rose again, and so we believe that God will take back with Jesus those who have died believing in him.

Voice 1   What we are teaching you now is the Lord's teaching: we who are alive on the day the Lord comes will not go ahead of those who have died.

Voice 1   There will be the shout of command, the archangel's voice, the sound of God's trumpet, and the Lord himself will come down from heaven.

Voice 1   Those who have died believing in Christ will rise to life first.

Voice 2   Then we who are living at that time will be gathered up along with them in the clouds to meet the Lord in the air.

Voice 1   And so we will always be with the Lord. So then—

Voices 1 and **2**   Encourage one another with these words.

Cast   [This is] the word of the Lord.
All   **Thanks be to God.**

Cast: **Voice 1, Voice 2.**

The great secret
From 1 Timothy 3.14–16

Paul   As I write this letter to you, I hope to come and see you soon. But if I am delayed, this letter will let you know how we should conduct ourselves in God's household, which is the church of the living God, the pillar and support of the truth. No one can deny how great is the secret of our religion:

Voice 1   He appeared in human form.

Voice 2   He was shown to be right by the Spirit.

Voice 3   He was seen by angels.

Voice 1   He was preached among the nations.

Voice 2   He was believed in throughout the world.

Voice 3   He was taken up to heaven.

Cast   [This is] the word of the Lord.
All   **Thanks be to God.**

Cast: **Paul, Voice 1, Voice 2, Voice 3.**

A living hope
1 Peter 1.3–12

Voices 1 and **2**   Let us give thanks to the God and Father of our Lord Jesus Christ!

Voice 1   Because of his great mercy he gave us new life by raising Jesus Christ from death.

Voice 2   This fills us with a living hope, and so we look forward to possessing the rich blessings that God keeps for his people.

Voice 1   He keeps them for you in heaven, where they cannot decay or spoil or fade away.

Voice 2   They are for you, who through faith are kept safe by God's power for the salvation which is ready to be revealed at the end of time.

Voice 3   Be glad about this, even though it may now be necessary for you to be sad for a while because of the many kinds of trials you suffer.

Voice 1   Their purpose is to prove that your faith is genuine. Even gold, which can be destroyed, is tested by fire; and so your faith, which is much more precious than gold, must also be tested, so that it may endure.

Voice 3   Then you will receive praise and glory and honour on the Day when Jesus Christ is revealed.

Voice 1   You love him, although you have not seen him.

Voice 2   And you believe in him, although you do not now see him.

Voice 1   So you rejoice with a great and glorious joy which words cannot express, because you are receiving the salvation of your souls, which is the purpose of your faith in him.

Voice 2   It was concerning this salvation that the prophets made careful search and investigation, and they prophesied about this gift which God would give you.

Voice 3   They tried to find out when the time would be and how it would come. This was the time to which Christ's Spirit in them was pointing, in predicting the sufferings that Christ would have to endure and the glory that would follow.

Voice 2   God revealed to these prophets that their work was not for their own benefit, but for yours, as they spoke about those things which you have now heard from the messengers who announced the Good News by the power of the Holy Spirit sent from heaven.

Voice 1   These are things which even the angels would like to understand.

Cast   [This is] the word of the Lord.
All   **Thanks be to God.**

Cast: **Voice 1, Voice 2, Voice 3** (can be the same as Voice 1).

The glory of the Son of Man
Revelation 1.9–20

John

I am John, your brother, and as a follower of Jesus I am your partner in patiently enduring the suffering that comes to those who belong to his Kingdom. I was put on the island of Patmos because I had proclaimed God's word and the truth that Jesus revealed. On the Lord's day the Spirit took control of me, and I heard a loud voice, that sounded like a trumpet, speaking behind me. It said:

Voice

Write down what you see, and send the book to the churches in these seven cities: Ephesus, Smyrna, Pergamum, Thyatira, Sardis, Philadelphia, and Laodicea.

John

I turned round to see who was talking to me, and I saw seven gold lampstands, and among them there was what looked like a human being, wearing a robe that reached to his feet, and a gold belt round his chest. His hair was white as wool, or as snow, and his eyes blazed like fire; his feet shone like brass that has been refined and polished, and his voice sounded like a roaring waterfall. He held seven stars in his right hand, and a sharp two-edged sword came out of his mouth. His face was as bright as the midday sun. When I saw him, I fell down at his feet like a dead man. He placed his right hand on me and said:

Voice

Don't be afraid! I am the first and the last. I am the living one! I was dead, but now I am alive for ever and ever. I have authority over death and the world of the dead. Write, then, the things you see, both the things that are now and the things that will happen afterwards. This is the secret meaning of the seven stars that you see in my right hand, and of the seven gold lamp-stands: the seven stars are the angels of the seven churches, and the seven lamp-stands are the seven churches.

Cast   [This is] the word of the Lord.
All   **Thanks be to God.**

Cast: **John, Voice.**

PENTECOST
(WHITSUN)

Joseph interprets the prisoners' dreams
Genesis 40.1–23

Narrator	[Some time later] the king of Egypt's wine steward and his chief baker offended the king. He was angry with these two officials and put them in prison in the house of the captain of the guard, in the same place where Joseph was being kept. They spent a long time in prison, and the captain assigned Joseph as their servant. (PAUSE)
	One night there in prison the wine steward and the chief baker each had a dream, and the dreams had different meanings. (PAUSE)
	When Joseph came to them in the morning, he saw that they were upset. [He asked them:]
Joseph	Why do you look so worried today?
[Narrator	They answered:]
Baker	Each of us had a dream, and there is no one here to explain what the dreams mean.
Joseph	It is God who gives the ability to interpret dreams. Tell me your dreams.
Narrator	So the wine steward said:
Steward	In my dream there was a grapevine in front of me with three branches on it. As soon as the leaves came out, the blossoms appeared, and the grapes ripened. I was holding the king's cup; so I took the grapes and squeezed them into the cup and gave it to him.
Joseph	This is what it means: the three branches are three days. In three days the king will release you, pardon you, and restore you to your position. You will give him his cup as you did before when you were his wine steward. But please remember me when everything is going well for you, and please be kind enough to mention me to the king and help me to get out of this prison. After all, I was kidnapped from the land of the Hebrews, and even here in Egypt I didn't do anything to deserve being put in prison.
Narrator	When the chief baker saw that the interpretation of the wine steward's dream was favourable, he said to Joseph:
Baker	I had a dream too, I was carrying three bread-baskets on my head. In the top basket there were all kinds of pastries for the king, and the birds were eating them.
Joseph	This is what it means: the three baskets are three days. In three days the king will release you—and have your head cut off! Then he will hang your body on a pole, and the birds will eat your flesh.
Narrator	On his birthday three days later the king gave a banquet for all his officials; he released his wine steward and his chief baker and brought them before his officials. He restored the wine steward to

121

his former position, but he executed the chief baker. It all happened just as Joseph had said. (PAUSE)

But the wine steward never gave Joseph another thought—he forgot all about him.

Cast	[This is] the word of the Lord.
All	**Thanks be to God.**

Cast: **Narrator, Joseph, Baker, Steward.**

Restoration
Isaiah 27.2–6

Isaiah   The Lord will say of his pleasant vineyard:

The Lord   I watch over it and water it continually. I guard it night and day so that no one will harm it. I am no longer angry with the vineyard. If only there were thorns and briars to fight against, then I would burn them up completely. But if the enemies of my people want my protection, let them make peace with me. Yes, let them make peace with me.

Isaiah   In days to come the people of Israel, the descendants of Jacob, will take root like a tree, and they will blossom and bud. The earth will be covered with the fruit they produce.

Cast	[This is] the word of the Lord.
All	**Thanks be to God.**

Cast: **Isaiah, The Lord.**

The good news of deliverance
Isaiah 61.1–11

Isaiah   The Sovereign Lord has filled me with his spirit. He has chosen me and sent me to bring good news to the poor, to heal the broken-hearted, to announce release to captives and freedom to those in prison. He has sent me to proclaim that the time has come when the Lord will save his people and defeat their enemies. He has sent me to comfort all who mourn, to give to those who mourn in Zion joy and gladness instead of grief, a song of praise instead of sorrow. They will be like trees that the Lord himself has planted. They will all do what is right, and God will be praised for what he has done. They will rebuild cities that have long been in ruins.
My people, foreigners will serve you. They will take care of your flocks and farm your land and tend your vineyards. And you will be known as the priests of the Lord, the servants of our God. You will enjoy the wealth of the nations and be proud that it is yours. Your shame and disgrace are ended. You will live in your own land, and your wealth will be doubled; your joy will last for ever.

The Lord says:

The Lord	I love justice and I hate oppression and crime. I will faithfully reward my people and make an eternal covenant with them. They will be famous among the nations; everyone who sees them will know that they are a people whom I have blessed.
Isaiah	Jerusalem rejoices because of what the Lord has done. She is like a bride dressed for her wedding. God has clothed her with salvation and victory. As surely as seeds sprout and grow, the Sovereign Lord will save his people, and all the nations will praise him.
Cast	[This is] the word of the Lord.
All	**Thanks be to God.**

Cast: **Isaiah, The Lord.**

New names
From Isaiah 62.1–12

Isaiah	I will speak out to encourage Jerusalem; I will not be silent until she is saved, and her victory shines like a torch in the night. Jerusalem, the nations will see you victorious! All their kings will see your glory. You will by called by a new name, a name given by the Lord himself. You will be like a beautiful crown for the Lord. No longer will you be called:
Sad voice	'Forsaken'—
Isaiah	Or your land be called:
Sad voice	'The Deserted Wife.'
Isaiah	Your new name will be:
Joyful voice	'God Is Pleased with Her.'
Isaiah	Your land will be called:
Joyful voice	'Happily Married'—
Isaiah	Because the Lord is pleased with you and will be like a husband to your land. Like a young man taking a virgin as his bride, he who formed you will marry you. As a groom is delighted with his bride, so your God will delight in you.
	[People of Jerusalem, go out of the city and build a road for your returning people! Prepare a highway; clear it of stones! Put up a signal so that the nations can know that the Lord is announcing to all the earth:
The Lord	Tell the people of Jerusalem that the Lord is coming to save you, bringing with him the people he has rescued.]
Isaiah	You will be called:
Joyful voice	'God's Holy People,' 'The People the Lord Has Saved.'
Isaiah	Jerusalem will be called:

123

Joyful voice	'The City That God Loves,' 'The City That God Did Not Forsake.'

Cast	[This is] the word of the Lord.
All	**Thanks be to God.**

Cast: **Isaiah, Sad voice, Joyful voice [The Lord].**

The valley of dry bones
From Ezekiel 37.1–14

Ezekiel	I felt the powerful presence of the Lord, and his spirit took me and set me down in a valley where the ground was covered with bones. He led me all round the valley, and I could see that there were very many bones and that they were very dry. [He said to me:]
The Lord	Mortal man, can these bones come back to life?
Ezekiel	[I replied:] Sovereign Lord, only you can answer that! [He said:]
The Lord	Prophesy to the bones. Tell these dry bones to listen to the word of the Lord. Tell them that I, the Sovereign Lord, am saying to them, 'I am going to put breath into you and bring you back to life. I will give you sinews and muscles, and cover you with skin. I will put breath into you and bring you back to life. Then you will know that I am the Lord.'
Ezekiel	So I prophesied as I had been told. While I was speaking, I heard a rattling noise, and the bones began to join together. While I watched, the bones were covered with sinews and muscles, and then with skin. But there was no breath in the bodies.
	God said to me:
The Lord	Mortal man, prophesy to the wind. Tell the wind that the Sovereign Lord commands it to come from every direction, to breathe into these dead bodies, and to bring them back to life.
Ezekiel	So I prophesied as I had been told. Breath entered the bodies, and they came to life and stood up. There were enough of them to form an army.
	God said to me:
The Lord	Mortal man, the people of Israel are like these bones. They say that they are dried up, without any hope and with no future. So prophesy to my people Israel and tell them that I, the Sovereign Lord, am going to open their graves. I am going to take them out and bring them back to the land of Israel. When I open the graves where my people are buried and bring them out, they will know that I am the Lord. I will put my breath in them, bring them back to life, and let them live in their own land. Then they will know that I am the Lord.
(deliberately)	I have promised that I would do this—and I will. (PAUSE) I, the Lord, have spoken!

| Cast | [This is] the word of the Lord. |
| All | **Thanks be to God.** |

Cast: **Ezekiel, The Lord**.

The Day of the Lord
Joel 2.28–32

The Lord	I will pour out my spirit on everyone: your sons and daughters will proclaim my message; your old men will have dreams, and your young men will see visions. At that time I will pour out my spirit even on servants, both men and women. (PAUSE)
	I will give warnings of that day in the sky and on the earth; there will be bloodshed, fire, and clouds of smoke.
Joel	The sun will be darkened, and the moon will turn red as blood before the great and terrible day of the Lord comes. But all who ask the Lord for help will be saved. As the Lord has said:
The Lord	Some in Jerusalem will escape; those whom I choose will survive.
Cast	[This is] the word of the Lord.
All	**Thanks be to God.**

Cast: **The Lord, Joel**.

A song of praise
From Psalm 40.1–3 (LIT)

Leader	I waited patiently for the Lord:
All	**he turned and heard my cry.**
Leader	He pulled me out of the slimy pit:
All	**out of the mud and mire.**
Leader	He set my feet upon a rock:
All	**and made my step secure.**
Leader	He put a new song in my mouth:
All	**a hymn of praise to God.**
All	**Many will see it and fear; and put their trust in the Lord.**
All	**Glory to the Father, and to the Son, and to the Holy Spirit: as it was in the beginning, is now, and shall be for ever. Amen.**

Cast: **Leader, All** (two or more persons/congregation).

In praise of the Creator
From Psalm 104.1–4, 29–30 (LIT)

| Leader | O Lord our God, you are very great: |
| All | **You are clothed with splendour and majesty.** |

All (group 1)	**You make winds your messengers:**
All (group 2)	**and flashes of fire your servants.**
All (group 1)	**How many are your works:**
All (group 2)	**the earth is full of your creatures!**

Leader	When you hide your face, they are afraid:
All (group I)	**when you take away their breath, they die.**

Leader	When you send your Spirit they are created:
All	**and you renew the face of the earth.**

All   Glory to the Father, and to the Son, and to the Holy Spirit:
as it was in the beginning, is now, and shall be for ever. Amen.

Cast: **Leader, All** (group 1—two or more persons/part of congregation), **All** (group 2—two or more persons/part of congregation).

Prayer for the help of God's Spirit
From Psalm 143.6-10 and Psalm 51.6-12 (LIT)

Leader	O Lord, I spread my hands out to you:
All	**I thirst for you like dry ground.**

Leader	Teach me to do your will, for you are my God:
All	**let your good Spirit lead me in safety.**

Leader	You require sincerity and truth in me:
All	**fill my mind with your wisdom.**

Leader	Create in me a pure heart, O God:
All	**and renew a faithful spirit in me.**

Leader	Do not cast me from your presence:
All	**or take your Holy Spirit from me.**

Leader	Give me again the joy of your salvation:
All	**and make me willing to obey.**

All   Glory to the Father, and to the Son, and to the Holy Spirit:
as it was in the beginning, is now, and shall be for ever. Amen

Cast: **Leader, All** (two or more persons/congregation). (Verses from Psalms 51 and 143 have been grouped together to make provision for an occasion when the person and work of the Holy Spirit is being considered.)

Jesus and Beelzebul
From Matthew 12.22-32

Narrator	Some people brought to Jesus a man who was blind and could not talk because he had a demon. Jesus healed the man, so that he was able to talk and see. The crowds were all amazed at what Jesus had done [and asked]:
Person(s)	Could he be the Son of David?
Narrator	When the Pharisees heard this, they replied:

Pharisee	He drives out demons only because their ruler Beelzebul gives him power to do so.
Narrator	Jesus knew what they were thinking, so he said to them:
Jesus	Any country that divides itself into groups which fight each other will not last very long. And any town or family that divides itself into groups which fight each other will fall apart. So if one group is fighting another in Satan's kingdom, this means that it is already divided into groups and will soon fall apart! You say that I drive out demons because Beelzebul gives me the power to do so. Well, then, who gives your followers the power to drive them out? What your own followers do proves that you are wrong! No, it is not Beelzebul, but God's Spirit, who gives me the power to drive out demons, which proves that the Kingdom of God has already come upon you.
	I tell you that people can be forgiven any sin and any evil thing they say; but whoever says evil things against the Holy Spirit will not be forgiven. Anyone who says something against the Son of Man can be forgiven; but whoever says something against the Holy Spirit will not be forgiven—now or ever.

Cast [This is] the word of the Lord.   OR   **This is the Gospel of Christ**/*This is the Gospel of the Lord.*
All   **Thanks be to God.**   **Praise to Christ our Lord**/*Praise to you, Lord Jesus Christ.*

Cast: **Narrator, Person(s), Pharisee, Jesus**.

Jesus talks to his disciples
From John 14.1–26 [27–31]

Jesus	Believe in God and believe also in me. There are many rooms in my Father's house, and I am going to prepare a place for you. I would not tell you this if it were not so. And after I go and prepare a place for you, I will come back and take you to myself, so that you will be where I am. You know the way that leads to the place where I am going.
Thomas	Lord, we do not know where you are going, so how can we know the way to get there?
Jesus	I am the way, the truth, and the life; no one goes to the Father except by me. Now that you have known me, you will know my Father also, and from now on you do know him and you have seen him.
Philip	Lord, show us the Father; that is all we need.
Jesus	For a long time I have been with you all; yet you do not know me, Philip? Whoever has seen me has seen the Father. Why, then, do you say, 'Show us the Father'? Do you not believe, Philip, that I am in the Father and the Father is in me? The words that I have spoken to you do not come from me. The Father, who remains in me, does his own work. Believe me when I say that I am in the

Father and the Father is in me. And I will do whatever you ask for in my name, so that the Father's glory will be shown through the Son. If you ask me for anything in my name, I will do it.

I will ask the Father, and he will give you another Helper, who will stay with you for ever. He is the Spirit who reveals the truth about God. When I go, you will not be left all alone; I will come back to you. When that day comes, you will know that I am in my Father and that you are in me, just as I am in you.

My Father will love whoever loves me; I too will love him and reveal myself to him.

Judas   Lord, how can it be that you will reveal yourself to us and not to the world?

Jesus   Whoever loves me will obey my teaching. My Father will love him, and my Father and I will come to him and live with him.

I have told you this while I am still with you. The Helper, the Holy Spirit, whom the Father will send in my name, will teach you everything and make you remember all that I have told you.

[Peace is what I leave with you; it is my own peace that I give you. I do not give it as the world does. Do not be worried and upset; do not be afraid. You heard me say to you, 'I am leaving, but I will come back to you.' If you loved me, you would be glad that I am going to the Father; for he is greater than I. I have told you this now before it all happens so that when it does happen, you will believe. I cannot talk with you much longer, because the ruler of this world is coming. He has no power over me, but the world must know that I love the Father; that is why I do everything he commands me.

Come, let us go from this place.]

Cast   [This is] the word of the Lord.   OR   This is the Gospel of Christ/*This is the Gospel of the Lord.*
All   **Thanks be to God**.   **Praise to Christ our Lord**/*Praise to you, Lord Jesus Christ.*

Cast: **Jesus, Thomas, Philip, Judas** (Thomas, Philip and Judas can all be the same).

Jesus appears to his disciples
John 20.19–23

Narrator   It was late that Sunday evening, and the disciples were gathered together behind locked doors, because they were afraid of the Jewish authorities. Then Jesus came and stood among them. [He said:]

Jesus   Peace be with you.

Narrator   After saying this, he showed them his hands and his side. The disciples were filled with joy at seeing the Lord. [Jesus said to them again:]

Jesus   Peace be with you. As the Father sent me, so I send you.

Narrator	Then he breathed on them [and said]:
Jesus	Receive the Holy Spirit. If you forgive people's sins, they are forgiven; if you do not forgive them, they are not forgiven.

Cast [This is] the word of the Lord.   OR   This is the Gospel of Christ/*This is the Gospel of the Lord.*
All   **Thanks be to God.**   **Praise to Christ our Lord**/*Praise to you, Lord Jesus Christ.*

Cast: **Narrator, Jesus**.

The coming of the Holy Spirit
From Acts 2.1–21

Narrator	When the day of Pentecost came, all the believers were gathered together in one place. Suddenly there was a noise from the sky which sounded like a strong wind blowing, and it filled the whole house where they were sitting. Then they saw what looked like tongues of fire which spread out and touched each person there. They were all filled with the Holy Spirit and began to talk in other languages, as the Spirit enabled them to speak. There were Jews living in Jerusalem, religious men who had come from every country in the world. When they heard this noise, a large crowd gathered. They were all excited, because each one of them heard the believers speaking in his own language. [In amazement and wonder they exclaimed:]
Person 1 (amazed)	These people who are talking like this are Galileans! How is it, then, that all of us hear them speaking in our own native languages about the great things that God has done?
Narrator	Amazed and confused, they kept asking each other:
Persons 1 and **2**	What does this mean?
Narrator	Others made fun of the believers:
Person 2	These people are drunk!
Narrator	Then Peter stood up with the other eleven apostles and in a loud voice began to speak to the crowd:
Peter	Fellow-Jews and all of you who live in Jerusalem, listen to me and let me tell you what this means. These people are not drunk, as you suppose; it is only nine o'clock in the morning. Instead, this is what the prophet Joel spoke about:
Joel	This is what I will do in the last days, God says: I will pour out my Spirit on everyone. Your sons and daughters will proclaim my message: your young men will see visions, and your old men will have dreams. Yes, even on my servants, both men and women, I will pour out my Spirit in those days, and they will proclaim my message. I will perform miracles in the sky above and wonders on the earth below. There will be blood, fire, and thick smoke; the sun will be darkened, and the moon will turn red as blood, before the

great and glorious Day of the Lord comes. And then, whoever calls
out to the Lord for help will be saved.

Cast   [This is] the word of the Lord.
All   **Thanks be to God.**

Cast: **Narrator, Person 1, Person 2, Peter, Joel** (can be the same as Peter).

The early church
Acts 2.36–47

Narrator   Peter said:

Peter   All the people of Israel, then, are to know for sure that this
                  Jesus, whom you crucified, is the one that God has made Lord
                  and Messiah!

Narrator   When the people heard this, they were deeply troubled and said
                  to Peter and the other apostles:

Person   What shall we do, brothers?

Peter   Each one of you must turn away from his sins and be baptized in
                  the name of Jesus Christ, so that your sins will be forgiven; and
                  you will receive God's gift, the Holy Spirit. For God's promise was
                  made to you and your children, and to all who are far away—all
                  whom the Lord our God calls to himself.

Narrator   Peter made his appeal to them and with many other words he
                  urged them:

Peter   Save yourselves from the punishment coming on this wicked people!

Narrator   Many of them believed his message and were baptized, and about
                  three thousand people were added to the group that day. They
                  spent their time in learning from the apostles, taking part in the
                  fellowship, and sharing in the fellowship meals and the prayers.
                  (PAUSE)

                  Many miracles and wonders were being done through the apostles,
                  and everyone was filled with awe. All the believers continued
                  together in close fellowship and shared their belongings with one
                  another. They would sell their property and possessions, and dis-
                  tribute the money among all, according to what each one needed.
                  Day after day they met as a group in the Temple, and they had
                  their meals together in their homes, eating with glad and humble
                  hearts, praising God, and enjoying the good will of all the people.
                  And every day the Lord added to their group those who were
                  being saved.

Cast: [This is] the word of the Lord.
All   **Thanks be to God.**

Cast: **Narrator, Peter, Person**.

The church at Antioch
Acts 11.19–30

Narrator 1   Some of the believers who were scattered by the persecution which took place when Stephen was killed went as far as Phoenicia, Cyprus, and Antioch, telling the message to Jews only.

Narrator 2   But other believers, men from Cyprus and Cyrene, went to Antioch and proclaimed the message to Gentiles also, telling them the Good News about the Lord Jesus. The Lord's power was with them, and a great number of people believed and turned to the Lord. The news about this reached the church in Jerusalem, so they sent Barnabas to Antioch.

Narrator 1   When he arrived and saw how God had blessed the people, he was glad and urged them all to be faithful and true to the Lord with all their hearts.

Narrator 3   Barnabas was a good man, full of the Holy Spirit and faith, and many people were brought to the Lord.

Narrator 1   Then Barnabas went to Tarsus to look for Saul. When he found him, he took him to Antioch, and for a whole year the two met with the people of the church and taught a large group. It was at Antioch that the believers were first called Christians.

Narrator 2   About that time some prophets went from Jerusalem to Antioch. One of them, named Agabus, stood up and by the power of the Spirit predicted that a severe famine was about to come over all the earth.

Narrator 3   It came when Claudius was emperor.

Narrator 2   The disciples decided that each of them would send as much as he could to help their fellow-believers who lived in Judaea. They did this, then, and sent the money to the church elders by Barnabas and Saul.

Cast   [This is]the word of the Lord.
All   **Thanks be to God.**

Cast: **Narrator 1, Narrator 2, Narrator 3**.

Paul in Ephesus
Acts 19.1–10

Narrator   Paul arrived in Ephesus. There he found some disciples [and asked them:]

Paul   Did you receive the Holy Spirit when you became believers?

[Narrator   They answered:]

Believer 1   We have not even heard that there *is* a Holy Spirit.

Paul   Well, then, what kind of baptism did you receive?

Believer 2   The baptism of John.

Paul   The baptism of John was for those who turned from their sins; and he told the people of Israel to believe in the one who was coming after him—that is, in Jesus.

Narrator   When they heard this, they were baptized in the name of the Lord Jesus. Paul placed his hands on them, and the Holy Spirit came upon them; they spoke in strange tongues and also proclaimed God's message. They were about twelve men in all.

Paul went into the synagogue and during three months spoke boldly with the people, holding discussions with them and trying to convince them about the Kingdom of God. But some of them were stubborn and would not believe, and before the whole group they said evil things about the Way of the Lord. So Paul left them and took the believers with him, and every day he held discussions in the lecture hall of Tyrannus. This went on for two years, so that all the people who lived in the province of Asia, both Jews and Gentiles, heard the word of the Lord.

Cast   [This is]the word of the Lord.
All   **Thanks be to God.**

Cast: **Narrator, Paul, Believer 1, Believer 2**.

Life in the Spirit
Romans 8.1–11

Voice 1   There is no condemnation now for those who live in union with Christ Jesus. For the law of the Spirit, which brings us life in union with Christ Jesus, has set me free from the law of sin and death. What the Law could not do, because human nature was weak, God did. He condemned sin in human nature by sending his own Son, who came with a nature like man's sinful nature, to do away with sin. God did this so that the righteous demands of the Law might be fully satisfied in us who live according to the Spirit, and not according to human nature.

Voice 2   Those who live as their human nature tells them to, have their minds controlled by what human nature wants.

Voice 1   Those who live as the Spirit tells them to, have their minds controlled by what the Spirit wants.

Voice 2   To be controlled by human nature results in death.

Voice 1   To be controlled by the Spirit results in life and peace.

Voice 2   And so a person becomes an enemy of God when he is controlled by his human nature; for he does not obey God's law, and in fact he cannot obey it. Those who obey their human nature cannot please God.

Voice 1   But you do not live as your human nature tells you to; instead, you live as the Spirit tells you to—if, in fact, God's Spirit lives in you.

Voice 2	Whoever does not have the Spirit of Christ does not belong to him.
Voice 1	But if Christ lives in you, the Spirit is life for you because you have been put right with God, even though your bodies are going to die because of sin. If the Spirit of God, who raised Jesus from death, lives in you, then he who raised Christ from death will also give life to your mortal bodies by the presence of his Spirit in you.
Cast	[This is] the word of the Lord.
All	**Thanks be to God.**

Cast: **Voice 1** (triumphant), **Voice 2** (serious).

Led by God's Spirit
Romans 8.14–17

Reader	Those who are led by God's Spirit are God's sons. For the Spirit that God has given you does not make you slaves and cause you to be afraid; instead, the Spirit makes you God's children, and by the Spirit's power we cry out to God:
Person 1	Father!
Person 2	My Father!
Reader	God's Spirit joins himself to our spirits to declare that we are God's children.
Person 1	Since we are his children, we will possess the blessings he keeps for his people.
Person 2	And we will also possess with Christ what God has kept for him.
Person 1	For if we share Christ's suffering, we will also share his glory.
Cast	[This is] the word of the Lord.
All	**Thanks be to God.**

Cast: **Reader, Person 1, Person 2.**

One body
Romans 12.4–13

Person 1	We have many parts in the one body, and all these parts have different functions.
Person 2	In the same way, though we are many, we are one body in union with Christ, and we are all joined to each other as different parts of one body.
Person 3	So we are to use our different gifts in accordance with the grace that God has given us.
Person 1	If our gift is to speak God's message, we should do it according to the faith that we have.

133

Person 2	If it is to serve, we should serve.
Person 3	If it is to teach, we should teach.
Person 1	If it is to encourage others, we should do so.
Person 2	Whoever shares with others should do it generously.
Person 3	Whoever has authority should work hard.
Person 1	Whoever shows kindness to others should do it cheerfully.
Teacher	Love must be completely sincere. Hate what is evil, hold on to what is good. Love one another warmly as Christian brothers, and be eager to show respect for one another. Work hard and do not be lazy. Serve the Lord with a heart full of devotion. Let your hope keep you joyful, be patient in your troubles, and pray at all times. Share your belongings with your needy fellow-Christians, and open your homes to strangers.
Cast	[This is] the word of the Lord.
All	**Thanks be to God.**

Cast: **Person 1, Person 2, Person 3, Teacher** (may be divided between Persons 1–3).

One body with many parts
From 1 Corinthians 12.12–27

Paul	Christ is like a single body, which has many parts; it is still one body, even though it is made up of different parts. In the same way, all of us, whether Jews or Gentiles, whether slaves or free, have been baptized into the one body by the same Spirit, and we have all been given the one Spirit to drink.
	For the body itself is not made up of only one part, but of many parts. If the foot were to say:
Foot	Because I am not a hand, I don't belong to the body.
Paul	That would not keep it from being a part of the body. And if the ear were to say:
Ear	Because I am not an eye, I don't belong to the body.
Paul	That would not keep it from being a part of the body. If the whole body were just an eye, how could it hear? And if it were only an ear, how could it smell? As it is, however, God put every different part in the body just as he wanted it to be. There would not be a body if it were all only one part! As it is, there are many parts but one body.
	So then, the eye cannot stay to the hand:
Eye	I don't need you!
Paul	Nor can the head say to the feet:
Head	Well, I don't need *you*!

Paul	On the contrary, we cannot do without the parts of the body that seem to be weaker.
Cast	All of you are Christ's body, and each one is a part of it.
Cast	[This is] the word of the Lord.
All	**Thanks be to God.**

Cast: **Paul, Foot, Ear, Eye, Head.**

Tongues
1 Corinthians 14.18–25

Paul

I thank God that I speak in strange tongues much more than any of you. But in church worship I would rather speak five words that can be understood, in order to teach others, than speak thousands of words in strange tongues.

Do not be like children in your thinking, my brothers; be children so far as evil is concerned, but be grown-up in your thinking. In the Scriptures it is written:

Scripture

By means of men speaking strange languages
I will speak to my people, says the Lord.
I will speak through lips of foreigners,
but even then my people will not listen to me.

Paul

So then, the gift of speaking in strange tongues is proof for unbelievers, not for believers, while the gift of proclaiming God's message is proof for believers, not for unbelievers.

If, then, the whole church meets together and everyone starts speaking in strange tongues—and if some ordinary people or unbelievers come in, won't they say that you are all crazy? But if everyone is proclaiming God's message when some unbeliever or ordinary person comes in, he will be convinced of his sin by what he hears. He will be judged by all he hears, his secret thoughts will be brought into the open, and he will bow down and worship God, confessing:

Person

Truly God is here among you!

Cast	[This is] the word of the Lord.
All	**Thanks be to God.**

Cast: **Paul, Scripture, Person.**

Spiritual blessings in Christ
Ephesians 1.2–14

Voices 1 and **2**

May God our Father and the Lord Jesus Christ give you grace and peace.

Voice 1

Let us give thanks to the God and Father of our Lord Jesus Christ! For in our union with Christ he has blessed us by giving us every spiritual blessing in the heavenly world.

135

Voice 2   Even before the world was made, God had already chosen us to be his through our union with Christ, so that we would be holy and without fault before him.

Voice 1   Because of his love God had already decided that through Jesus Christ he would make us his sons—this was his pleasure and purpose.

Voices 1 and 2   Let us praise God for his glorious grace.

Voice 2   For the free gift he gave us in his dear Son!

Voice 1   For by the sacrificial death of Christ we are set free, that is, our sins are forgiven.

Voice 2   How great is the grace of God, which he gave to us in such large measure!

Voice 1   In all his wisdom and insight God did what he had purposed, and made known to us the secret plan he had already decided to complete by means of Christ. This plan, which God will complete when the time is right, is to bring all creation together, everything in heaven and on earth, with Christ as head.

Voice 2   All things are done according to God's plan and decision; and God chose us to be his own people in union with Christ because of his own purpose, based on what he had decided from the very beginning.

Voices 1 and 2   Let us, then, who were the first to hope in Christ, praise God's glory!

Voice 1   And you also became God's people when you heard the true message, the Good News that brought you salvation. You believed in Christ, and God put his stamp of ownership on you by giving you the Holy Spirit he had promised.

Voice 2   The Spirit is the guarantee that we shall receive what God has promised his people, and this assures us that God will give complete freedom to those who are his.

Voices 1 and 2   Let us praise his glory!

Cast   [This is] the word of the Lord.
All   **Thanks be to God.**

Cast: **Voice 1, Voice 2.**

Gifts and unity in the church
Ephesians 4.1–16

Voice 1   Live a life that measures up to the standard God set when he called you.

Voice 2   Be always humble, gentle, and patient. Show your love by being tolerant with one another.

Voice 3   Do your best to preserve the unity which the Spirit gives by means of the peace that binds you together.

Voice 1   There is one body and one Spirit, just as there is one hope to which God has called you.

Voice 2   There is one Lord, one faith, one baptism.

Voice 3   There is one God and Father of all mankind, who is Lord of all, works through all, and is in all.

Voice 1   Each one of us has received a special gift in proportion to what Christ has given. As the scripture says:

Psalmist   When he went up to the very heights,
                   he took many captives with him;
                   he gave gifts to mankind.

Voice 2   Now, what does 'he went up' mean?

Voice 1   It means that first he came down to the lowest depths of the earth.

Voice 3   So the one who came down is the same one who went up, above and beyond the heavens, to fill the whole universe with his presence.

Voice 1   It was he who 'gave gifts to mankind'; he appointed some to be apostles, others to be prophets, others to be evangelists, others to be pastors and teachers. He did this to prepare all God's people for the work of Christian service, in order to build up the body of Christ.

Voice 2   And so we shall all come together to that oneness in our faith and in our knowledge of the Son of God.

Voice 3   We shall become mature people, reaching to the very height of Christ's full stature. Then we shall no longer be children, carried by the waves and blown about by every shifting wind of the teaching of deceitful men, who lead others into error by the tricks they invent.

Voice 1   Instead, by speaking the truth in a spirit of love, we must grow up in every way to Christ, who is the head.

Voice 2   Under his control all the different parts of the body fit together, and the whole body is held together by every joint with which it is provided.

Voice 3   So when each separate part works as it should, the whole body grows and builds itself up through love.

Cast   [This is] the word of the Lord.
All   **Thanks be to God.**

Cast: **Voice 1, Voice 2, Voice 3, Psalmist** (can be the same as Voice 3).

Instructions to the church
From 1 Thessalonians 5.12–28

Voice 1   Respect those who work hard among you, who are over you in the Lord and who admonish you.

Voice 2   Hold them in the highest regard in love because of their work.

Voice 3   Live in peace with each other.

Voice 1   And we urge you . . .

Voice 2   Warn those who are idle.

Voice 3   Encourage the timid.

Voice 1   Help the weak.

Voice 2   Be patient with everyone.

Voice 3   Make sure that nobody pays back wrong for wrong, but always try to be kind to each other and to everyone else.

Voice 1   Be joyful always.

Voice 2   Pray continually; give thanks in all circumstances—

Voice 3   For this is God's will for you in Christ Jesus.

Voice 1   Do not put out the Spirit's fire; do not treat prophecies with contempt.

Voice 2   Test everything.

Voice 3   Hold on to the good.

Voice 1   Avoid every kind of evil.

Voice 2   May God himself, the God of peace, sanctify you through and through.

Voice 3   May your whole spirit, soul and body be kept blameless at the coming of our Lord Jesus Christ.

Voice 1   The one who calls you is faithful and he will do it.

Voices 1–3   The grace of our Lord Jesus Christ be with you.

Cast   [This is] the word of the Lord.
All   **Thanks be to God.**

Cast: **Voice 1, Voice 2, Voice 3.**

The grace of Christ
From Titus 2.11–3.7

Voice 1   The grace of God that brings salvation has appeared to all. It teaches us to say:

Voices 1–3   No!

Voice 1	. . . to ungodliness and worldly passions, and to live self-controlled, upright and godly lives in this present age, while we wait for the blessed hope—
Voice 2	The glorious appearing of our great God and Saviour, Jesus Christ, who gave himself for us to redeem us from all wickedness—
Voice 3	And to purify for himself a people that are his very own, eager to do what is good.
Voice 1	At one time we too were foolish . . .
Voice 2	Disobedient . . .
Voice 3	Deceived and enslaved by all kinds of passions and pleasures.
Voice 1	We lived in malice and envy, being hated and hating one another.
Voice 2	But when the kindness and love of God our Saviour appeared, he saved us—
Voice 3	Not because of righteous things we had done, but because of his mercy.
Voice 2	He saved us through the washing of rebirth and renewal by the Holy Spirit, whom he poured out on us generously through Jesus Christ our Saviour.
Voice 1	So that, having been justified by his grace, we might become heirs having the hope of eternal life.
Cast	[This is] the word of the Lord.
All	**Thanks be to God.**

Cast: **Voice 1, Voice 2, Voice 3.**

HARVEST

Laws about the harvest

From Leviticus 23.15–22; Deuteronomy 14.22–29, 16.9–12

eviticus Count seven full weeks from the day after the Sabbath on which you bring your sheaf of corn to present to the Lord. On the fiftieth day, the day after the seventh Sabbath, present to the Lord another new offering of corn. Each family is to bring two loaves of bread and present them to the Lord as a special gift. Each loaf shall be made of two kilogrammes of flour baked with yeast and shall be presented to the Lord as an offering of the first corn to be harvested . . . On that day do none of your daily work, but gather for worship. Your descendants are to observe this regulation for all time to come, no matter where they live.

Deuteronomy Set aside a tithe—a tenth of all that your fields produce each year. Then go to the one place where the Lord your God has chosen to be worshipped; and there in his presence eat the tithes of your corn, wine, and olive-oil, and the first-born of your cattle and sheep. Do this so that you may learn to honour the Lord your God always . . . Do not neglect the Levites who live in your towns; they have no property of their own. At the end of every third year bring the tithe of all your crops and store it in your towns. This food is for the Levites, since they own no property, and for the foreigners, orphans, and widows who live in your towns. They are to come and get all they need. Do this, and the Lord your God will bless you in everything you do.

eviticus When you harvest your fields, do not cut the corn at the edges of the fields, and do not go back to cut the ears of corn that were left; leave them for poor people and foreigners. The Lord is your God.

Deuteronomy Count seven weeks from the time that you begin to harvest the corn, and then celebrate the Harvest Festival, to honour the Lord your God, by bringing him a freewill offering in proportion to the blessing he has given you. Be joyful in the Lord's presence, together with your children, your servants, and the Levites, foreigners, orphans, and widows who live in your towns. Do this at the one place of worship. Be sure that you obey these commands; do not forget that you were slaves in Egypt.

Cast [This is] the word of the Lord.
All **Thanks be to God.**

Cast: **Leviticus, Deuteronomy**.

Harvest offerings
Moses speaks to the people
Deuteronomy 26. 1–15

Moses   After you have occupied the land that the Lord your God is giving you and have settled there, each of you must place in a basket the first part of each crop that you harvest and you must take it with you to the one place of worship. Go to the priest in charge at that time and say to him:

Worshipper   I now acknowledge to the Lord my God that I have entered the land that he promised our ancestors to give us.

Moses   The priest will take the basket from you and place it before the altar of the Lord your God. Then, in the Lord's presence you will recite these words:

Worshipper   My ancestor was a wandering Aramean, who took his family to Egypt to live. They were few in number when they went there, but they became a large and powerful nation. The Egyptians treated us harshly and forced us to work as slaves. Then we cried out for help to the Lord, the God of our ancestors. He heard us and saw our suffering, hardship, and misery. By his great power and strength he rescued us from Egypt. He worked miracles and wonders, and caused terrifying things to happen. He brought us here and gave us this rich and fertile land. So now I bring to the Lord the first part of the harvest that he has given me.

Moses   Then set the basket down in the Lord's presence and worship there. Be grateful for the good things that the Lord your God has given you and your family; and let the Levites and the foreigners who live among you join in the celebration. Every third year give the tithe—a tenth of your crops—to the Levites, the foreigners, the orphans, and the widows, so that in every community they will have all they need to eat. When you have done this, say to the Lord:

Worshipper   None of the sacred tithe is left in my house; I have given it to the Levites, the foreigners, the orphans, and the widows, as you commanded me to do. I have not disobeyed or forgotten any of your commands concerning the tithe. I have not eaten any of it when I was mourning; I have not taken any of it out of my house when I was ritually unclean; and I have not given any of it as an offering for the dead. I have obeyed you, O Lord; I have done everything you commanded concerning the tithe. Look down from your holy place in heaven and bless your people Israel; bless also the rich and fertile land that you have given us, as you promised our ancestors.

Cast   [This is] the word of the Lord.
All   **Thanks be to God.**

Cast: **Moses, Worshipper**.

144

God appears to Solomon again
2 Chronicles 7.11–22

Chronicler   After King Solomon had finished the Temple and the palace, successfully completing all his plans for them, the Lord appeared to him at night [He said to him]:

The Lord   I have heard your prayer, and I accept this Temple as the place where sacrifices are to be offered to me. Whenever I hold back the rain or send locusts to eat up the crops or send an epidemic on my people, if they pray to me and repent and turn away from the evil they have been doing, then I will hear them in heaven, forgive their sins, and make their land prosperous again. I will watch over this Temple and be ready to hear all the prayers that are offered here, because I have chosen it and consecrated it as the place where I will be worshipped for ever. I will watch over it and protect it for all time. If you serve me faithfully as your father David did, obeying my laws and doing everything I have commanded you, I will keep the promise I made to your father David when I told him that Israel would always be ruled by his descendants. But if you and your people ever disobey the laws and commands I have given you, and worship other gods, then I will remove you from the land that I gave you, and I will abandon this Temple that I have consecrated as the place where I am to be worshipped. People everywhere will ridicule it and treat it with contempt.

The Temple is now greatly honoured, but then everyone who passes by it will be amazed and will ask:

Person 1   Why did the Lord do this to this land and this Temple?

The Lord   People will answer:

Person 2   It is because they abandoned the Lord their God, who brought their ancestors out of Egypt.

Person 3   They gave their allegiance to other gods and worshipped *them*.

Person 2   That is why the Lord has brought this disaster on them.

Cast   [This is] the word of the Lord.
All   **Thanks be to God**.

Cast: **Chronicler, The Lord, Person 1, Person 2, Person 3** (can be the same as Person 2).

At the Festival of Unleavened Bread
From 2 Chronicles 30.26–31.21

Chronicler 1   The city of Jerusalem was filled with joy, because nothing like the Festival of Unleavened Bread had happened since the days of King Solomon, the son of David. The priests and the Levites asked the Lord's blessing on the people. In his home in heaven God heard their prayers and accepted them.

145

Chronicler 2   After the festival ended, all the people of Israel went to every city in Judah and broke the stone pillars, cut down the symbols of the goddess Asherah, and destroyed the altars and the pagan places of worship. They did the same thing throughout the rest of Judah, and the territories of Benjamin, Ephraim, and Manasseh; then they all returned home.

Chronicler 1   King Hezekiah re-established the organization of the priests and Levites, under which they each had specific duties. In addition, the king told the people of Jerusalem to bring the offerings to which the priests and the Levites were entitled, so that they could give all their time to the requirements of the Law of the Lord. As soon as the order was given, the people of Israel brought gifts of their finest corn, wine, olive-oil, honey, and other farm produce, and they also brought the tithes of everything they had.

Chronicler 2   The gifts started arriving in the third month and continued to pile up for the next four months. When King Hezekiah and his officials saw how much had been given, they praised the Lord and praised his people Israel. The king spoke to the priests and the Levites about these gifts, and Azariah the High Priest, a descendant of Zadok, said to him:

Azariah   Since the people started bringing their gifts to the Temple, there has been enough to eat and a large surplus besides. We have all this because the Lord has blessed his people.

Chronicler 1   Throughout all Judah, King Hezekiah did what was right and what was pleasing to the Lord his God. He was successful, because everything he did for the Temple or in observance of the Law, he did in a spirit of complete loyalty and devotion to his God.

Cast   [This is] the word of the Lord.
All: **Thanks to God.**

Cast: **Chronicler 1, Chronicler 2, Azariah**.

The Festival of Shelters
Nehemiah 8.13–18

Nehemiah   The heads of the clans, together with the priests and the Levites, went to Ezra to study the teachings of the Law. They discovered that the Law, which the Lord gave through Moses, ordered the people of Israel to live in temporary shelters during the Festival of Shelters. So they gave the following instructions and sent them all through Jerusalem and the other cities and towns:

Leader 1   Go out to the hills and get branches from pines, olives, myrtles, palms, and other trees—

Leader 2   To make shelters according to the instructions written in the Law.

Nehemiah   So the people got branches and built shelters on the flat roofs of their houses, in their yards, in the temple courtyard, and in the public squares by the Water Gate and by the Ephraim Gate. All the people who had come back from captivity built shelters and lived in them. This was the first time it had been done since the days of Joshua son of Nun, and everybody was excited and happy. From the first day of the festival to the last they read a part of God's Law every day. They celebrated for seven days, and on the eighth day there was a closing ceremony, as required in the Law.

Cast	[This is] the word of the Lord.
All	**Thanks be to God.**

Cast: **Nehemiah, Leader 1, Leader 2** (can be the same as Leader 1).

God and humanity
Psalm 8.1–9 (LIT)

Leader	O Lord, our Lord:
All	**how great is your name in all the world!**
All (group 1)	**Your glory fills the skies.**
All (group 2)	**Your praise is sung by children.**
All (group 3)	**You silence your enemies.**
Leader	I look at the sky your hands have made, the moon and stars you put in place:
All	**Who are we that you care for us?**
Leader	You made us less than gods:
All	**to crown us with glory and honour.**
Leader	You put us in charge of creation:
All (group 1)	**the beasts of the field.**
All (group 2)	**the birds of the air.**
All (group 3)	**the fish of the sea.**
Leader	O Lord, our Lord,
All	**how great is your name in all the world!**
All	**Glory to the Father, and to the Son, and to the Holy Spirit: as it was in the beginning, is now, and shall be for ever. Amen.**

Cast: **Leader, All** (group 1—two or more persons / part of congregation), **All** (group 2—two or more persons / part of congregation), **All** (group 3—two or more persons / part of congregation)

Praise for the harvest
From Psalm 65.1–13 (LIT)

Leader 2	O God, it is right for us to praise you, because you answer our prayers:
Leader 1	You care for the land and water it:
All (group 1)	**and make it rich and fertile.**
Leader 2	You fill the running streams with water:
All (group 2)	**and irrigate the land.**

| Leader 1 | You soften the ground with showers: |
| All (group 1) | **and make the young crops grow**. |

| Leader 2 | You crown the year with goodness: |
| All (group 2) | **and give us a plentiful harvest**. |

| Leader 1 | The pastures are filled with flocks: |
| All (group 1) | **the hillsides are clothed with joy**. |

| Leader 2 | The fields are covered with grain: |
| All | **they shout for joy and sing**. |

| All | **Glory to the Father, and to the Son, and to the Holy Spirit: as it was in the beginning, is now, and shall be for ever. Amen.** |

Cast: **Leader 2, Leader 1**, **All** (group 1—two or more persons / part of congregation), **All** (group 2—two or more persons / part of congregation).

A song of thanksgiving
Psalm 67.1–7 (LIT)

| Leader 1 | May God be gracious to us and bless us: |
| All (group 1) | **and make his face to shine upon us**. |

| Leader 2 | Let your ways be known upon earth: |
| All (group 2) | **your saving grace to every nation**. |

| Leaders 1 and 2 | Let the peoples praise you, O God: |
| All | **let the peoples praise you**. |

| Leader 1 | Let the nations be glad: |
| All (group 1) | **and sing aloud for joy**. |

| Leader 2 | Because you judge the peoples justly: |
| All (group 2) | **and guide the nations of the earth**. |

| Leaders 1 and 2 | Let the peoples praise you, O God: |
| All | **let all the peoples praise you**. |

| Leader 1 | Then the land will yield its harvest: |
| All (group 1) | **and God, our God, will bless us**. |

Leader 2	God will bless us:
All (group 2)	**and people will fear him**
All	**to the ends of the earth**.

| All | **Glory to the Father, and to the Son, and to the Holy Spirit: as it was in the beginning, is now, and shall be for ever. Amen.** |

Cast: **Leader 1**, **All** (group 1—two or more persons / part of congregation), **Leader 2**, **All** (group 2—two or more persons / part of congregation).

Invitation to worship
From Psalm 95.1–7 (LIT)

| Leader 1 | Come, let's joyfully praise our God, acclaiming the Rock of our salvation. |

Leader 2	Come before him with thanksgiving, and greet him with melody.
All (group 1)	**Our God is a great God:**
All (group 2)	**a king above all other gods!**
All (group 1)	**The depths of the earth are in his hands:**
All (group 2)	**the mountain peaks belong to him.**
All (group 1)	**The sea is his—he made it!**
All (group 2)	**his hands have fashioned all the earth.**
Leader 1	Come, bow down to worship him.
Leader 2	Kneel before the Lord who made us.
All (groups 1 & 2)	**We are his people: the sheep of his flock.**
Leader 1	Let us trust in him today.
Leader 2	Please listen to his voice!
All	**Glory to the Father, and to the Son, and to the Holy Spirit: as it was in the beginning, is now, and shall be for ever. Amen.**

Cast: **Leader 1, Leader 2, All** (group 1—two or more persons / part of congregation), **All** (group 2—two or more persons / part of congregation).

In praise of the Creator
From Psalm 104.1–4, 29–30 (LIT)

Leader	O Lord our God, you are very great:
All	**you are clothed with splendour and majesty.**
All (group 1)	**You make winds your messengers:**
All (group 2)	**and flashes of fire your servants.**
All (group 1)	**How many are your works:**
All (group 2)	**the earth is full of your creatures!**
Leader	When you hide your face, they are afraid:
All (group 1)	**when you take away their breath, they die.**
Leader	When you send your Spirit they are created:
All	**and you renew the face of the earth.**
All	**Glory to the Father, and to the Son, and to the Holy Spirit: as it was in the beginning, is now, and shall be for ever. Amen.**

Cast: **Leader, All** (group 1—two or more persons / part of congregation), **All** (group 2—two or more persons / part of congregation). (See also choral verson below.)

A prayer for deliverance
From Psalm 126.1–6 (LIT)

Leader	When the Lord brought us back from slavery:
All (group 1)	**we were like those who dream.**

149

Leader	Our mouths were filled with laughter:
All (group 2)	**our tongues with songs of joy**.
Leader	Then those around us said, 'The Lord has done great things for them':
All (group 1)	**The Lord has done great things for us, and we are filled with joy**.
Leader	Those who sow in tears.
All (group 2)	**shall reap with songs of joy**.
All	**Glory to the Father, and to the Son, and to the Holy Spirit: as it was in the beginning, is now, and shall be for ever. Amen.**

Cast: **Leader, All** (group 1—two or more persons / part of congregation), **All** (group 2—two or more persons / part of congregation).

In praise of God the almighty
From Psalm 147.1–20 (LIT)

Leader	O praise the Lord, sing out to God:
All	**such praise is right and good**.
Leader	The Lord restores Jerusalem:
All (group 1)	**he brings the exiles home**.
Leader	He heals all those with broken hearts:
All (group 2)	**he bandages their wounds**.
Leader	He counts the number of the stars:
All (group 3)	**he calls them each by name**.
Leader	How great and mighty is the Lord:
All (group 1)	**immeasurably wise!**
Leader	He raises up the humble ones:
All (group 2)	**and brings the mighty down**.
Leader	Sing hymns of triumph to his name
All (group 3)	**make music to our God!**
Leader	He spreads the clouds across the sky:
All (group 1)	**he showers the earth with rain**.
Leader	He sends the animals their food:
All (group 2)	**he feeds the hungry birds**.
Leader	His true delight is not the strong:
All (group 3)	**but those who trust his love**.
Leader	Extol the Lord, Jerusalem:
All (group 1)	**let Zion worship God!**
Leader	For God shall keep your people safe:
All (group 2)	**and bring your harvest home**.
Leader	He gives commandment to the earth:
All (group 3)	**his will is quickly done**.

| Leader | He spreads like wool the falling snow: |
| **All** (group 1) | **how cold the frosty air!** |

| Leader | He sends the wind, the warming rain: |
| **All** (group 2) | **and melts the ice away**. |

| Leader | His laws he gives to Israel: |
| **All** (group 3) | **and Judah hears his word**. |

| Leader | He does not favour other lands: |
| **All** | **so, praise the Lord. Amen!** |

| All | **Glory to the Father, and to the Son, and to the Holy Spirit: as it was in the beginning, is now, and shall be for ever. Amen.** |

Cast: **Leader, All** (group 1—two or more persons / part of congregation), **All** (group 2—two or more persons / part of congregation), **All** (group 3 – two or more persons / part of congregation).

Let the universe praise God!
From Psalm 148.1–14 (LIT)

| **All** | **Praise the Lord!** |

| Leader 1 | Praise the Lord from the heavens: |
| **All** (group 1) | **praise him in the heights above**. |

| Leader 2 | Praise him, all his angels: |
| **All** (group 2) | **praise him, all his heavenly host**. |

| Leader 1 | Praise him, sun and moon: |
| **All** (group 1) | **praise him, all you shining stars**. |

| Leader 2 | Let them praise the name of the Lord: |
| **All** | **Praise the Lord!** |

| Leader 1 | Praise the Lord from the earth: |
| **All** (group 1) | **praise him, great sea creatures**. |

| Leader 2 | Praise him, storms and clouds: |
| **All** (group 2) | **praise him, mountains and hills**. |

| Leader 1 | Praise him, fields and woods: |
| **All** (group 1) | **praise him, animals and birds**. |

| Leader 2 | Praise him, rulers and nations: |
| **All** (group 2) | **praise him, old and young**. |

| Leader 1 | Let them praise the name of the Lord: |
| **All** | **Praise the Lord! Amen**. |

| All | **Glory to the Father, and to the Son, and to the Holy Spirit: as it was in the beginning, is now, and shall be for ever. Amen.** |

Cast: **Leader 1, Leader 2, All** (group 1—two or more persons / part of congregation), **All** (group 2—two or more persons / part of congregation).

A hymn of praise
Psalm 149.1–9 (LIT)

Leader | Praise the Lord:
All | **praise the Lord!**

Leader | Sing a new song to the Lord:
All | **let the people shout his name!**

Leader | Praise your maker, Israel:
All (group 1) | **hail, your king, Jerusalem.**

Leader | Sing and dance to honour him:
All (group 2) | **praise him with the strings and drums.**

Leader | God takes pleasure in his saints:
All (group 1) | **crowns the meek with victory.**

Leader | Rise, you saints, in triumph now:
All (group 2) | **sing the joyful night away!**

Leader | Shout aloud and praise your God!
All (group 1) | **Hold aloft the two-edged sword!**

Leader | Let the judgement now begin:
All (group 2) | **kings shall fail and tyrants die.**

Leader | Through his people, by his word:
All | **God shall have the victory!**

Leader | Praise the Lord!
All | **Praise the Lord!**

All | **Glory to the Father, and to the Son, and to the Holy Spirit: as it was in the beginning, is now, and shall be for ever. Amen.**

Cast: **Leader, All** (group 1—two or more persons / part of congregation), **All** (group 2—two or more persons / part of congregation).

God will bless his people
Isaiah 30.19–26

Isaiah — You people who live in Jerusalem will not weep any more. The Lord is compassionate, and when you cry to him for help, he will answer you. The Lord will make you go through hard times, but he himself will be there to teach you, and you will not have to search for him any more. If you wander off the road to the right or the left, you will hear his voice behind you saying:

The Lord — Here is the road. Follow it.

Isaiah — You will take your idols plated with silver and your idols covered with gold, and will throw them away like filth, shouting:

Person — Out of my sight!

Isaiah — Whenever you sow your seeds, the Lord will send rain to make them grow and will give you a rich harvest, and your livestock will have plenty of pasture. The oxen and donkeys that plough your fields will eat the finest and best fodder. On the day when the forts of your enemies are captured and their people are killed, streams of water will flow from every mountain and every hill. The moon will be as bright as the sun, and the sun will be seven times brighter than usual, like the light of seven days in one. This will all happen when the Lord bandages and heals the wounds he has given his people.

Cast   [This is] the word of the Lord.
All   **Thanks be to God**.

Cast: **Isaiah, The Lord, Person.**

Jeremiah's sorrow for his people
Jeremiah 8.18–9.16

Jeremiah   My sorrow cannot be healed; I am sick at heart. Listen! Throughout the land I hear my people crying out:

Person 1   Is the Lord no longer in Zion?

Person 2   Is Zion's king no longer there? (PAUSE)

Jeremiah   The Lord, their king, replies:

The Lord   Why have you made me angry by worshipping your idols and by bowing down to your useless foreign gods?

Jeremiah   The people cry out:

Person 1   The summer is gone.

Person 2   The harvest is over.

Persons 1 and **2** But we have not been saved.

Jeremiah   My heart has been crushed because my people are crushed; I mourn; I am completely dismayed. Is there no medicine in Gilead? Are there no doctors there? Why, then, have my people not been healed? I wish my head were a well of water, and my eyes a fountain of tears, so that I could cry day and night for my people who have been killed. I wish I had a place to stay in the desert where I could get away from my people. They are all unfaithful, a mob of traitors. They are always ready to tell lies; dishonesty instead of truth rules the land. [The Lord says:]

The Lord   My people do one evil thing after another, and do not acknowledge me as their God.

Jeremiah   Everyone must be on guard against his friend, and no one can trust his brother; for every brother is as deceitful as Jacob, and everyone slanders his friends. They all mislead their friends, and no one tells the truth; they have taught their tongues to lie and will not give up their sinning. They do one violent thing after another, and one deceitful act follows another.

       The Lord says that his people reject him. [Because of this the Lord Almighty says:]

153

| **The Lord** | I will refine my people like metal and put them to the test. My people have done evil—what else can I do with them? Their tongues are like deadly arrows; they always tell lies. Everyone speaks friendly words to his neighbour, but is really setting a trap for him. Will I not punish them for these things? Will I not take revenge on a nation like this? I, the Lord, have spoken. |

Jeremiah

I said:
'I will mourn for the mountains
and weep for the pastures,
because they have dried up,
and no one travels through them.
The sound of livestock is no longer heard;
birds and wild animals have fled and gone.'

The Lord says:

The Lord

I will make Jerusalem a pile of ruins, a place where jackals live; the cities of Judah will become a desert, a place where no one lives.

Jeremiah

I asked: 'Lord, why is the land devastated and dry as a desert, so that no one travels through it? Who is wise enough to understand this? To whom have you explained it so that he can tell others?'

The Lord answered:

The Lord

This has happened because my people have abandoned the teaching that I gave them. They have not obeyed me or done what I told them. Instead, they have been stubborn and have worshipped the idols of Baal as their fathers taught them to do. So then, listen to what I, the Lord Almighty, the God of Israel, will do: I will give my people bitter plants to eat and poison to drink. I will scatter them among nations that neither they nor their ancestors have heard about, and I will send armies against them until I have completely destroyed them.

Cast   [This is] the word of the Lord.
All   **Thanks be to God**.

Cast: **Jeremiah, Person 1, Person 2** (can be the same as Person 1), **The Lord**.

The Lord's love for his people
Hosea 2.14–23

Prophet

I am going to take your mother into the desert again; there I will win her back with words of love. I will give back to her the vineyards she had and make Trouble Valley a door of hope. She will respond to me there as she did when she was young, when she came from Egypt. Then once again she will call me her husband—she will no longer call me her Baal. I will never let her speak the name of Baal again. At that time I will make a covenant with all the wild animals and birds, so that they will not harm my people. I will also remove all weapons of war from the land, all swords and bows, and will let my people live in peace and safety.

Poet	Israel, I will make you my wife; I will be true and faithful; I will show you constant love and mercy and make you mine for ever. I will keep my promise and make you mine, and you will acknowledge me as Lord. At that time I will answer the prayers of my people Israel. I will make rain fall on the earth, and the earth will produce corn and grapes and olives. I will establish my people in the land and make them prosper. I will show love to those who were called 'Unloved', and to those who were called 'Not-My-People'. I will say, 'You are my people,' and they will answer, 'You are our God.'
Cast All	[This is] the word of the Lord. **Thanks be to God.**

Cast: **Prophet, Poet.**

The fruit of repentance
Hosea 14.1–9

Prophet	Return to the Lord your God, people of Israel. Your sin has made you stumble and fall. Return to the Lord, and let this prayer be your offering to him:
Israelite 1	Forgive all our sins and accept our prayer, and we will praise you as we have promised.
Israelite 2	Assyria can never save us, and war-horses cannot protect us.
Israelite 1	We will never again say to our idols that they are our God.
Israelite 2	O Lord, you show mercy to those who have no one else to turn to.
Prophet	The Lord says:
The Lord	I will bring my people back to me. I will love them with all my heart; no longer am I angry with them. I will be to the people of Israel like rain in a dry land. They will blossom like flowers; they will be firmly rooted like the trees of Lebanon. They will be alive with new growth, and beautiful like olive-trees. They will be fragrant like the cedars of Lebanon. Once again they will live under my protection. They will flourish like a garden and be fruitful like a vineyard.

	They will be as famous as the wine of Lebanon.
	The people of Israel will have nothing more to do with idols;
	I will answer their prayers and take care of them;
	like an evergreen tree I will shelter them;
	I am the source of all their blessings.

Prophet   May those who are wise understand what is written here, and may they take it to heart. The Lord's ways are right, and righteous people live by following them, but sinners stumble and fall because they ignore them.

Cast   [This is] the word of the Lord.
All   **Thanks be to God.**

Cast: **Prophet, Israelite 1, Israelite 2** (can be the same as Israelite 1), **The Lord**.

God restores fertility to the land
From Joel 2.18–27

Joel   When the people assembled and the priests wept and prayed, then the Lord showed concern for his land; he had mercy on his people. He answered them:

The Lord   Now I am going to give you corn and wine and olive-oil, and you will be satisfied. Other nations will no longer despise you. [I will remove the locust army that came from the north and will drive some of them into the desert. Their front ranks will be driven into the Dead Sea, their rear ranks into the Mediterranean. Their dead bodies will stink. I will destroy them because of all they have done to you.]

Joel   Fields, don't be afraid, but be joyful and glad because of all the Lord has done for you. Animals, don't be afraid. The pastures are green; the trees bear their fruit, and there are plenty of figs and grapes. Be glad, people of Zion, rejoice at what the Lord your God has done for you. He has given you the right amount of autumn rain; he has poured down the winter rain for you and the spring rain as before.

The Lord   The threshing-places will be full of corn; the pits beside the presses will overflow with wine and olive-oil. I will give you back what you lost in the years when swarms of locusts ate your crops. It was I who sent this army against you.

Joel   Now you will have plenty to eat, and be satisfied. You will praise the Lord your God, who has done wonderful things for you.

The Lord   Then, Israel, you will know that I am among you, and that I, the Lord, am your God and there is no other. My people will never be despised again.

Cast   [This is] the word of the Lord.
All   **Thanks be to God.**

Cast: **Joel, The Lord.**

156

The future restoration of Israel
Amos 9.11–15

Amos
(with flourish)   The Lord says:

The Lord   A day is coming when I will restore the kingdom of David, which is like a house fallen into ruins. I will repair its walls and restore it. I will rebuild it and make it as it was long ago. And so the people of Israel will conquer what is left of the land of Edom and all the nations that were once mine.

Amos
(with flourish)   So says the Lord, who will cause this to happen!

The Lord says:

The Lord   The days were coming
when corn will grow faster than it can be harvested,
and grapes will grow faster than the wine can be made.
The mountains will drip with sweet wine,
and the hills will flow with it.
I will bring my people back to their land.
They will rebuild their ruined cities and live there;
they will plant vineyards and drink the wine;
they will plant gardens and eat what they grow.
I will plant my people on the land I gave them,
and they will not be pulled up again.

Amos
(with flourish)   The Lord your God has spoken!

Cast   [This is] the word of the Lord.
All   **Thanks be to God**.

Cast: **Amos, The Lord**.

The restoration of God's people
From Zechariah 9.11–17

Zechariah
(with flourish)   The Lord says:

The Lord   Because of my covenant with you that was sealed by the blood of sacrifices, I will set your people free—from the waterless pit of exile. Return, you exiles who now have hope; return to your place of safety. I tell you now, I will repay you twice over with blessing for all you have suffered. I will use Judah like a soldier's bow and Israel like the arrows. I will use the men of Zion like a sword, to fight the men of Greece.

Zechariah   When that day comes, the Lord will save his people, as a shepherd saves his flock from danger. They will shine in his land like the jewels of a crown. How good and beautiful the land will be! The young people will grow strong on its corn and wine.

Cast	[This is] the word of the Lord.
All	**Thanks be to God**.

Cast: **Zechariah, The Lord.**

Jesus' parable of the weeds
Matthew 13.24–30, 37–43

Story-teller	The Kingdom of heaven is like this. A man sowed good seed in his field.
Interpreter	The man who sowed the good seed is the Son of Man; the field is the world; the good seed is the people who belong to the Kingdom.
Story-teller	One night, when everyone was asleep, an enemy came and sowed weeds among the wheat and went away.
Interpreter	The weeds are the people who belong to the Evil One; and the enemy who sowed the weeds is the Devil.
Story-teller	When the plants grew and the ears of corn began to form, then the weeds showed up. The man's servants came to him [and said]:
Servant	Sir, it was good seed you sowed in your field; where did the weeds come from?
[Story-teller	He answered:]
Man	It was some enemy who did this.
Servant	Do you want us to go and pull up the weeds?
Man	No, because as you gather the weeds you might pull up some of the wheat along with them. Let the wheat and the weeds both grow together until harvest. Then I will tell the harvest workers to pull up the weeds first, tie them in bundles and burn them, and then to gather in the wheat and put it in my barn.
Interpreter	The harvest is the end of the age, and the harvest workers are angels. Just as the weeds are gathered up and burnt in the fire, so the same thing will happen at the end of the age: the Son of Man will send out his angels to gather up out of his Kingdom all those who cause people to sin and all others who do evil things, and they will throw them into the fiery furnace where they will cry and grind their teeth. Then God's people will shine like the sun in their Father's Kingdom. Listen, then, if you have ears!

Cast	[This is] the word of the Lord. OR This is the Gospel of Christ / *This is the Gospel of the Lord.*
All	**Thanks be to God.** **Praise to Christ our Lord** / *Praise to you, Lord Jesus Christ.*

Cast: **Story-teller, Interpreter, Servant, Man.**

The parable of the sower
From Mark 4.1–20

Narrator   Jesus began to teach beside Lake Galilee. The crowd that gathered round him was so large that he got into a boat and sat in it. The boat was out in the water and the crowd stood on the shore at the water's edge. He used parables to teach them many things:

Jesus   Listen! Once there was a man who went out to sow corn. As he scattered the seed in the field, some of it fell along the path, and the birds came and ate it up. Some of it fell on rocky ground, where there was little soil. The seeds soon sprouted, because the soil wasn't deep. Then, when the sun came up, it burnt the young plants; and because the roots had not grown deep enough, the plants soon dried up. Some of the seed fell among thorn bushes, which grew up and choked the plants, and they didn't produce any corn. But some seeds fell in good soil, and the plants sprouted, grew, and produced corn: some had thirty grains, others sixty, and others a hundred.

Narrator   And Jesus concluded:

Jesus   Listen, then, if you have ears!

Narrator   When Jesus was alone, some of those who had heard him came to him with the twelve disciples and asked him to explain the parables. [Jesus answered:]

Jesus   You have been given the secret of the Kingdom of God. But the others, who are on the outside, hear all things by means of parables, so that, as Isaiah says:

Isaiah   They may look and look, yet not see; they may listen and listen, yet not understand. For if they did, they would turn to God, and he would forgive them.

[Narrator   Then Jesus asked them:]

Jesus   Don't you understand this parable? How, then, will you ever understand any parable? The sower sows God's message. Some people are like the seeds that fall along the path; as soon as they hear the message, Satan comes and takes it away.

Other people are like the seeds that fall on rocky ground. As soon as they hear the message, they receive it gladly. But it does not sink deep into them, and they don't last long. So when trouble or persecution comes because of the message, they give up at once.

Other people are like the seeds sown among the thorn bushes. These are the ones who hear the message, but the worries about this life, the love for riches, and all other kinds of desires crowd in and choke the message, and they don't bear fruit.

But other people are like the seeds sown in good soil. They hear the message, accept it, and bear fruit: some thirty, some sixty, and some a hundred.

Cast [This is] the word of the Lord. OR This is the Gospel of Christ / *This is the Gospel of the Lord.*
All   **Thanks be to God.**   **Praise to Christ our Lord** / *Praise to you, Lord Jesus Christ.*

Cast: **Narrator, Jesus, Isaiah.**

The parable of the rich man (longer version)
Luke 12.13–21

Narrator	A man in the crowd said to Jesus:
Man (angrily)	Teacher, tell my brother to divide with me the property our father left us.
[Narrator	Jesus answered him:]
Jesus (to the Man)	My friend, who gave me the right to judge or to divide the property between you two?
Narrator	And he went on to say to them all:
Jesus (to everyone)	Watch out and guard yourselves from every kind of greed; because a person's true life is not made up of the things he owns, no matter how rich he may be.
Narrator	Then Jesus told them this parable:
Jesus	There was once a rich man who had land which bore good crops. He began to think to himself:
Rich man	I haven't anywhere to keep all my crops. What can I do? (PAUSE TO THINK)
	This is what I will do; I will tear down my barns and build bigger ones, where I will store my corn and all my other goods. Then I will say to myself, 'Lucky man! You have all the good things you need for many years. Take life easy, eat, drink, and enjoy yourself!'
Jesus	But God said to him:
God	You fool! This very night you will have to give up your life; then who will get all these things you have kept for yourself?
Narrator	And Jesus concluded:
Jesus	This is how it is with those who pile up riches for themselves but are not rich in God's sight.

Cast [This is] the word of the Lord. OR This is the Gospel of Christ / *This is the Gospel of the Lord.*
All   **Thanks be to God.**   **Praise to Christ our Lord**/ *Praise to you, Lord Jesus Christ.*

Cast: **Narrator, Man, Jesus, Rich man, God.**

The parable of the rich man (shorter version)
Luke 12.16–21

Jesus	There was once a rich man who had land which bore good crops. He began to think to himself:

160

Rich man	I haven't anywhere to keep all my crops. What can I do?
Jesus	He told himself:
Rich man	This is what I will do; I will tear down my barns and build bigger ones, where I will store my corn and all my other goods. Then I will say to myself, 'Lucky man! You have all the good things you need for many years. Take life easy, eat, drink, and enjoy yourself!'
Jesus	But God said to him:
God	You fool! This very night you will have to give up your life; then who will get all these things you have kept for yourself?
Jesus	This is how it is with those who pile up riches for themselves but are not rich in God's sight.

Cast [This is] the word of the Lord.   OR   This is the Gospel of Christ / *This is the Gospel of the Lord.*
All   **Thanks be to God.**   **Praise to Christ our Lord** / *Praise to you, Lord Jesus Christ.*

Cast: **Jesus, Rich man, God.**

Jesus and the Samaritan woman
From John 4.5–42

Narrator	In Samaria Jesus came to a town named Sychar, which was not far from the field that Jacob had given to his son Joseph. Jacob's well was there, and Jesus, tired out by the journey, sat down by the well. It was about noon. A Samaritan woman came to draw some water, and Jesus said to her:
Jesus	Give me a drink of water.
Narrator	His disciples had gone into town to buy food. Now Jews will not use the same cups and bowls that Samaritans use. [So the woman answered:]
Woman	You are a Jew, and I am a Samaritan—so how can you ask me for a drink?
Jesus	If only you knew what God gives and who it is that is asking you for a drink, you would ask him, and he would give you life-giving water.
Woman	Sir, you haven't got a bucket, and the well is deep. Where would you get that life-giving water? It was our ancestor Jacob who gave us this well; he and his sons and his flocks all drank from it. You don't claim to be greater than Jacob, do you?
Jesus	Whoever drinks this water will be thirsty again, but whoever drinks the water that I will give him will never be thirsty again. The water that I will give him will become in him a spring which will provide him with life-giving water and give him eternal life.
Woman	Sir, give me that water! Then I will never be thirsty again, nor will I have to come here to draw water.

Jesus	Go and call your husband, and come back.
Woman	I haven't got a husband.
Jesus	You are right when you say you haven't got a husband. You have been married to five men, and the man you live with now is not really your husband. You have told me the truth.
[Woman	I see you are a prophet, sir. My Samaritan ancestors worshipped God on this mountain, but you Jews say that Jerusalem is the place where we should worship God.
Jesus	Believe me, woman, the time will come when people will not worship the Father either on this mountain or in Jerusalem. You Samaritans do not really know whom you worship; but we Jews know whom we worship, because it is from the Jews that salvation comes. But the time is coming and is already here, when by the power of God's Spirit people will worship the Father as he really is, offering him the true worship that he wants. God is Spirit, and only by the power of his Spirit can people worship him as he really is.
Woman	I know that the Messiah will come, and when he comes, he will tell us everything. (PAUSE)
Jesus (slowly)	I am he, I who am talking with you.
Narrator	At that moment Jesus' disciples returned, and they were greatly surprised to find him talking with a woman. But none of them said to her, 'What do you want?' or asked him, 'Why are you talking with her?' (PAUSE)]
	Then the woman left her water jar, went back to the town, and said to the people there:
Woman	Come and see the man who told me everything I have ever done. Could he be the Messiah?
Narrator	So they left the town and went to Jesus. Many of the Samaritans in that town believed in Jesus because the woman had said:
[Woman]	He told me everything I have ever done.
Narrator	So when the Samaritans came to him, they begged him to stay with them, and Jesus stayed there two days. Many more believed because of his message, and they said to the woman:
Person 1	We believe now, not because of what you said, but because we ourselves have heard him.
Person 2	And we know that he really is the Saviour of the world.

Cast	[This is] the word of the Lord. OR	This is the Gospel of Christ / *This is the Gospel of the Lord.*
All	**Thanks be to God.**	**Praise to Christ our Lord** / *Praise to you, Lord Jesus Christ.*

Cast: **Narrator, Jesus, Woman, Person 1, Person 2** (can be the same as Person 1).

Jesus the bread of life
John 6.25–35

Narrator   When the people found Jesus on the other side of the lake, they said to him:

Person 1   Teacher!

Person 2   When did you get here?

Jesus   I am telling you the truth: you are looking for me because you ate the bread and had all you wanted, not because you understood my miracles. Do not work for food that goes bad; instead, work for the food that lasts for eternal life. This is the food which the Son of Man will give you, because God, the Father, has put his mark of approval on him.

Person 1   What can we do in order to do what God wants?

Jesus   What God wants you to do is to believe in the one he sent.

Person 2   What miracle will you perform so that we may see it and believe you?

Person 1   What will you do? Our ancestors ate manna in the desert, just as the scripture says, 'He gave them bread from heaven to eat.'

Jesus   I am telling you the truth. What Moses gave you was not the bread from heaven; it is my Father who gives you the real bread from heaven. For the bread that God gives is he who comes down from heaven and gives life to the world.

Persons 1 and 2   Sir, give us this bread always.

Jesus   I am the bread of life. He who comes to me will never be hungry; he who believes in me will never be thirsty.

Cast   [This is] the word of the Lord.   OR   This is the Gospel of Christ / *This is the Gospel of the Lord.*
All   **Thanks be to God**.   **Praise to Christ our Lord** / *Praise to you, Lord Jesus Christ.*

Cast: **Narrator, Person 1, Person 2, Jesus**.

Paul and Barnabas in Lystra and Derbe
Acts 14.8–20

Narrator   In Lystra there was a man who had been lame from birth and had never been able to walk. He sat there and listened to Paul's words. Paul saw that he believed and could be healed, so he looked straight at him:

Paul (loudly)   Stand up straight on your feet!

Narrator   The man jumped up and started walking around. When the crowds saw what Paul had done, they started shouting in their own Lycaonian language:

Person 1	The gods have become like men.
Person 2	They have come down to us!
Narrator	They gave Barnabas the name Zeus, and Paul the name Hermes, because he was the chief speaker. The priest of the god Zeus, whose temple stood just outside the town, brought bulls and flowers to the gate, for he and the crowds wanted to offer sacrifice to the apostles.
	When Barnabas and Paul heard what they were about to do, they tore their clothes and ran into the middle of the crowd [shouting:]
Barnabas	Why are you doing this? We ourselves are only human beings like you!
Paul	We are here to announce the Good News.
Barnabas	To turn you away from these worthless things to the living God, who made heaven, earth, sea, and all that is in them.
Paul	In the past he allowed all people to go their own way. But he has always given evidence of his existence by the good things he does: he gives you rain from heaven and crops at the right times; he gives you food and fills your hearts with happiness.
Narrator	Even with these words the apostles could hardly keep the crowd from offering a sacrifice to them. (PAUSE)
	Some Jews came from Antioch in Pisidia and from Iconium; they won the crowd over to their side, stoned Paul and dragged him out of the town, thinking that he was dead. But when the believers gathered round him, he got up and went back into the town. The next day he and Barnabas went to Derbe.
Cast	[This is] the word of the Lord.
All	**Thanks be to God.**

Cast: **Narrator, Paul, Person 1, Person 2**, (can be the same as Person 1), **Barnabas.**

The harvest of the earth
Revelation 14.14–19

John	Then I looked, and there was a white cloud, and sitting on the cloud was what looked like a human being, with a crown of gold on his head and a sharp sickle in his hand. Then another angel came out from the temple and cried out in a loud voice to the one who was sitting on the cloud:
Angel 1	Use your sickle and reap the harvest, because the time has come; the earth is ripe for the harvest!
John	Then the one who sat on the cloud swung his sickle on the earth, and the earth's harvest was reaped. Then I saw another angel come out of the temple in heaven, and he also had a sharp sickle. Then another angel, who is in charge of the fire, came from the altar. He shouted in a loud voice to the angel who had the sharp sickle:

Angel 2   Use your sickle, and cut the grapes from the vineyard of the earth, because the grapes are ripe!

John   So the angel swung his sickle on the earth, cut the grapes from the vine, and threw them into the winepress of God's furious anger.

Cast   [This is] the word of the Lord.
All   **Thanks be to God.**

Cast: **John, Angel 1, Angel 2.**

THE CHURCH
ANNIVERSARY/
LOCAL CHURCH
FESTIVALS

Jacob's dream at Bethel
Genesis 28.10–22

Narrator   Jacob left Beersheba and started towards Haran. At sunset he came to a holy place and camped there. He lay down to sleep, resting his head on a stone. He dreamt that he saw a stairway reaching from earth to heaven, with angels going up and coming down on it. And there was the Lord standing beside him:

The Lord   I am the Lord, the God of Abraham and Isaac, I will give to you and to your descendants this land on which you are lying. They will be as numerous as the specks of dust on the earth. They will extend their territory in all directions, and through you and your descendants I will bless all the nations. Remember, I will be with you and protect you wherever you go, and I will bring you back to this land. I will not leave you until I have done all that I have promised you.

Narrator   Jacob woke up:

Jacob (startled)   The Lord is here! He is in this place, and I didn't know it!

Narrator   He was afraid.

Jacob (afraid)   What a terrifying place this is! It must be the house of God; it must be the gate that opens into heaven.

Narrator   Jacob got up early next morning, took the stone that was under his head, and set it up as a memorial. Then he poured olive-oil on it to dedicate it to God. He named the place Bethel. Then Jacob made a vow to the Lord:

Jacob   If you will be with me and protect me on the journey I am making and give me food and clothing, and if I return safely to my father's home, then you will be my God. This memorial stone which I have set up will be the place where you are worshipped, and I will give you a tenth of everything you give me.

Cast   [This is] the word of the Lord.
All   **Thanks be to God.**

Cast: **Narrator, The Lord, Jacob.**

Solomon prepares to build the Temple
1 Kings 5.1–12

Narrator   King Hiram of Tyre had always been a friend of David's, and when he heard that Solomon had succeeded his father David as king he sent ambassadors to him. Solomon sent back this message to Hiram:

Solomon   You know that because of the constant wars my father David had to fight against the enemy countries all round him, he could not build a temple for the worship of the Lord his God until the Lord had given him victory over all his enemies. But now the Lord my God

	has given me peace on all my borders. I have no enemies, and there is no danger of attack. The Lord promised my father David:
[The Lord]	Your son, whom I will make king after you, will build a temple for me.
Solomon	And I have now decided to build that temple for the worship of the Lord my God. So send your men to Lebanon to cut down cedars for me. My men will work with them, and I will pay your men whatever you decide. As you well know, my men don't know how to cut down trees as well as yours do.
Narrator	Hiram was extremely pleased when he received Solomon's message [and he said]:
Hiram	Praise the Lord today for giving David such a wise son to succeed him as king of that great nation!
Narrator	Then Hiram sent Solomon the following message:
Hiram	I have received your message and I am ready to do what you ask. I will provide the cedars and the pine-trees. My men will bring the logs down from Lebanon to the sea, and will tie them together in rafts to float them down the coast to the place you choose. There my men will untie them, and your men will take charge of them. On your part, I would like you to supply the food for my men.
Narrator	So Hiram supplied Solomon with all the cedar and pine logs that he wanted, and Solomon provided Hiram with two thousand tons of wheat and four hundred thousand litres of pure olive-oil every year to feed his men. The Lord kept his promise and gave Solomon wisdom. There was peace between Hiram and Solomon, and they made a treaty with each other.
Cast	[This is] the word of the Lord.
All	**Thanks be to God**.

Cast: **Narrator, Solomon, The Lord** (can be the same as Solomon), **Hiram**.

The Covenant Box is brought to the Temple
From 1 Kings 8.1–13

Narrator 1	King Solomon summoned all the leaders of the tribes and clans of Israel to come to him in Jerusalem in order to take the Lord's Covenant Box from Zion, David's City, to the Temple.
Narrator 2	The Levites and the priests also moved the Tent of the Lord's presence and all its equipment to the Temple.
Narrator 1	Then the priests carried the Covenant Box into the Temple and put it in the Most Holy Place, beneath the winged creatures. Their outstretched wings covered the box and the poles it was carried by.
Narrator 2	There was nothing inside the Covenant Box except the two stone tablets which Moses had placed there at Mount Sinai, when the Lord made a covenant with the people of Israel as they were coming from Egypt.

Narrator 1   As the priests were leaving the Temple, it was suddenly filled with a cloud shining with the dazzling light of the Lord's presence, and they could not go back in to perform their duties.

Narrator 2   Then Solomon prayed:

Solomon   You, Lord, have placed the sun in the sky, yet you have chosen to live in clouds and darkness. Now I have built a majestic temple for you, a place for you to live in for ever.

Cast   [This is] the word of the Lord.
All   **Thanks be to God**.

Cast: **Narrator 1, Narrator 2, Solomon.**

Solomon's address to the people
1 Kings 8.14–21

Narrator   As the people stood in the Temple, King Solomon turned to face them, and he asked God's blessing on them. He said:

Solomon   Praise the Lord God of Israel! He has kept the promise he made to my father David [when he said]:

The Lord   From the time I brought my people out of Egypt, I have not chosen any city in all the land of Israel in which a temple should be built where I would be worshipped. But I chose you, David, to rule my people.

Narrator   And Solomon continued:

Solomon   My father David planned to build a temple for the worship of the Lord God of Israel, but the Lord said to him:

The Lord   You were right in wanting to build a temple for me, but *you* will never build it. It is your son, your own son, who will build my temple.

Solomon   And now the Lord has kept his promise. I have succeeded my father as king of Israel, and I have built the Temple for the worship of the Lord God of Israel. I have also provided a place in the Temple for the Covenant Box containing the stone tablets of the covenant which the Lord made with our ancestors when he brought them out of Egypt.

Cast   [This is] the word of the Lord.
All   **Thanks be to God.**

Cast: **Narrator, Solomon, The Lord** (preferably unseen).

God appears to Solomon again
1 Kings 9.1–9

Narrator   After King Solomon had finished building the Temple and the palace and everything else he wanted to build, the Lord appeared to him again, as he had in Gibeon. [The Lord said to him:]

The Lord	I have heard your prayer. I consecrate this Temple which you have built as the place where I shall be worshipped for ever. I will watch over it and protect it for all time. If you will serve me in honesty and integrity, as your father David did, and if you obey my laws and do everything I have commanded you, I will keep the promise I made to your father David when I told him that Israel would always be ruled by his descendants. But if you or your descendants stop following me, if you disobey the laws and commands I have given you, and worship other gods, then I will remove my people Israel from the land that I have given them. I will also abandon this Temple which I have consecrated as the place where I am to be worshipped. People everywhere will ridicule Israel and treat her with contempt. This Temple will become a pile of ruins, and everyone who passes by will be shocked and amazed. [They will ask:]
Person 1	Why did the Lord do this to this land and this Temple?
[The Lord	People will answer:]
Person 2	It is because they abandoned the Lord their God, who brought their ancestors out of Egypt.
Person 3	They gave their allegiance to other gods and worshipped them.
Person 1	That is why the Lord has brought this disaster on them.
Cast	[This is] the word of the Lord.
All	**Thanks be to God**.

Cast: **Narrator, The Lord, Person 1, Person 2, Person 3** (Persons 1–3 can be the same).

Solomon's agreement with Hiram
1 Kings 9.10–14

Narrator	It took Solomon twenty years to build the Temple and his palace. King Hiram of Tyre had provided him with all the cedar and pine and with all the gold he wanted for this work. After it was finished, King Solomon gave Hiram twenty towns in the region of Galilee. Hiram went to see them, and he did not like them. So he said to Solomon:
Hiram	So these, my brother, are the towns you have given me!
Narrator	For this reason the area is still called Cabul. Hiram had sent Solomon more than four thousand kilogrammes of gold.
Cast	[This is] the word of the Lord.
All	**Thanks be to God.**

Cast: **Narrator, Hiram**

David's prayer of thanksgiving
1 Chronicles 17.16–27

Chronicler King David went into the Tent of the Lord's presence, sat down, and prayed:

David I am not worthy of what you have already done for me, Lord God, nor is my family. Yet now you are doing even more; you have made promises about my descendants in the years to come, and you, Lord God, are already treating me like a great man. What more can I say to you! You know me well, and yet you honour me, your servant. It was your will and purpose to do this for me and to show me my future greatness. Lord, there is none like you; we have always known that you alone are God. There is no other nation on earth like Israel, whom you rescued from slavery to make them your own people. The great and wonderful things you did for them spread your fame throughout the world. You rescued your people from Egypt and drove out other nations as your people advanced. You have made Israel your own people for ever, and you, Lord, have become their God.

And now, O Lord, fulfil for all time the promise you made about me and my descendants, and do what you said you would. Your fame will be great, and people will for ever say:

Persons 1 and **2** The Lord Almighty is God over Israel.

David And you will preserve my dynasty for all time. I have the courage to pray this prayer to you, my God, because you have revealed all this to me, your servant, and have told me that you will make my descendants kings. You, Lord, are God, and you have made this wonderful promise to me. I ask you to bless my descendants so that they will continue to enjoy your favour. You, Lord, have blessed them, and your blessing will rest on them for ever.

Cast [This is] the word of the Lord.
All **Thanks be to God.**

Cast: **Chronicler, David, Person 1, Person 2** (can be the same as Person 1).

David's preparations for building the Temple
From 1 Chronicles 22.2–23.1

Chronicler King David gave orders for all the foreigners living in the land of Israel to assemble, and he put them to work. Some of them prepared stone blocks for building the Temple. He supplied a large amount of iron for making nails and clamps for the wooden gates, and so much bronze that no one could weigh it. He arranged for the people of Tyre and Sidon to bring him a large number of cedar logs. David thought:

David The Temple that my son Solomon is to build must be splendid and world-famous. But he is young and inexperienced, so I must make preparations for it.

Chronicler   So David got large amounts of the materials ready before he died. He sent for his son Solomon and commanded him to build a temple for the Lord, the God of Israel:

David   My son, I wanted to build a temple to honour the Lord my God. But the Lord told me that I had killed too many people and fought too many wars. And so, because of all the bloodshed I have caused, he would not let me build a temple for him. He did, however, make me a promise. [He said:]

[The Lord]   You will have a son who will rule in peace, because I will give him peace from all his enemies. His name will be Solomon, because during his reign I will give Israel peace and security. He will build a temple for me. He will be my son, and I will be his father. His dynasty will rule Israel for ever.

[Chronicler   David continued:]

David   Now, my son, may the Lord your God be with you, and may he keep his promise to make you successful in building a temple for him. And may the Lord your God give you insight and wisdom so that you may govern Israel according to his Law. If you obey all the laws which the Lord gave to Moses for Israel, you will be successful. Be determined and confident, and don't let anything make you afraid. Now begin the work, and may the Lord be with you.

Chronicler   David commanded all the leaders of Israel to help Solomon. [He said]:

David   The Lord your God has been with you and given you peace on all sides. He let me conquer all the people who used to live in this land, and they are now subject to you and to the Lord. Now serve the Lord your God with all your heart and soul. Start building the Temple, so that you can place in it the Covenant Box of the Lord and all the other sacred objects used in worshipping him.

Chronicler   When David was very old, he made his son Solomon king of Israel.

Cast   [This is] the word of the Lord.
All   **Thanks be to God.**

Cast: **Chronicler, David, [The Lord** (preferably unseen)].

David's instructions for the Temple
1 Chronicles 28.1–21

Chronicler   King David commanded all the officials of Israel to assemble in Jerusalem. So all the officials of the tribes, the officials who administered the work of the kingdom, the leaders of the clans, the supervisors of the property and livestock that belonged to the king and his sons—indeed all the palace officials, leading soldiers, and important men—gathered in Jerusalem. David stood before them and addressed them:

David	My countrymen, listen to me. I wanted to build a permanent home for the Covenant Box, the footstool of the Lord our God. I have made preparations for building a temple to honour him, but he has forbidden me to do it, because I am a soldier and have shed too much blood. The Lord, the God of Israel, chose me and my descendants to rule Israel for ever. He chose the tribe of Judah to provide leadership, and out of Judah he chose my father's family. From all that family it was his pleasure to take me and make me king over all Israel. He gave me many sons, and out of them all he chose Solomon to rule over Israel, the Lord's kingdom. The Lord said to me:
The Lord]	Your son Solomon is the one who will build my Temple. I have chosen him to be my son, and I will be his father. I will make his kingdom last for ever if he continues to obey carefully all my laws and commands as he does now.
David	So now, my people, in the presence of our God and of this assembly of all Israel, the Lord's people, I charge you to obey carefully everything that the Lord our God has commanded us, so that you may continue to possess this good land and so that you may hand it on to succeeding generations for ever.
Chronicler	And to Solomon he said:
David	My son, I charge you to acknowledge your father's God and to serve him with an undivided heart and a willing mind. He knows all our thoughts and desires. If you go to him, he will accept you; but if you turn away from him, he will abandon you for ever. You must realize that the Lord has chosen you to build his holy Temple. Now do it—and do it with determination.
Chronicler	David gave Solomon the plans for all the temple buildings, for the storerooms and all the other rooms, and for the Most Holy Place, where sins are forgiven. He also gave him the plans for all he had in mind for the courtyards and the rooms around them, and for the storerooms for the temple equipment and the gifts dedicated to the Lord. David also gave him the plans for organizing the priests and Levites to perform their duties, to do the work of the Temple, and to take care of all the temple utensils. He gave instructions as to how much silver and gold was to be used for making the utensils, for each lamp and lampstand, for the silver tables, and for each gold table on which were placed the loaves of bread offered to God. He also gave instructions as to how much pure gold was to be used in making forks, bowls, and jars, how much silver and gold in making dishes, and how much pure gold in making the altar on which incense was burnt and in making the chariot for the winged creatures that spread their wings over the Lord's Covenant Box. King David said:
David	All this is contained in the plan written according to the instructions which the Lord himself gave me to carry out.
Chronicler	King David said to his son Solomon:

175

David	Be confident and determined. Start the work and don't let anything stop you. The Lord God, whom I serve, will be with you. He will not abandon you, but he will stay with you until you finish the work to be done on his Temple. The priests and the Levites have been assigned duties to perform in the Temple. Workmen with every kind of skill are eager to help you, and all the people and their leaders are at your command.
Cast	[This is] the word of the Lord.
All	**Thanks be to God.**

Cast: **Chronicler, David, [The Lord** (preferably unseen)].

Gifts for building the Temple
1 Chronicles 29.1–9

Chronicler	King David announced to the whole assembly:
David	My son Solomon is the one whom God has chosen, but he is still young and lacks experience. The work to be done is tremendous, because this is not a palace for men but a temple for the Lord God. I have made every effort to prepare materials for the Temple—gold, silver, bronze, iron, timber, precious stones and gems, stones for mosaics, and quantities of marble. Over and above all this that I have provided, I have given silver and gold from my personal property because of my love for God's Temple. I have given more than a hundred tons of the finest gold and almost two hundred and forty tons of pure silver for decorating the walls of the Temple and for all the objects which the craftsmen are to make. Now who else is willing to give a generous offering to the Lord?
Chronicler	Then the heads of the clans, the officials of the tribes, the commanders of the army, and the administrators of the royal property volunteered to give the following for the work on the Temple: more than 170 tons of gold, over 340 tons of silver, almost 620 tons of bronze, and more than 3,400 tons of iron. Those who had precious stones gave them to the temple treasury which was administered by Jehiel of the Levite clan of Gershon. The people had given willingly to the Lord, and they were happy that so much had been given. King David also was extremely happy.
Cast	[This is] the word of the Lord.
All	**Thanks be to God.**

Cast: **Chronicler, David.**

David praises God
1 Chronicles 29.9–20

Chronicler	[*The people had given willingly to the Lord for the building of the Temple, and they were happy that so much had been given. King David also was extremely happy.] There in front of the whole assembly King David praised the Lord:

176

David	Lord God of our ancestor Jacob, may you be praised for ever and ever! You are great and powerful, glorious, splendid, and majestic. Everything in heaven and earth is yours, and you are king, supreme ruler over all. All riches and wealth come from you; you rule everything by your strength and power; and you are able to make anyone great and strong. Now, our God, we give you thanks, and we praise your glorious name.

Yet my people and I cannot really give you anything, because everything is a gift from you, and we have only given back what is yours already. You know, O Lord, that we pass through life like exiles and strangers, as our ancestors did. Our days are like a passing shadow, and we cannot escape death. O Lord, our God, we have brought together all this wealth to build a temple to honour your holy name, but it all came from you and all belongs to you. I know that you test everyone's heart and are pleased with people of integrity. In honesty and sincerity I have willingly given all this to you, and I have seen how your people who are gathered here have been happy to bring offerings to you. Lord God of our ancestors Abraham, Isaac, and Jacob, keep such devotion for ever strong in your people's hearts and keep them always faithful to you. Give my son Solomon a wholehearted desire to obey everything that you command and to build the Temple for which I have made these preparations.

Chronicler   Then David commanded the people:

David   Praise the Lord your God!

Chronicler   And the whole assembly praised the Lord, the God of their ancestors, and they bowed low and gave honour to the Lord and also to the king.

Last   [This is] the word of the Lord.
All   **Thanks be to God**.

Last: **Chronicler, David**. (*Please note: this section overlaps with the previous reading.)

The glory of the Lord
2 Chronicles 5.11–14

Chronicler   All the priests present, regardless of the group to which they belonged, had consecrated themselves. And all the Levite musicians—Asaph, Heman, and Jeduthun, and the members of their clans—were wearing linen clothing. The Levites stood near the east side of the altar with cymbals and harps, and with them were a hundred and twenty priests playing trumpets. The singers were accompanied in perfect harmony by trumpets, cymbals, and other instruments, as they praised the Lord, singing:

Singer 1   Praise the Lord because he is good—

Singer 2   And his love is eternal.

177

Chronicler	As the priests were leaving the Temple, it was suddenly filled wit a cloud shining with the dazzling light of the Lord's presence, an they could not continue the service of worship.

Cast	[This is] the word of the Lord.
All	**Thanks be to God**.

Cast: **Chronicler, Singer 1, Singer 2** (can be the same as Singer 1).

Solomon's address to the people
2 Chronicles 6.1–11

Chronicler	King Solomon prayed:
Solomon	Lord, you have chosen to live in clouds and darkness. Now I hav built a majestic temple for you, a place for you to live in for ever
Chronicler	All the people of Israel were standing there. The king turned t face them and asked God's blessing on them. He said:
Solomon	Praise the Lord God of Israel! He has kept the promise he mad to my father David when he said to him:
[The Lord]	From the time I brought my people out of Egypt until now, I did no choose any city in the land of Israel as the place to build a templ where I would be worshipped, and I did not choose anyone to lea my people Israel. But now I have chosen Jerusalem as the plac where I will be worshipped, and you, David, to rule my people.
Chronicler	And Solomon continued:
Solomon	My father David planned to build a temple for the worship of th Lord God of Israel, but the Lord said to him:
[The Lord]	You were right in wanting to build a temple for me, but yo will never build it. It is your son, your own son, who will buil my temple.
Solomon	Now the Lord has kept his promise: I have succeeded my fathe as king of Israel, and I have built a temple for the worship of th Lord God of Israel. I have placed in the Temple the Covenant Box which contains the stone tablets of the covenant which the Lor made with the people of Israel.

Cast	[This is] the word of the Lord.
All	**Thanks be to God**.

Cast: **Chronicler, Solomon, [The Lord** (preferably unseen)].

Solomon's prayer (i)
2 Chronicles 6.12–21

Chronicler	In the presence of the people Solomon went and stood in front o the altar and raised his arms in prayer.

[Commentator]	Solomon had made a bronze platform and put it in the middle of the courtyard. It was 2.2 metres square and 1.3 metres high. He mounted this platform, knelt down where everyone could see him, and raised his hands towards heaven.
Chronicler	Solomon prayed:
Solomon	Lord God of Israel, in all heaven and earth there is no god like you. You keep your covenant with your people and show them your love when they live in wholehearted obedience to you. You have kept the promise you made to my father David; today every word has been fulfilled. Now, Lord God of Israel, keep the other promise you made to my father when you told him that there would always be one of his descendants ruling as king of Israel, provided that they carefully obeyed your Law just as he did. So now, Lord God of Israel, let everything come true that you promised to your servant David.
	But can you, O God, really live on earth among men and women? Not even all heaven is large enough to hold you, so how can this Temple that I have built be large enough? Lord my God, I am your servant. Listen to my prayer and grant the requests I make to you. Watch over this Temple day and night. You have promised that this is where you will be worshipped, so hear me when I face this Temple and pray. Hear my prayers and the prayers of your people Israel when they face this place and pray. In your home in heaven hear us and forgive us.
Cast	[This is] the word of the Lord.
All	**Thanks be to God**.

Cast: **Chronicler, [Commentator], Solomon**.

Solomon's prayer (ii)
2 Chronicles 6.22–31

Voice 1	When a person is accused of wronging another and is brought to your altar in this Temple to take an oath that he is innocent—
Voice 2	O Lord, listen in heaven and judge your servants. Punish the guilty one as he deserves and acquit the one who is innocent.
Voice 1	When your people Israel are defeated by their enemies because they have sinned against you and then when they turn to you and come to this Temple, humbly praying to you for forgiveness—
Voice 2	Listen to them in heaven. Forgive the sins of your people and bring them back to the land which you gave to them and to their ancestors.
Voice 1	When you hold back the rain because your people have sinned against you and then when they repent and face this Temple, humbly praying to you—
Voice 2	O Lord, listen to them in heaven and forgive the sins of your

servants, the people of Israel, and teach them to do what is right. Then, O Lord, send rain on this land of yours, which you gave to your people as a permanent possession.

Voice 1   When there is famine in the land or an epidemic or the crops are destroyed by scorching winds or swarms of locusts, or when your people are attacked by their enemies, or when there is disease or sickness among them—

Voice 2   Listen to their prayers.

Voice 1   If any of your people Israel, out of heartfelt sorrow, stretch out their hands in prayer towards this Temple—

Voice 2   Hear their prayer. Listen to them in your home in heaven and forgive them. You alone know the thoughts of the human heart. Deal with each person as he deserves, so that your people may honour you and obey you all the time they live in the land which you gave to our ancestors.

Cast   [This is] the word of the Lord.
All   **Thanks be to God**.

Cast: **Voice 1, Voice 2**.

Solomon's prayer (iii)
2 Chronicles 6.32–40

Voice 1   When a foreigner who lives in a distant land hears how great and powerful you are and how you are always ready to act, and then comes to pray at this Temple—

Voice 2   Listen to his prayer. In heaven, where you live, hear him and do what he asks you to do, so that all the peoples of the world may know you and obey you, as your people Israel do. Then they will know that this Temple I have built is where you are to be worshipped.

Voice 1   When you command your people to go into battle against their enemies and they pray to you, wherever they are, facing this city which you have chosen and this Temple which I have built for you—

Voice 2   Listen to their prayers. Hear them in heaven and give them victory.

Voice 1   When your people sin against you—and there is no one who does not sin—and in your anger you let their enemies defeat them and take them as prisoners to some other land, even if that land is far away—

Voice 2   Listen to your people's prayers.

Voice 1   If there in that land they repent and pray to you, confessing how sinful and wicked they have been—

Voice 2	Hear their prayers, O Lord.
Voice 1	If in that land they truly and sincerely repent and pray to you as they face towards this land which you gave to our ancestors, this city which you have chosen, and this Temple which I have built for you—
Voice 2	Then listen to their prayers. In your home in heaven hear them and be merciful to them and forgive all the sins of your people.
	Now, O my God—
Voices 1 and **2**	Look on us and listen to the prayers offered in this place.
Cast	[This is] the word of the Lord.
All	**Thanks be to God.**

Cast: **Voice 1, Voice 2**.

God appears to Solomon
2 Chronicles 7.11–22

Chronicler	After King Solomon had finished the Temple and the palace, successfully completing all his plans for them, the Lord appeared to him at night [He said to him]:
The Lord	I have heard your prayer, and I accept this Temple as the place where sacrifices are to be offered to me. Whenever I hold back the rain or send locusts to eat up the crops or send an epidemic on my people, if they pray to me and repent and turn away from the evil they have been doing, then I will hear them in heaven, forgive their sins, and make their land prosperous again. I will watch over this Temple and be ready to hear all the prayers that are offered here, because I have chosen it and consecrated it as the place where I will be worshipped for ever. I will watch over it and protect it for all time. If you serve me faithfully as your father David did, obeying my laws and doing everything I have commanded you, I will keep the promise I made to your father David when I told him that Israel would always be ruled by his descendants. But if you and your people ever disobey the laws and commands I have given you, and worship other gods, then I will remove you from the land that I gave you, and I will abandon this Temple that I have consecrated as the place where I am to be worshipped. People everywhere will ridicule it and treat it with contempt.
	The Temple is now greatly honoured, but then everyone who passes by it will be amazed and will ask:
Person 1	Why did the Lord do this to this land and this Temple?
The Lord	People will answer:
Person 2	It is because they abandoned the Lord their God, who brought their ancestors out of Egypt.
Person 3	They gave their allegiance to other gods and worshipped *them*.

Person 2   That is why the Lord has brought this disaster on them.

Cast   [This is] the word of the Lord.
All   **Thanks be to God**.

Cast: **Chronicler, The Lord, Person 1, Person 2, Person 3** (can be the same as Person 2).

King Hezekiah of Judah
From 2 Chronicles 29.1–17

Chronicler   Hezekiah became king of Judah at the age of twenty-five, and he ruled in Jerusalem for twenty-nine years. His mother was Abijah, the daughter of Zechariah. Following the example of his ancestor King David, he did what was pleasing to the Lord. (PAUSE)

In the first month of the year after Hezekiah became king, he re-opened the gates of the Temple and had them repaired. He assembled a group of priests and Levites in the east courtyard of the Temple and spoke to them there:

Hezekiah   You Levites are to consecrate yourselves and purify the Temple of the Lord, the God of your ancestors. Remove from the Temple everything that defiles it. Our ancestors were unfaithful to the Lord our God and did what was displeasing to him. They abandoned him and turned their backs on the place where he dwells. They closed the doors of the Temple, let the lamps go out, and failed to burn incense or offer burnt-offerings in the Temple of the God of Israel. Because of this the Lord has been angry with Judah and Jerusalem, and what he has done to them has shocked and frightened everyone. You know this very well. Our fathers were killed in battle, and our wives and children have been taken away as prisoners. I have now decided to make a covenant with the Lord, the God of Israel, so that he will no longer be angry with us. My sons, do not lose any time. You are the ones that the Lord has chosen to burn incense to him and to lead the people in worshipping him.

Chronicler   The Levites all made themselves ritually clean. Then, as the king had commanded them to do, they began to make the Temple ritually clean, according to the Law of the Lord. The priests went inside the Temple to purify it, and they carried out into the Temple courtyard everything that was ritually unclean. From there the Levites took it all outside the city to the valley of the Kidron. The work was begun on the first day of the first month, and by the eighth day they had finished it all, including the entrance room to the Temple. Then they worked for the next eight days, until the sixteenth of the month, preparing the Temple for worship.

Cast   [This is] the word of the Lord.
All   **Thanks be to God**.

Cast: **Chronicler, Hezekiah**.

The Temple is rededicated
From 2 Chronicles 29.18–36

Chronicler   The Levites made the following report to King Hezekiah:

Levite 1   We have completed the ritual purification of the whole Temple, including the altar for burnt-offerings, the table for the sacred bread, and all their equipment.

Levite 2   We have also brought back all the equipment which King Ahaz took away during those years he was unfaithful to God, and we have rededicated it.

Levite 1   It is all in front of the Lord's altar.

Chronicler   Without delay King Hezekiah assembled the leading men of the city, and together they went to the Temple. As an offering to take away the sins of the royal family and of the people of Judah and to purify the Temple, they took seven bulls, seven sheep, seven lambs, and seven goats. The king told the priests, who were descendants of Aaron, to offer the animals as sacrifices on the altar. The priests killed the bulls first, then the sheep, and then the lambs, and sprinkled the blood of each sacrifice on the altar. Finally they took the goats to the king and to the other worshippers, who laid their hands on them. Then the priests killed the goats and poured their blood on the altar as a sacrifice to take away the sin of all the people, for the king had commanded burnt-offerings and sin-offerings to be made for all Israel.

Then King Hezekiah and all the people knelt down and worshipped God. The king and the leaders of the nation told the Levites to sing to the Lord the songs of praise that were written by David and by Asaph the prophet. So everyone sang with great joy as they knelt and worshipped God. And so worship in the Temple was begun again. King Hezekiah and the people were happy, because God had helped them to do all this so quickly.

Cast   [This is] the word of the Lord.
All   **Thanks be to God.**

Cast: **Chronicler, Levite 1, Levite 2** (can be the same as Levite 1).

Cyrus commands the Jews to return
Ezra 1.1–11

Narrator 1   In the first year that Cyrus of Persia was emperor, the Lord made what he had said through the prophet Jeremiah come true. He prompted Cyrus to issue the following command and send it out in writing to be read aloud everywhere in his empire:

Cyrus   This is the command of Cyrus, Emperor of Persia. The Lord, the God of Heaven, has made me ruler over the whole world and has given me the responsibility of building a temple for him in Jerusalem in Judah. May God be with all of you who are his people. You are to go to Jerusalem and rebuild the Temple of the Lord, the God of Israel, the God who is worshipped in Jerusalem. If any of his people in exile need help to return, their neighbours are to give them this help. They are to provide them with silver and gold, supplies and pack animals, as well as offerings to present in the Temple of God in Jerusalem.

Narrator 2 Then the heads of the clans of the tribes of Judah and Benjamin, the priests and Levites, and everyone else whose heart God had moved got ready to go and rebuild the Lord's Temple in Jerusalem. All their neighbours helped them by giving them many things: silver utensils, gold, supplies, pack animals, other valuables, and offerings for the Temple.

Narrator 1 Cyrus gave them back the bowls and cups that King Nebuchadnezzar had taken from the Temple in Jerusalem and had put in the temple of his gods. He handed them over to Mithredath, chief of the royal treasury, who made an inventory of them for Sheshbazzar, the governor of Judah, as follows:

Gold bowls for offerings—

Narrator 2 30

Narrator 1 Silver bowls for offerings—

Narrator 2 1,000

Narrator 1 Other bowls—

Narrator 2 29

Narrator 1 Small gold bowls—

Narrator 2 30

Narrator 1 Small silver bowls—

Narrator 2 410

Narrator 1 Other utensils—

Narrator 2 1,000. In all there were 5,400 gold and silver bowls and other articles which Sheshbazzar took with him when he and the other exiles went from Babylon to Jerusalem.

Cast [This is]the word of the Lord.
All **Thanks be to God.**

Cast: **Narrator 1, Cyrus, Narrator 2.**

The rebuilding of the Temple begins
Ezra 3.7–13

Narrator 1 The people of Israel gave money to pay the stonemasons and the carpenters and gave food, drink, and olive-oil to be sent to the cities of Tyre and Sidon in exchange for cedar-trees from Lebanon, which were to be brought by sea to Joppa. All this was done with the permission of Cyrus, emperor of Persia.

Narrator 2	So in the second month of the year after they came back to the site of the Temple in Jerusalem, they began work. Zerubbabel, Joshua, and the rest of their fellow-countrymen, the priests, and the Levites—
Commentator	In fact all the exiles who had come back to Jerusalem—
Narrator 2	Joined in the work. All the Levites twenty years of age or older were put in charge of the work of rebuilding the Temple.
Narrator 1	The Levite Jeshua and his sons and relatives, and Kadmiel and his sons—
Commentator	The clan of Hodaviah—
Narrator 1	Joined together in taking charge of the rebuilding of the Temple.
Commentator	They were helped by the Levites of the clan of Henadad.
Narrator 2	When the men started to lay the foundation of the Temple, the priests in their robes took their places with trumpets in their hands, and the Levites of the clan of Asaph stood there with cymbals. They praised the Lord according to the instructions handed down from the time of King David. They sang the Lord's praises, repeating the refrain:
Singers 1 and 2	The Lord is good.
Singer 1	And his love for Israel is eternal.
Narrator 1	Everyone shouted with all his might, praising the Lord because the work on the foundation of the Temple had been started.
Narrator 2	Many of the older priests, Levites, and heads of clans had seen the first Temple, and as they watched the foundation of this Temple being laid, they cried and wailed.
Narrator 1	But the others who were there shouted for joy.
Narrator 2	No one could distinguish between the joyful shouts and the crying, because the noise they made was so loud that it could be heard far and wide.
Cast All	[This is] the word of the Lord. **Thanks be to God.**

Cast: **Narrator 1, Narrator 2, Commentator, Singer 1, Singer 2** (can be the same as Commentator).

Opposition to the rebuilding of the Temple
Ezra 4.1–5

Narrator	The enemies of the people of Judah and Benjamin heard that those who had returned from exile were rebuilding the Temple of the Lord, the God of Israel. So they went to see Zerubbabel and the heads of the clans and said:
Enemy 1	Let us join you in building the Temple.

Enemy 2	We worship the same God you worship, and we have been offering sacrifices to him ever since Esarhaddon, emperor of Assyria, sent us here to live.
Narrator	Zerubbabel, Joshua, and the heads of the clans said to them:
Zerubbabel	We don't need your help to build a temple for the Lord our God.
Joshua	We will build it ourselves, just as Cyrus, emperor of Persia, commanded us.
Narrator	Then the people who had been living in the land tried to discourage and frighten the Jews and keep them from building. They also bribed Persian government officials to work against them. They kept on doing this throughout the reign of Cyrus and into the reign of Darius.
Cast All	[This is] the word of the Lord. **Thanks be to God.**

Cast: **Narrator, Enemy 1, Enemy 2** (can be the same as Enemy 1), **Zerubbabel, Joshua** (can be the same as Enemy 1).

Work on the Temple begins again
Ezra 4.24–5.17

Narrator	Work on the Temple had been stopped and had remained at a standstill until the second year of the reign of Darius, emperor of Persia. At that time two prophets, Haggai and Zechariah son of Iddo, began to speak in the name of the God of Israel to the Jews who lived in Judah and Jerusalem. When Zerubbabel son of Shealtiel and Joshua son of Jehozadak heard their messages, they began to rebuild the Temple in Jerusalem, and the two prophets helped them. Almost at once Tattenai, governor of West Euphrates, Shethar Bozenai, and their fello-officials came to Jerusalem and demanded:
Tattenai	Who gave you orders to build this Temple and equip it?
Narrator	They also asked for the names of all the men who were helping to build the Temple. But God was watching over the Jewish leaders, and the Persian officials decided to take no action until they could write to Darius and receive a reply. This is the report that they sent to the emperor:
Official	To Emperor Darius, may you rule in peace. Your Majesty should know that we went to the province of Judah and found that the Temple of the great God is being rebuilt with large stone blocks and with wooden beams set in the wall. The work is being done with great care and is moving ahead steadily. We then asked the leaders of the people to tell us who had given them authority to rebuild the Temple and to equip it. We also asked them their names so that we could inform you who the leaders of this work are. They answered:

186

Leader 1	We are servants of the God of heaven and earth, and we are rebuilding the Temple which was originally built and equipped many years ago by a powerful king of Israel.
Leader 2	Because our ancestors made the God of Heaven angry, he let them be conquered by King Nebuchadnezzar of Babylonia, a king of the Chaldean dynasty.
Leader 1	The Temple was destroyed, and the people were taken into exile in Babylonia.
Leader 3	Then in the first year of the reign of King Cyrus as emperor of Babylonia, Cyrus issued orders for the Temple to be rebuilt.
Leader 2	He restored the gold and silver temple utensils which Nebuchadnezzar had taken from the Temple in Jerusalem and had placed in the temple in Babylon.
Leader 3	Cyrus handed these utensils over to a man named Sheshbazzar, whom he appointed governor of Judah.
Leader 1	The emperor told him to take them and return them to the Temple in Jerusalem, and to rebuild the Temple where it had stood before.
Leader 2	So Sheshbazzar came and laid its foundation; construction has continued from then until the present, but the Temple is still not finished.
Official	Now, if it please Your Majesty, let a search be made in the royal records in Babylon to find whether or not Cyrus gave orders for this Temple in Jerusalem to be rebuilt, and then inform us what your will is in this matter.
Cast	[This is] the word of the Lord.
All	**Thanks be to God.**

Cast: **Narrator, Tattenai, Official, Leader 1, Leader 2, Leader 3** (Leaders 1–3 can be the same).

Cyrus' order is rediscovered
Ezra 6.1–12

Narrator	Darius the emperor issued orders for a search to be made in the royal records that were kept in Babylon. But it was in the city of Ecbatana in the province of Media that a scroll was found, containing the following record:
Reader	In the first year of his reign Cyrus the emperor commanded that the Temple in Jerusalem be rebuilt as a place where sacrifices are made and offerings are burnt. The Temple is to be twenty-seven metres high and twenty-seven metres wide. The walls are to be built with one layer of wood on top of every three layers of stone. All expenses are to be paid by the royal treasury. Also the gold and silver utensils which King Nebuchadnezzar brought to Babylon from the Temple in Jerusalem are to be returned to their proper place in the Jerusalem Temple.

Narrator	Then Darius sent the following reply:
Darius	To Tattenai, governor of West Euphrates, Shethar Bozenai, and your fellow-officials in West Euphrates.
	Stay away from the Temple and do not interfere with its construction. Let the governor of Judah and the Jewish leaders rebuild the Temple of God where it stood before. I hereby command you to help them rebuild it. Their expenses are to be paid promptly out of the royal funds received from taxes in West Euphrates, so that the work is not interrupted. Day by day, without fail, you are to give the priests in Jerusalem whatever they tell you they need: young bulls, sheep, or lambs to be burnt as offerings to the God of Heaven, or wheat, salt, wine, or olive-oil. This is to be done so that they can offer sacrifices that are acceptable to the God of Heaven and pray for his blessing on me and my sons. [I further command that if anyone disobeys this order, a wooden beam is to be torn out of his house, sharpened at one end, and then driven through his body. And his house is to be made a rubbish heap.] May the God who chose Jerusalem as the place where he is to be worshipped overthrow any king or nation that defies this command and tries to destroy the Temple there. I, Darius, have given this order. It is to be fully obeyed.
Cast	[This is]the word of the Lord
All	**Thanks be to God**.

Cast: **Narrator, Reader, Darius**.

Nehemiah talks to the Emperor
Nehemiah 2.1–8

Old Nehemiah	One day, when Emperor Artaxerxes was dining, I took the wine to him. He had never seen me look sad before, so he asked:
Emperor	Why are you looking so sad? You aren't ill, so it must be that you're unhappy.
Old Nehemiah	I was startled and answered:
Young Nehemiah	May Your Majesty live for ever! How can I help looking sad when the city where my ancestors are buried is in ruins and its gates have been destroyed by fire?
Emperor	What is it that you want?
Old Nehemiah	I prayed to the God of Heaven, and then I said to the emperor:
Young Nehemiah	If Your Majesty is pleased with me and is willing to grant my request, let me go to the land of Judah, to the city where my ancestors are buried, so that I can rebuild the city.
Old Nehemiah	The emperor, with the empress sitting at his side, approved my request. He asked me how long I would be gone and when I would return, and I told him. (PAUSE)

Then I asked him to grant me the favour of giving me letters to the governors of West Euphrates Province, instructing them to let me travel to Judah. I asked also for a letter to Asaph, keeper of the royal forests, instructing him to supply me with timber for the gates of the fort that guards the Temple, for the city walls, and for the house I was to live in. The emperor gave me all I asked for, because God was with me.

Cast	[This is] the word of the Lord.
All	**Thanks be to God.**

Cast: **Old Nehemiah, Emperor, Young Nehemiah.**

God and humanity
Psalm 8.1–9 (LIT)

Leader	O Lord, our Lord:
All	**how great is your name in all the world!**
All (group 1)	**Your glory fills the skies.**
All (group 2)	**Your praise is sung by children.**
All (group 3)	**You silence your enemies.**
Leader	I look at the sky your hands have made, the moon and stars you put in place:
All	**Who are we that you care for us?**
Leader	You made us less than gods:
All	**to crown us with glory and honour.**
Leader	You put us in charge of creation:
All (group 1)	**the beasts of the field.**
All (group 2)	**the birds of the air.**
All (group 3)	**the fish of the sea.**
Leader	O Lord, our Lord,
All	**how great is your name in all the world!**
All	**Glory to the Father, and to the Son, and to the Holy Spirit: as it was in the beginning, is now, and shall be for ever. Amen.**

Cast: **Leader, All** (group 1—two or more persons/part of congregation), **All** (group 2—two or more persons/part of congregation), **All** (group 3—two or more persons/part of congregation)

The great king
Psalm 24.1–10 (LIT)

Leader	The earth is the Lord's, and everything in it:
All	**the world, and all who live here.**
Leader	He founded it upon the seas:
All	**and established it upon the waters.**
Enquirer	Who has the right to go up the Lord's hill; who may enter his holy temple?

All	**Those who have clean hands and a pure heart,** **who do not worship idols** **or swear by what is false.**
Leader **All**	They receive blessing continually from the Lord: **and righteousness from the God of their salvation.**
Leader **All**	Such are the people who seek for God: **who enter the presence of the God of Jacob.**
Director **All**	Fling wide the gates, open the ancient doors: **that the king of glory may come in.**
Enquirer **All**	Who is the king of glory? **The Lord, strong and mighty,** **the Lord mighty in battle.**
Director **All**	Fling wide the gates, open the ancient doors: **that the king of glory may come in.**
Enquirer **All**	Who is he, this king of glory? **The Lord almighty, he is the king of glory.**
All	**Glory to the Father, and to the Son, and to the Holy Spirit:** **as it was in the beginning, is now, and shall be for ever. Amen.**

Cast: **Leader, All** (two or more persons/congregation), **Enquirer, Director.**

A song of praise
From Psalm 33.1–22 (LIT)

Leader **All**	Sing joyfully to the Lord, you righteous: **it is right that his people should praise him.**
Leader **All** (group 1)	Praise the Lord with the harp: **make music to him on the strings.**
Leader **All** (group 2)	Sing to the Lord a new song: **play skilfully, and shout for joy.**
Leader **All**	For the word of the Lord is right and true: **and all his work is faithfulness.**
Leader **All** (group 1)	The Lord loves righteousness and justice: **his endless love fills the earth.**
Leader **All** (group 2)	By the word of the Lord the skies were formed: **his breath created moon and stars.**
Leader **All**	Let all the earth fear the Lord: **the people of the world revere him.**
Leader **All** (group 1)	For he spoke, and it came to be: **he commanded, and all was made.**
Leader **All** (group 2)	The Lord holds back the nations: **he thwarts their evil intent.**

Leader	God's purposes are sure:
All	**his plans endure for ever.**

Leader	Happy is the nation whose God is the Lord:
All (group 1)	**happy the people he makes his own.**

Leader	The eyes of the Lord are on those who fear him:
All (group 2)	**who trust in his unfailing love.**

Leader	We wait in hope for the Lord:
All (group 1)	**he is our help and shield.**

Leader	In him our hearts rejoice:
All (group 2)	**we trust his holy name.**

Leader	May your constant love be with us, Lord:
All	**as we put our hope in you.**

All	**Glory to the Father, and to the Son, and to the Holy Spirit:**
	as it was in the beginning, is now, and shall be for ever. Amen.

Cast: **Leader, All** (group 1—two or more persons/part of congregation), **All** (group 2—two or more persons/part of congregation).

The goodness of God
From Psalm 36.5–9 (LIT)

Leader 1	Your love, O Lord, reaches the heavens:
All (group 1)	**your faithfulness extends to the skies.**

Leader 2	Your righteousness is towering like the mountains:
All (group 2)	**your justice is like the great deep.**

Leader 1	How precious is your love, O God:
All (group 1)	**we find shelter beneath your wings!**

Leader 2	We feast on the food you provide:
All (group 2)	**we drink from the river of your goodness:**

Leader 1	For with you is the fountain of life:
All	**in your light we see light.**

All	**Glory to the Father, and to the Son, and to the Holy Spirit:**
	as it was in the beginning, is now, and shall be for ever. Amen.

Cast: **Leader 1, Leader 2** (can be the same as Leader 1), **All** (group 1—two or more persons/part of congregation), **All** (group 2—two or more persons/part of congregation).

A song of praise (i)
From Psalm 40.1–3 (LIT)

Leader	I waited patiently for the Lord:
All	**he turned and heard my cry.**

Leader	He pulled me out of the slimy pit:
All	**out of the mud and mire.**

Leader	He set my feet upon a rock:
All	**and made my step secure.**

Leader	He put a new song in my mouth:
All	**a hymn of praise to God.**

All	**Many will see it and fear;**
	and put their trust in the Lord.

All	**Glory to the Father, and to the Son, and to the Holy Spirit:**
	as it was in the beginning, is now, and shall be for ever. Amen.

Cast: **Leader, All** (two or more persons/congregation).

A song of praise (ii)
From Psalm 40.4–16 (LIT)

Leader 1	Happy are those who trust in God:
All	**who do not worship idols.**

Leader 1	Sacrifice and offering you do not desire:
All	**but you want my ears to be open.**

Leader 2	So I said, 'Lord I come:
All	**obedient to your word.'**

Leader 2	I delight to do your will, O God:
All	**and keep your teaching in my heart.**

Leader 2	I'll tell the world your saving news:
All	**you know my lips will not be sealed.**

Leader 2	I have not hid your righteousness:
All	**but speak of your salvation, Lord.**

Leader 2	I do not hide your faithful love:
All	**but share your mercy with them all.**

Leader 1	May all who come to you be glad—

Leader 2	May all who know your saving power for ever say:
All	**How great is the Lord!**

All	**Glory to the Father, and to the Son, and to the Holy Spirit:**
	as it was in the beginning, is now, and shall be for ever. Amen.

Cast: **Leader 1, Leader 2, All** (two or more persons/congregation).

God is with us
From Psalm 46.1–11 (LIT)

Leader	God is our refuge and strength:
All	**an ever-present help in trouble.**

Leader	Therefore we will not fear:
All (group 1)	**though the earth should shake,**

192

All (group 2)	**though the mountains fall into the sea,**
All (group 1)	**though the waters surge and foam,**
All (group 2)	**though the mountains shake and roar.**
All	**The Lord Almighty is with us:**
	the God of Jacob is our fortress.
Leader	There is a river whose streams make glad the city of God: the holy place where the Most High dwells.
All (group 1)	**God is within her, she will not fall:**
All (group 2)	**God will help her at break of day.**
Leader	Nations are in uproar, kingdoms fall:
All	**God lifts his voice—the earth melts away.**
All (group 1)	**The Lord Almighty is with us:**
All (group 2)	**the God of Jacob is our fortress.**
Leader	Come and see what God has done:
All	**his devastation on the earth!**
Leader	He stops the wars throughout the world:
All (group 1)	**he breaks the bow and shatters the spear—**
All (group 2)	**he sets the shield on fire.**
Voice of God	Be still, and know that I am God: I will be exalted over the nations,
	I will be exalted over the earth.
All	**The Lord Almighty is with us:**
	the God of Jacob is our fortress.
All	**Glory to the Father, and to the Son, and to the Holy Spirit:**
	as it was in the beginning, is now, and shall be for ever. Amen.

Cast: **Leader, All** (group 1—two or more persons/part of congregation), **All** (group 2—two or more persons/part of congregation), **Voice of God** (preferably unseen).

The supreme ruler
From Psalm 47.1–9 (LIT)

Leader	Clap your hands, all you nations:
All	**shout to God with cries of joy.**
Leader	How awesome is the Lord most high:
All (group 1)	**the King who rules the whole wide earth!**
Leader	God has ascended to his throne:
All (group 2)	**with shouts of joy and sound of trumpets.**
Leader	Sing praises to our God, sing praises:
All (group 1)	**sing praises to our King, sing praises.**
Leader	For God is King of all the earth:
All (group 2)	**sing to him a psalm of praise.**
Leader	God is seated on his throne:
All (group 1)	**he rules the nations of the world.**

Leader	The leaders of the nations come:
All (group 2)	**as subjects of our holy God.**

Leader	The lords of earth belong to God:
All	**he reigns supreme.**

All	**Glory to the Father, and to the Son, and to the Holy Spirit:**
	as it was in the beginning, is now, and shall be for ever. Amen.

Cast: **Leader, All** (group 1—two or more persons/part of congregation), **All** (group 2—two or more persons/part of congregation).

Prayer for the help of God's Spirit
From Psalm 51.6–12 and Psalm 143.6–10 (LIT)

Leader	O Lord, I spread my hands out to you:
All	**I thirst for you like dry ground.**

Leader	Teach me to do your will, for you are my God:
All	**let your good Spirit lead me in safety.**

Leader	You require sincerity and truth in me:
All	**fill my mind with your wisdom.**

Leader	Create in me a pure heart, O God:
All	**and renew a faithful spirit in me.**

Leader	Do not cast me from your presence:
All	**or take your Holy Spirit from me.**

Leader	Give me again the joy of your salvation:
All	**and make me willing to obey.**

All	**Glory to the Father, and to the Son, and to the Holy Spirit:**
	as it was in the beginning, is now, and shall be for ever. Amen.

Cast: **Leader, All** (two or more persons/congregation). (Verses from Psalms 51 and 143 have been grouped together to make provision for an occasion when the person and work of the Holy Spirit is being considered.)

A song of praise and thanksgiving
From Psalm 66.1–20 (LIT)

Leader	Praise your God with shouts of joy:
All	**all the earth sing praise to him.**

Leader	Sing the glory of his name:
All (group 1)	**offer him your highest praise.**

Leader	Say to him: How great you are:
All (group 2)	**wonderful the things you do!**

Leader	All your enemies bow down:
All (group 3)	**all the earth sings praise to you.**

Leader	Come and see what God has done:

All (group 1)	**causing mortal men to fear;**
All (group 2)	**how he turned the sea to land,**
All (group 3)	**led his people safely through.**
Leader	We rejoice at what he does—
All (group 1)	**ruling through eternity,**
All (group 2)	**watching over all the world,**
All (group 3)	**keeping every rebel down.**
Leader	Praise our God, O nations, praise:
All (group 1)	**let the sound of praise be heard!**
All (group 2)	**God sustains our very lives:**
All (group 3)	**keeps our feet upon the way.**
Leader	Once, you tested us, O God—
All (group 1)	**silver purified by fire—**
Leader	Let us fall into a trap,
All (group 2)	**placed hard burdens on our backs—**
Leader	Sent us through the flame and flood:
All (group 3)	**now you bring us safely home.**
Leader	I will come to worship you:
All (group 1)	**bring to you my offering,**
All (group 2)	**give you what I said I would,**
All (group 3)	**when the troubles threatened me.**
Leader	All who love and honour God:
All (group 1)	**come and listen, while I tell**
All (group 2)	**what great things he did for me**
All (group 3)	**when I cried to him for help,**
All (group 1)	**when I praised him with my songs,**
All (group 2)	**when my heart was free from sin,**
All (group 3)	**then he listened to my prayer.**
Leader	Praise the Lord who heard my cry:
All	**God has shown his love to me!**
All	**Glory to the Father, and to the Son, and to the Holy Spirit: as it was in the beginning, is now, and shall be for ever. Amen.**

Cast: **Leader, All** (group 1—two or more persons/part of congregation), **All** (group 2—two or more persons/part of congregation), **All** (group 3—two or more persons/part of congregation).

A song of thanksgiving
Psalm 67.1–7 (LIT)

Leader 1	May God be gracious to us and bless us:
All (group 1)	**and make his face to shine upon us.**
Leader 2	Let your ways be known upon earth:
All (group 2)	**your saving grace to every nation.**
Leaders 1 and 2	Let the peoples praise you, O God:
All	**let the peoples praise you.**

| Leader 1 | Let the nations be glad: |
| **All** (group 1) | **and sing aloud for joy.** |

| Leader 2 | Because you judge the peoples justly: |
| **All** (group 2) | **and guide the nations of the earth.** |

| Leaders 1 and 2 | Let the peoples praise you, O God: |
| **All** | **let all the peoples praise you.** |

| Leader 1 | Then the land will yield its harvest: |
| **All** (group 1) | **and God, our God, will bless us.** |

Leader 2	God will bless us:
All (group 2)	**and people will fear him**
All	**to the ends of the earth.**

| **All** | **Glory to the Father, and to the Son, and to the Holy Spirit: as it was in the beginning, is now, and shall be for ever. Amen.** |

Cast: **Leader 1, All** (group 1—two or more persons/part of congregation), **Leader 2, All** (group 2—two or more persons/part of congregation).

A prayer for restoration
From Psalm 80.1–19 (LIT)

Leader 1	Hear us, O Shepherd of Israel, leader of your flock.
Leader 2	Hear us from your throne above the cherubim.
Leader 3	Shine forth, awaken your strength, and come to save us.
All	**Bring us back, O God, and save us, make your face to shine upon us.**

Leader 1	O Lord God almighty, how long will you be angry with your people's prayers?
Leader 2	You have given us sorrow to eat and tears to drink.
Leader 3	You have made us a source of contention to our neighbours, and our enemies insult us.
All	**Bring us back, O God, and save us, make your face to shine upon us.**

Leader 1	Return to us, O God Almighty, look down from heaven and see.
Leader 2	Look on this vine that you planted with your own hand, this child you raised for yourself.
Leader 3	Let your hand rest upon the people you have chosen, then we will not turn away from you; revive us, and we shall praise your name.
All	**Bring us back, O God, and save us, make your face to shine upon us.**

| **All** | **Glory to the Father, and to the Son, and to the Holy Spirit: as it was in the beginning is now, and shall be for ever. Amen.** |

Cast: **Leader 1, Leader 2, Leader 3** (can be the same as Leader 1), **All** (two or more persons/congregation).

Longing for God's House
Psalm 84.1–12

Worshipper 1   How I love your Temple, Lord Almighty!
How I want to be there!

Worshipper 2   I long to be in the Lord's Temple.
With my whole being I sing for joy
to the living God.

Worshipper 1   Even the sparrows have built a nest,
and the swallows have their own home;
they keep their young near your altars,
Lord Almighty, my king and my God.

Worshipper 2   How happy are those who live in your Temple,
always singing praise to you.

Worshipper 1   How happy are those whose strength comes from you,
who are eager to make the pilgrimage to Mount Zion.
As they pass through the dry valley of Baca,
it becomes a place of springs;
the autumn rain fills it with pools.
They grow stronger as they go;
they will see the God of gods on Zion.

Worshipper 2   Hear my prayer, Lord God Almighty.
Listen, O God of Jacob!
Bless our king, O God,
the king you have chosen.

Worshipper 1   One day spent in your Temple
is better than a thousand anywhere else.

Worshipper 2   I would rather stand at the gate of the house of my God
than live in the homes of the wicked.

Worshipper 1   The Lord is our protector and glorious king,
blessing us with kindness and honour.
He does not refuse any good thing
to those who do what is right.

Worshippers
 1 and **2**   Almighty Lord, how happy are those who trust in you!

Cast [This is] the word of the Lord. OR **All Glory to the Father, and to the Son, and to the Holy Spirit:**
All   **Thanks be to God.**   **as it was in the beginning, is now, and shall be for ever. Amen.**

Cast: **Worshipper 1, Worshipper 2.**

God is king
From Psalm 93.1–5 (LIT)

Leader   The Lord reigns, robed in majesty:
All (group 1)   **he arms himself with power.**

Leader   The earth is firmly set in place:
All (group 2)   **it never can be moved.**

Leader   Your throne was founded long ago:
All (group 1)   **before all time began.**

Leader   The oceans raise their voice, O Lord:
All (group 2)   **and lift their roaring waves.**

Leader   The Lord is mightier than the sea:
All (group 1)   **he rules supreme on high.**

Leader   His laws stand firm through endless days:
All (group 2)   **his praise for evermore.**

All   Amen.

All   **Glory to the Father, and to the Son, and to the Holy Spirit:
                          as it was in the beginning, is now, and shall be for ever. Amen.**

Cast: **Leader, All** (group 1—two or more persons/part of congregation), **All** (group 2—two or more persons/part of congregation).

Invitation to worship
From Psalm 95.1–7 (LIT)

Leader 1   Come, let's joyfully praise our God,
                          acclaiming the Rock of our salvation.

Leader 2   Come before him with thanksgiving,
                          and greet him with melody.

All (group 1)   **Our God is a great God:**
All (group 2)   **a king above all other gods!**

All (group 1)   **The depths of the earth are in his hands:**
All (group 2)   **the mountain peaks belong to him.**

All (group 1)   **The sea is his—he made it!**
All (group 2)   **his hands have fashioned all the earth.**

Leader 1   Come, bow down to worship him.
Leader 2   Kneel before the Lord who made us.

All (groups   **We are his people:**
1 & 2)   **the sheep of his flock.**

Leader 1   Let us trust in him today.

Leader 2   Please listen to his voice!

All   **Glory to the Father, and to the Son, and to the Holy Spirit:
                          as it was in the beginning, is now, and shall be for ever. Amen.**

Cast: **Leader 1, Leader 2, All** (group 1—two or more persons/part of congregation), **All** (group 2—two or more persons/part of congregation).

God, the supreme king
From Psalm 96.1–13 (LIT)

Leader   Sing to the Lord a new song:
All (group 1)   **sing to the Lord, all the earth.**

Leader   Sing to the Lord, praise his name:
All (group 2)   **proclaim his salvation each day.**

Leader   Declare his glory among the nations:
All (group 1)   **his marvellous deeds among the peoples.**

Leader   Great is the Lord, and worthy of praise:
All (group 2)   **honour him above all gods.**

Leader   Splendour and majesty surround him:
All (group 1)   **power and beauty fill his temple.**

Leader   Praise the Lord all people on earth:
All (group 2)   **praise his glory and might.**

Leader   Give him the glory due to his name:
All (group 1)   **bring an offering into his temple.**

Leader   Worship the Lord in his beauty and holiness:
All (group 2)   **tremble before him all the earth.**

Leader   Say to the nations:
All   **The Lord is king!**

Leader   Let the heavens rejoice and the earth be glad:
All (group 1)   **let all creation sing for joy.**

Leader   For God shall come to judge the world:
All (group 2)   **and rule the people with his truth.**

All   **Glory to the Father, and to the Son, and to the Holy Spirit:
as it was in the beginning, is now, and shall be for ever. Amen.**

Cast: **Leader, All** (group 1–two or more persons/part of congregation), **All** (group 2–two or more persons/part of congregation).

God, the supreme ruler
From Psalm 97.1–12 (LIT)

Leader   The Lord is king:
All   **the Lord is king!**

Leader   Let the whole wide earth rejoice:
All (group 1)   **let the islands all be glad.**

Leader   Thunder-clouds encircle him:
All (group 2)   **truth and justice are his throne.**

Leader   Fire shall go before the Lord:
All (group 3)   **burning up his enemies.**

Leader   Lightning strikes the darkened world:

All (group 1)	**all the people see and fear.**
Leader	Mountains melt before our God:
All (group 2)	**he is Lord of all the earth.**
Leader	Skies proclaim his righteousness:
All (group 3)	**nations see his glory now.**
Leader	Idol-worshippers are shamed:
All (group 1)	**gods bow down before the Lord.**
Leader	Let Jerusalem rejoice:
All (group 2)	**in your faithful judgements, Lord!**
Leader	Sovereign of the universe:
All (group 3)	**mightier still than all the gods!**
Leader	Yet you help your saints, O Lord:
All (group 1)	**saving them from wicked men.**
Leader	Light will shine upon the good:
All (group 2)	**gladness fill the righteous heart.**
Leader	Now recall what God has done:
All (group 3)	**thank him,**
All (group 2)	**praise him,**
All	**and rejoice!**
All	**Glory to the Father, and to the Son, and to the Holy Spirit: as it was in the beginning, is now, and shall be for ever. Amen.**

Cast: **Leader, All** (group 1-two or more persons/part of congregation), **All** (group 2-two or more persons/part of congregation) **All**, (group 3-two or more persons/part of congregation).

God, the ruler of the world
From Psalm 98.1–9 (LIT)

Leader	Sing to the Lord a new song:
All	**for he has done marvellous things.**
Leader	His right hand and his holy arm:
All	**have brought a great triumph to us.**
All (group 1)	**He lets his salvation be known:**
All (group 2)	**his righteousness shines in the world.**
All (group 1)	**To us he continues his love:**
All (group 2)	**his glory is witnessed by all.**
Leader	Shout for joy to the Lord, all the earth:
All	**and burst into jubilant song.**
All (group 1)	**Make music to God with the harp:**
All (group 2)	**with songs and the sound of your praise.**
All (group 1)	**With trumpets and blast of the horn:**
All (group 2)	**sing praises to God as your king.**
Leader	Let rivers and streams clap their hands:

All	**the mountains together sing praise.**
Leader	The Lord comes to judge the whole earth:
All	**in righteousness God rules the world.**
All	**Glory to the Father, and to the Son, and to the Holy Spirit:** **as it was in the beginning, is now, and shall be for ever. Amen.**

Cast: **Leader, All** (group 1–two or more persons/part of congregation), **All** (group 2–two or more persons/part of congregation).

God, the supreme king
From Psalm 99.1–9 (LIT)

Leader 1	The Lord reigns:
All (group 1)	**let the nations tremble!**
Leader 2	He sits enthroned on high:
All (group 2)	**let the earth shake!**
Leader 1	Great is the Lord our God:
All (group 1)	**exalted over all the world.**
Leader 2	Let the nations praise his awesome name, and say:
All (group 2)	**God is holy!**
Leader 1	Praise the Lord our God, and worship at his feet:
All (group 1)	**God is holy!**
Leader 2	Exalt the Lord our God, and worship on his holy mountain:
All	**The Lord our God is holy!**
All	**Glory to the Father, and to the Son, and to the Holy Spirit:** **as it was in the beginning, is now, and shall be for ever. Amen.**

Cast: **Leader 1, Leader 2, All** (group 1—two or more persons/part of congregation), **All** (group 2—two or more persons/part of congregation).

A hymn of praise
From Psalm 100.1–5 (LIT)

Leader	Rejoice in the Lord, all the earth:
All	**worship the Lord with gladness.**
Leader	Remember the Lord is our God:
All	**we are his flock and he made us.**
Leader	Come to his temple with praise:
All	**enter his gates with thanksgiving.**
Leader	The love of the Lord will not fail:
All	**God will be faithful for ever.**
All	**Glory to the Father, and to the Son, and to the Holy Spirit:** **as it was in the beginning, is now, and shall be for ever. Amen.**

Cast: **Leader, All** (two or more persons/congregation).

The love of God
From Psalm 103.1–22 (LIT)

Leader	Praise the Lord, my soul:
All	**all my being, praise his holy name!**
Leader	Praise the Lord, my soul:
All	**and do not forget how generous he is.**
All (group 1)	**He forgives all my sins:**
All (group 2)	**and heals all my diseases.**
All (group 1)	**He keeps me from the grave:**
All (group 2)	**and blesses me with love and mercy.**
Leader	The Lord is gracious and compassionate:
All (group 1)	**slow to become angry,**
All (group 2)	**and full of constant love.**
All (group 1)	**He does not keep on rebuking:**
All (group 2)	**he is not angry for ever.**
All (group 1)	**He does not punish us as we deserve:**
All (group 2)	**or repay us for our wrongs.**
All (group 1)	**As far as the east is from the west:**
All (group 2)	**so far does he remove our sins from us.**
Leader	As kind as a Father to his children:
All (group 1)	**so kind is the Lord to those who honour him.**
Leader	Praise the Lord, all his creation:
All	**praise the Lord, my soul!**
All	**Glory to the Father, and to the Son, and to the Holy Spirit: as it was in the beginning, is now, and shall be for ever. Amen.**

Cast: **Leader, All** (group 1—two or more persons/part of congregation), **All** (group 2—two or more persons/part of congregation).

In praise of the Creator
From Psalm 104. 1–4, 29–30 (LIT)

Leader	O Lord our God, you are very great:
All	**you are clothed with splendour and majesty.**
All (group 1)	**You make winds your messengers:**
All (group 2)	**and flashes of fire your servants.**
All (group 1)	**How many are your works:**
All (group 2)	**the earth is full of your creatures!**
Leader	When you hide your face, they are afraid:
All (group 1)	**when you take away their breath, they die.**
Leader	When you send your Spirit they are created:
All	**and you renew the face of the earth.**
All	**Glory to the Father, and to the Son, and to the Holy Spirit: as it was in the beginning, is now, and shall be for ever. Amen.**

Cast: **Leader, All** (group 1—two or more persons/part of congregation), **All** (group 2—two or more persons/part of congregation).

God and his people
From Psalm 105. 1–45 (LIT)

Leader 1	Give thanks to the Lord, praise his name:
All (group 1)	**tell the nations what he has done.**
Leader 2	Sing to him, sing praise to him:
All (group 2)	**tell of all his wonderful deeds.**
Leader 1	Glory in his holy name:
All (group 1)	**let all who worship him rejoice.**
Leader 2	Go to the Lord for help:
All (group 2)	**and worship him for ever.**
Leader 1	Remember the wonders he does:
All (group 1)	**the miracles be performs.**
Leader 2	He is the Lord our God:
All (group 2)	**he judges the whole wide earth.**
Leader 1	He keeps his word and covenant:
All (group 1)	**for a thousand generations.**
Leader 2	The covenant he made with Abraham:
All (group 2)	**the oath he swore to Israel.**
Leader 1	He brought them out of Egypt:
All (group 1)	**and none of them was lost.**
Leader 2	He gave a cloud for covering:
All (group 2)	**a pillar of fire by night.**
Leader 1	He gave them bread from heaven:
All (group 1)	**and water from the rock.**
Leader 2	He brought his people out rejoicing:
All (group 2)	**his chosen ones with shouts of joy.**
All	**Praise the Lord!**
All	**Glory to the Father, and to the Son, and to the Holy Spirit: as it was in the beginning, is now, and shall be for ever. Amen.**

Cast: **Leader 1, All** (group 1—two or more persons/part of congregation), **Leader 2, All** (group 2—two or more persons/part of congregation).

In praise of God's goodness
From Psalm 107.1–31 (LIT)

Leader	Give thanks to the Lord, for he is good:
All	**his love endures for ever.**
Leader	Repeat these words in praise to the Lord:
All (group 1)	**all those he has redeemed.**
Leader	Some sailed the ocean in ships:
All (group 2)	**they earned their way on the seas.**

Leader	They saw what the Lord can do:
All (group 3)	**his wonderful deeds in the deep**.
Leader	For he spoke and stirred up a storm:
All (group 1)	**and lifted high the waves**.
Leader	Their ships were thrown in the air:
All (group 2)	**and plunged into the depths**.
Leader	Their courage melted away:
All (group 3)	**they reeled like drunken men**.
Leader	They came to the end of themselves:
All (group 1)	**and cried to the Lord in their trouble**.
Leader	He brought them out of distress:
All (group 2)	**and stilled the raging storm**.
Leader	They were glad because of the calm:
All (group 3)	**he brought them safely to harbour**.
Leader	Let them give thanks to the Lord:
All	**for his unfailing love**.
All	**Glory to the Father, and to the Son, and to the Holy Spirit: as it was in the beginning, is now, and shall be for ever. Amen.**

Cast: **Leader, All** (group 1—two or more persons/part of congregation), **All** (group 2—two or more persons/part of congregation), **All** (group 3—two or more persons/part of congregation).

In praise of the Lord
From Psalm 111.1–10 (LIT)

Leader 1	Praise the Lord:
All	**praise the Lord!**
Leader 2	With my whole heart I will thank the Lord: in the company of his people. Great are the works of the Lord:
All	**those who marvel seek them.**
Leader 2	Glorious and majestic are his deeds:
All	**his goodness lasts for ever.**
Leader 2	He reminds us of his works of grace:
All	**he is merciful and kind.**
Leader 2	He sustains those who fear him:
All	**he keeps his covenant always.**
Leader 2	All he does is right and just:
All	**all his words are faithful.**
Leader 2	They will last for ever and ever:
All	**and be kept in faith and truth.**
Leader 1	He provided redemption for his people, and made an eternal covenant with them:
All	**holy and awesome is his name!**

Leader 1	The fear of the Lord is the beginning of wisdom; he gives understanding to those who obey:
All	**to God belongs eternal praise!**

| **All** | **Glory to the Father, and to the Son, and to the Holy Spirit: as it was in the beginning, is now, and shall be for ever, Amen.** |

Cast: **Leader 1, Leader 2,** (can be the same as Leader 1), **All** (two or more persons/congregation).

In praise of the Lord's goodness
From Psalm 113.1–9 (LIT)

Leaders 1 and 2	Praise the Lord:
All	**praise the Lord!**

Leader 2	You servants of the Lord, praise his name:
All	**let the name of the Lord be praised, both now and for evermore!**

Leader 1	From the rising of the sun to the place where it sets:
All	**the name of the Lord be praised!**

Leader 2	The Lord is exalted above the earth:
All	**his glory over the heavens.**

Leader 1	Who is like the Lord our God?
All	**He is throned in the heights above—**

Leader 2	Yet he bends down:
All	**he stoops to look at our world.**

Leader 1	He raises the poor from the dust:
All	**and lifts the needy from their sorrow.**

Leader 2	He honours the childless wife in her home:
All	**he makes her happy, the mother of children.**

Leaders 1 and 2	Praise the Lord:
All	**Amen.**

| **All** | **Glory to the Father, and to the Son, and to the Holy Spirit: as it was in the beginning, is now, and shall be for ever. Amen.** |

Cast: **Leader 1, Leader 2, All** (two or more persons/congregation).

Praising God, who saves from death
From Psalm 116.1–19 (LIT)

Leader	I love the Lord because he heard my voice:
All (group 1)	**the Lord in mercy listened to my prayers.**

Leader	Because the Lord has turned his ear to me:
All (group 2)	**I'll call on him as long as I shall live.**

Leader	The cords of death entangled me around:
All (group 3)	**the horrors of the grave came over me.**

Leader	But then I called upon the Lord my God:
All (group 1)	**I said to him: 'O Lord, I beg you, save!'**

Leader	The Lord our God is merciful and good:
All (group 2)	**the Lord protects the simple-hearted ones.**

Leader	The Lord saved me from death and stopped my tears:
All (group 3)	**he saved me from defeat and picked me up.**

Leader	And so I walk before him all my days:
All (group 1)	**and live to love and praise his holy name.**

Leader	What shall I give the Lord for all his grace?
All (group 2)	**I'll take his saving cup, and pay my vows.**

Leader	Within the congregation of his saints:
All (group 3)	**I'll offer him my sacrifice of praise.**

Leader	Praise the Lord:
All	**Amen, amen!**

All	**Glory to the Father, and to the Son, and to the Holy Spirit:**
	as it was in the beginning, is now, and shall be for ever. Amen.

Cast: **Leader, All** (group 1–two or more persons/part of congregation), **All,** (group 2–two or more persons/part of congregation), **All** (group 3–two or more persons/part of congregation).

In praise of the Lord
From Psalm 117.1–2 (LIT)

Leader	Praise the Lord, all you nations:
All (group 1)	**praise him, all you people!**

Leader	Great is his love towards us:
All (group 2)	**his faithfulness shall last for ever.**

Leader	Praise the Lord:
All	**Amen.**

All	**Glory to the Father, and to the Son, and to the Holy Spirit:**
	as it was in the beginning, is now, and shall be for ever. Amen.

Cast: **Leader, All** (group 1–two or more person/part of congregation), **All** (group 2–two or more persons/part of congregation).

Thanking God for victory
From Psalm 118.1–29 (LIT)

Leader	Give thanks to the Lord, for he is good:
All	**his love endures for ever.**

Leader	All those who fear the Lord shall say:
All	**His love endures for ever.**

Worshipper	Open for me the gates of the temple; I will go in and give thanks to the Lord.

| Leader | This is the gate of the Lord, only the righteous can come in. |

| Worshipper | I will give thanks because you heard me; you have become my salvation. |

Choir	The stone which the builders rejected as worthless turned out to be the most important of all:
All (group 1)	**The Lord has done this—**
All (group 2)	**what a wonderful sight it is!**

Choir	This is the day of the Lord's victory—let us be happy, let us celebrate:
All (group 1)	**O Lord save us—**
All (group 2)	**O Lord, grant us success.**

Leader	May God bless the one who comes in the name of the Lord:
All (group 1)	**The Lord is God—**
All (group 2)	**he has been good to us!**

| Choir | From the temple of the Lord, we bless you. |

Director (in matter-of-fact tone)	With branches in your hands, start the procession and march round the altar:
All (group 1)	**You are my God and I will give you thanks.**
All (group 2)	**You are my God, and I will exalt you.**

| Leader | Give thanks to the Lord, for he is good: |
| All | **His love endures for ever.** |

| All | **Glory to the Father, and to the Son, and to the Holy Spirit: as it was in the beginning, is now, and shall be fore ever. Amen.** |

Cast: **Leader, Worshipper, Choir, Director** (can be the same as Leader), **All** (group 1—two or more persons/part of congregation), **All** (group 2—two or more persons/part of congregation).

In praise of Jerusalem
From Psalm 122.1–8 (LIT)

| Leader | I was glad when they said to me: |
| All | **let us go to the house of the Lord!** |

| Leader | **Pray** for the peace of Jerusalem: |
| All (group 1) | **may those who love our land be blessed.** |

| Leader | May there be peace in your homes: |
| All (group 2) | **and safety for our families.** |

| Leader | For the sake of those we love we say: |
| All | **Let there be peace!** |

| All | **Glory to the Father, and to the Son, and to the Holy Spirit: as it was in the beginning, is now, and shall be for ever. Amen.** |

Cast: **Leader, All** (group 1, preferably male voices—two or more persons/part of congregation. **All** (group 2, preferably female voices—two or more persons/part of congregation).

God, the protector of his people
Psalm 124.1–8 (LIT)

Leader	If the Lord had not been on our side—now let Israel say:
All	**If the Lord had not been on our side—**
All (group 1)	**when enemies attacked us,**
All (group 2)	**when their anger flared against us,**
All (group 3)	**they would have swallowed us alive.**
All (group 1)	**The flood would have engulfed us,**
All (group 2)	**the torrent would have swept over us,**
All (group 3)	**the waters would have drowned us.**
Leader	Praise the Lord:
All (group 1)	**who has not given us up to their teeth.**
All (group 2)	**We have escaped like a bird from the snare:**
All (group 3)	**the snare is broken and we are free.**
Leader	Our help is in the name of the Lord:
All	**who made heaven and earth.**
All	**Glory to the Father, and to the Son, and to the Holy Spirit:**
	as it was in the beginning, is now, and shall be for ever. Amen.

Cast: **Leader, All** (group 1—two or more persons/part of congregation), **All** (group 2—two or more persons/part of congregation), **All** (group 3—two or more persons/part of congregation).

A prayer for deliverance
From Psalm 126.1–6 (LIT)

Leader	When the Lord brought us back from slavery:
All (group 1)	**we were like those who dream.**
Leader	Our mouths were filled with laughter:
All (group 2)	**our tongues with songs of joy.**
Leader	Then those around us said, 'The Lord has done great things for them':
All (group 1)	**The Lord has done great things for us,**
	and we are filled with joy.
Leader	Those who sow in tears
All (group 2)	**shall reap with songs of joy.**
All	**Glory to the Father, and to the Son, and to the Holy Spirit:**
	as it was in the beginning, is now, and shall be for ever. Amen.

Cast: **Leader, All** (group 1—two or more persons/part of congregation), **All** (group 2—two or more persons/part of congregation).

The reward of obedience to the Lord
From Psalm 128.1–6 (LIT)

Leader	The pilgrims' song:
All (group 1)	**Blessed are those who fear the Lord,**

All (group 2)	**who walk in his ways.**
Leader	You will eat the fruit of your work; blessings and prosperity will be yours:
All (group 1)	**Blessed are those who fear the Lord,**
All (group 2)	**who walk in his ways.**
Leader	Your wife will be like a fruitful vine within your house; your children will be like young olive trees around your table:
All (group 1)	**Blessed are those who fear the Lord,**
All (group 2)	**who walk in his ways.**
Leader	May the Lord bless you all the days of your life; may you have prosperity; may you live to see your children's children:
All	**Peace be with you.**
All	**Glory to the Father, and to the Son, and to the Holy Spirit: as it was in the beginning, is now, and shall be for ever. Amen.**

Cast: **Leader, All** (group 1—two or more persons/part of congregation), **All** (group 2—two or more persons/part of congregation).

A call to praise the Lord
From Psalm 134.1–3 (LIT)

Leader	You servants of the Lord, who stand in his temple at night:
All (group 1)	**praise the Lord!**
Leader	Lift your hands in prayer to the Lord:
All (group 2)	**in his sanctuary, praise the Lord!**
Leader	May the Lord who made the heaven and earth bless you from Zion:
All	**Amen!**
All	**Glory to the Father, and to the Son, and to the Holy Spirit: as it was in the beginning, is now, and shall be for ever. Amen.**

Cast **Leader, All** (group 1—two or more persons/part of congregation), **All** (group 2—two or more persons/part of congregation).

A hymn of thanksgiving
From Psalm 136.1–26 (LIT)

Leader 1	Give thanks to God, for he is good:
All (group 1)	**his love shall last for ever!**
Leader 2	Give thanks to him, the God of gods:
All (group 2)	**his love shall last for ever!**
Leader 3	Give thanks to him, the Lord of lords:
All (group 3)	**his love shall last for ever!**
Leader 1	For God alone works miracles:

All (group 1)	**his love shall last for ever!**
Leader 2	The skies were made at his command:
All (group 2)	**his love shall last for ever!**
Leader 3	He spread the seas upon the earth:
All (group 3)	**his love shall last for ever!**
Leader 1	He made the stars to shine at night:
All (group 1)	**his love shall last for ever!**
Leader 2	He made the sun to shine by day:
All (group 2)	**his love shall last for ever!**
Leader 3	He brought us out from slavery:
All (group 3)	**his love shall last for ever!**
Leader 1	He leads us onward by his grace:
All (group 1)	**his love shall last for ever!**
Leader 2	He saves us from our enemies:
All (group 2)	**his love shall last for ever!**
Leader 3	Give thanks to God, for he is good:
All	**his love shall last for ever!**
All	**Glory to the Father, and to the Son, and to the Holy Spirit: as it was in the beginning, is now, and shall be for ever. Amen.**

Cast **Leader 1, Leader 2, Leader 3, All** (group 1—two or more persons/part of congregation), **All** (group 2—two or more persons/part of congregation). **All** (group 3—two or more persons/part of congregation) (This reading should not be used with a congregation unless it is divided into three parts.)

Prayer for the help of God's Spirit
From Psalm 143.6–10, and Psalm 51.6–12 (LIT)

Leader	O Lord, I spread my hands out to you:
All	**I thirst for you like dry ground.**
Leader	Teach me to do your will, for you are my God:
All	**let your good Spirit lead me in safety.**
Leader	You require sincerity and truth in me:
All	**fill my mind with your wisdom.**
Leader	Create in me a pure heart, O God:
All	**and renew a faithful spirit in me.**
Leader	Do not cast me from your presence:
All	**or take your Holy Spirit from me.**
Leader	Give me again the joy of your salvation:
All	**and make me willing to obey.**
All	**Glory to the Father, and to the Son, and to the Holy Spirit: as it was in the beginning, is now, and shall be for ever. Amen.**

Cast: **Leader, All** (two or more persons/congregation). (Psalms 143 and 51 have been grouped together to make provision for an occasion when the person and work of the Holy Spirit is being considered.)

In praise of God the almighty
From Psalm 147.1–20 (LIT)

Leader	O praise the Lord, sing out to God:
All	**such praise is right and good**.
Leader	The Lord restores Jerusalem:
All (group 1)	**he brings the exiles home**.
Leader	He heals all those with broken hearts:
All (group 2)	**he bandages their wounds**.
Leader	He counts the number of the stars:
All (group 3)	**he calls them each by name**.
Leader	How great and mighty is the Lord:
All (group 1)	**immeasurably wise!**
Leader	He raises up the humble ones:
All (group 2)	**and brings the mighty down**.
Leader	Sing hymns of triumph to his name:
All (group 3)	**make music to our God!**
Leader	He spreads the clouds across the sky:
All (group 1)	**he showers the earth with rain**.
Leader	He sends the animals their food:
All (group 2)	**he feeds the hungry birds**.
Leader	His true delight is not the strong:
All (group 3)	**but those who trust his love**.
Leader	Extol the Lord, Jerusalem:
All (group 1)	**let Zion worship God!**
Leader	For God shall keep your people safe:
All (group 2)	**and bring your harvest home**.
Leader	He gives commandment to the earth:
All (group 3)	**his will is quickly done**.
Leader	He spreads like wool the falling snow:
All (group 1)	**how cold the frosty air!**
Leader	He sends the wind, the warming rain:
All (group 2)	**and melts the ice away**.
Leader	His laws he gives to Israel:
All (group 3)	**and Judah hears his word**.
Leader	He does not favour other lands:
All	**so, praise the Lord. Amen!**
All	**Glory to the Father, and to the Son, and to the Holy Spirit: as it was in the beginning, is now, and shall be for ever. Amen!**

Cast: **Leader, All** (group 1—two or more persons/part of congregation), **All** (group 2—two or more persons/part of congregation), **All** (group 3—two or more persons/part of congregation).

Let the universe praise God!
From Psalm 148.1–14 (LIT)

All   **Praise the Lord!**

Leader 1   Praise the Lord from the heavens:
All (group 1) **praise him in the heights above.**

Leader 2   Praise him, all his angels:
All (group 2) **praise him, all his heavenly host.**

Leader 1   Praise him, sun and moon:
All (group 1) **praise him, all you shining stars.**

Leader 2   Let them praise the name of the Lord:
All   **Praise the Lord!**

Leader 1   Praise the Lord from the earth:
All (group 1) **praise him, great sea creatures.**

Leader 2   Praise him, storms and clouds:
All (group 2) **praise him, mountains and hills.**

Leader 1   Praise him, fields and woods:
All (group 1) **praise him, animals and birds.**

Leader 2   Praise him, rulers and nations:
All (group 2) **praise him, old and young.**

Leader 1   Let them praise the name of the Lord:
All   **Praise the Lord! Amen.**

All   **Glory to the Father, and to the Son, and to the Holy Spirit:
                  as it was in the beginning, is now, and shall be for ever. Amen.**

Cast: **Leader 1, Leader 2, All** (group 1—two or more persons/part of congregation), **All** (group 2—two or more persons/part of congregation).

A hymn of praise
Psalm 149.1–9 (LIT)

Leader   Praise the Lord:
All   **praise the Lord!**

Leader   Sing a new song to the Lord:
All   **let the people shout his name!**

Leader   Praise your maker, Israel:
All (group 1) **hail, your king, Jerusalem.**

Leader   Sing and dance to honour him:
All (group 2) **praise him with the strings and drums.**

Leader   God takes pleasure in his saints:
All (group 1) **crowns the meek with victory.**

Leader   Rise, you saints, in triumph now:
All (group 2) **sing the joyful night away!**

Leader	Shout aloud and praise your God!
All (group 1)	**Hold aloft the two-edged sword!**

Leader	Let the judgement now begin:
All (group 2)	**kings shall fail and tyrants die.**

Leader	Through his people, by his word:
All	**God shall have the victory!**

Leader	Praise the Lord!
All	**Praise the Lord!**

All   **Glory to the Father, and to the Son, and to the Holy Spirit:
as it was in the beginning, is now, and shall be for ever. Amen.**

Cast: **Leader, All** (group 1—two or more persons/part of congregation), **All** (group 2—two or more persons/part of congregation).

Praise the Lord
From Psalm 150.1–6 (LIT)

Leader	Praise the Lord!
All (group 1)	**praise God in his sanctuary:**
All (group 2)	**praise his strength beyond the skies.**

All (group 1)	**Praise him for his acts of power:**
All (group 2)	**praise him for his surpassing greatness.**

All (group 1)	**Praise him with the sounding of the trumpet:**
All (group 2)	**praise him with the harp and lyre.**

All (group 1)	**Praise him with tambourine and dancing:**
All (group 2)	**praise him with the strings and flute.**

All (group 1)	**Praise him with the clash of cymbals:**
All (group 2)	**praise him with resounding cymbals.**

Leader	Let everything that has breath praise the Lord:
All	**Praise the Lord!**

All   **Glory to the Father, and to the Son, and to the Holy Spirit:
as it was in the beginning, is now, and shall be for ever. Amen.**

Cast: **Leader, All** (group 1—two or more persons/part of congregation), **All** (group 2—two or more persons/part of congregation).

The song of the vineyard
Isaiah 5.1–7

Isaiah	Listen while I sing you this song, a song of my friend and his vineyard:
Singer	My friend had a vineyard on a very fertile hill. He dug the soil and cleared it of stones; he planted the finest vines. He built a tower to guard them,

dug a pit for treading the grapes.
He waited for the grapes to ripen,
but every grape was sour.

Isaiah   So now my friend says:

Friend   You people who live in Jerusalem and Judah, judge between my vineyard and me. Is there anything I failed to do for it? Then why did it produce sour grapes and not the good grapes I expected? This is what I am going to do to my vineyard; I will take away the hedge round it, break down the wall that protects it, and let wild animals eat it and trample it down. I will let it be overgrown with weeds. I will not prune the vines or hoe the ground; instead I will let briars and thorns cover it. I will even forbid the clouds to let rain fall on it.

Isaiah   Israel is the vineyard of the Lord Almighty; the people of Judah are the vines he planted. He expected them to do what was good, but instead they committed murder. He expected them to do what was right, but their victims cried out for justice.

Cast   [This is] the word of the Lord.
All   **Thanks be to God.**

Cast: **Isaiah, Singer** (can be the same as Isaiah), **Friend.**

Restoration
Isaiah 27.2–6

Isaiah   The Lord will say of his pleasant vineyard:

The Lord   I watch over it and water it continually. I guard it night and day so that no one will harm it. I am no longer angry with the vineyard. If only there were thorns and briars to fight against, then I would burn them up completely. But if the enemies of my people want my protection, let them make peace with me. Yes, let them make peace with me.

Isaiah   In days to come the people of Israel, the descendants of Jacob, will take root like a tree, and they will blossom and bud. The earth will be covered with the fruit they produce.

Cast   [This is] the word of the Lord.
All   **Thanks be to God.**

Cast: **Isaiah, The Lord.**

Jeremiah preaches in the Temple
Jeremiah 7.1–15

Jeremiah   The Lord sent me to the gate of the Temple where the people of Judah went in to worship. He told me to stand there and announce what the Lord Almighty, the God of Israel, had to say to them:

214

The Lord	Change the way you are living and the things you are doing, and I will let you go on living here. Stop believing those deceitful words:
Persons 1 and **2**	We are safe!
Person 1 (proudly)	This is the Lord's Temple!
Person 2	This is the Lord's Temple!
Persons 1 and **2**	This is the Lord's Temple!
The Lord	Change the way you are living and stop doing the things you are doing. Be fair in your treatment of one another. Stop taking advantage of aliens, orphans, and widows. Stop killing innocent people in this land. Stop worshipping other gods, for that will destroy you. If you change, I will let you go on living here in the land which I gave your ancestors as a permanent possession.
	Look, you put your trust in deceitful words. You steal, murder, commit adultery, tell lies under oath, offer sacrifices to Baal, and worship gods that you had not known before. You do these things I hate, and then you come and stand in my presence, in my own Temple, and say:
Persons 1 and **2** (complacently)	We are safe!
The Lord	Do you think that my Temple is a hiding place for robbers? I have seen what you are doing. Go to Shiloh, the first place where I chose to be worshipped, and see what I did to it because of the sins of my people Israel. You have committed all these sins, and even though I spoke to you over and over again, you refused to listen. You would not answer when I called you. And so, what I did to Shiloh I will do to this Temple of mine, in which you trust. Here in this place that I gave to your ancestors and to you, I will do the same thing that I did to Shiloh. I will drive you out of my sight as I drove out your relatives, the people of Israel. (PAUSE) I, the Lord, have spoken!
Cast	[This is] the word of the Lord.
All	**Thanks be to God.**

Cast: **Jeremiah, The Lord, Person 1, Person 2** (can be the same as Person 1).

A parable about a vine
Ezekiel 15.1–8

Ezekiel	The Lord spoke to me [He said]:
The Lord	Mortal man, how does a vine compare with a tree? What good is a branch of a grapevine compared with the trees of the forest? Can you use it to make anything? Can you even make a peg out of it to hang things on? It is only good for building a fire. And when

the ends are burnt up and the middle is charred, can you make anything out of it? It was useless even before it was burnt. Now that the fire has burnt it and charred it, it is even more useless.

Ezekiel   Now this is what the Sovereign Lord is saying:

The Lord   Just as a vine is taken from the forest and burnt, so I will take the people who live in Jerusalem and will punish them. They have escaped one fire, but now fire will burn them up. When I punish them, you will know that I am the Lord. They have been unfaithful to me, and so I will make the country a wilderness.

Ezekiel
(with flourish)   The Sovereign Lord has spoken!

Cast   [This is] the word of the Lord.
All   **Thanks be to God.**

Cast: **Ezekiel, The Lord.**

Ezekiel is taken to the Temple
From Ezekiel 40.1–41.22 [41.23–42.14]

Ezekiel   It was the tenth day of the new year, which was the twenty-fifth year after we had been taken into exile and the fourteenth year after Jerusalem was captured. On that day I felt the powerful presence of the Lord, and he carried me away. In a vision God took me to the land of Israel and put me on a high mountain. I saw in front of me a group of buildings that looked like a city. He took me closer, and I saw a man who shone like bronze. He was holding a linen tape-measure and a measuring-rod and was standing by a gateway. He said to me:

Man   Watch, mortal man. Listen carefully and pay close attention to everything I show you, because this is why you were brought here. You are to tell the people of Israel everything you see.

Ezekiel   What I saw was the Temple, and there was a wall round it. The man took his measuring-rod, which was three metres long, and measured the wall. It was three metres high and three metres thick.

The man took me through the gateway into the courtyard. There were thirty rooms built against the outer wall, and in front of them there was an area paved with stones, which extended round the courtyard.

Then the man measured the gateway on the north side that led into the outer courtyard.

Next, the man took me to the south side, and there we saw another gateway. He measured it, and it was the same as the others.

The man took me through the east gateway into the inner courtyard. He measured the gateway, and it was the same size as the others.

216

Then the man took me to the north gateway. He measured it, and it was the same size as the others.

The man measured the inner courtyard, and it was fifty metres square. The Temple was on the west side, and in front of it was an altar.

Next, the man took me into the central room, the Holy Place.

This room was beyond the central room. Then he said to me:

Man   This is the Most Holy Place.

Ezekiel   The man measured the outside of the Temple, and it was fifty metres long. And from the back of the Temple, across the open space to the far side of the building to the west, the distance was also fifty metres. The distance across the front of the Temple, including the open space on either side was also fifty metres. He measured the length of the building to the west, including its corridors on both sides, and it was also fifty metres.

The entrance room of the Temple, the Holy Place, and the Most Holy Place were all panelled with wood from the floor to the windows. These windows could be covered. The inside walls of the Temple, up as high as above the doors, were completely covered with carvings of palm-trees and winged creatures. Palm-trees alternated with creatures, one following the other, all the way round the room. Each creature had two faces: a human face that was turned towards the palm-tree on one side, and a lion's face that was turned towards the tree on the other side. It was like this all round the wall, from the floor to above the doors. The door-posts of the Holy Place were square.

In front of the entrance of the Most Holy Place there was something that looked like a wooden altar. It was one and a half metres high and one metre wide. Its corner-posts, its base, and its sides were all made of wood. The man said to me:

Man   This is the table which stands in the presence of the Lord.

[Ezekiel   There was a door at the end of the passage leading to the Holy Place and one also at the end of the passage leading to the Most Holy Place. They were double doors that swung open in the middle. There were palm-trees and winged creatures carved on the doors of the Holy Place, just as there were on the walls. And there was a wooden covering over the outside of the doorway of the entrance room. At the sides of this room there were windows, and the walls were decorated with palm-trees.

The man said to me:

Man   Both these buildings are holy. In them the priests who enter the Lord's presence eat the holiest offerings. Because the rooms are holy, the priests will place the holiest offerings there: the grain-offerings and the sacrifices offered for sin or as repayment-offerings. When priests have been in the Temple and want to go to the outer

217

courtyard, they must leave in these rooms the holy clothing they wore while serving the Lord. They must put on other clothes before going out to the area where the people gather.]

Cast   [This is] the word of the Lord.
All   **Thanks be to God.**

Cast: **Ezekiel, Man.**

The Lord returns to the Temple
Ezekiel 43.1–9

Ezekiel In my vision the man took me to the gate of the Temple that faces east, and there I saw coming from the east the dazzling light of the presence of the God of Israel. God's voice sounded like the roar of the sea, and the earth shone with the dazzling light. This vision was like the one I had seen when God came to destroy Jerusalem, and the one I saw by the River Chebar. Then I threw myself face downwards on the ground. The dazzling light passed through the east gate and went into the Temple.

The Lord's spirit lifted me up and took me into the inner courtyard, where I saw that the Temple was filled with the glory of the Lord. The man stood beside me there, and I heard the Lord speak to me out of the Temple:

The Lord Mortal man, here is my throne. I will live here among the people of Israel and rule over them for ever. Neither the people of Israel nor their kings will ever again disgrace my holy name by worshipping other gods or by burying the corpses of their kings in this place. The kings built the thresholds and door-posts of their palace right against the thresholds and door-posts of my Temple, so that there was only a wall between us. They disgraced my holy name by all the disgusting things they did, and so in my anger I destroyed them. Now they must stop worshipping other gods and remove the corpses of their kings. If they do, I will live among them for ever.

Cast   [This is] the word of the Lord.
All   **Thanks be to God.**

Cast: **Ezekiel, The Lord.**

What the Lord requires
Micah 6.6–16

Micah What shall I bring to the Lord, the God of heaven, when I come to worship him? Shall I bring the best calves to burn as offerings to him? Will the Lord be pleased if I bring him thousands of sheep or endless streams of olive-oil? Shall I offer him my first-born child to pay for my sins? No, the Lord has told us what is good. What he requires of us is this: to do what is just, to show constant love, and to live in humble fellowship with our God. It is wise to fear the Lord.

(with flourish)   He calls to the city:

The Lord   Listen, you people who assemble in the city! In the houses of
                       evil men are treasures which they got dishonestly. They use false
                       measures, a thing that I hate. How can I forgive men who use
                       false scales and weights? Your rich men exploit the poor, and all
                       of you are liars. So I have already begun your ruin and destruction
                       because of your sins. You will eat, but not be satisfied—in fact you
                       will still be hungry. You will carry things off, but you will not be able
                       to save them; anything you do save I will destroy in war. You will
                       sow corn, but not harvest the crop. You will press oil from olives,
                       but never be able to use it. You will make wine, but never drink
                       it. This will happen because you have followed the evil practices of
                       King Omri and of his son, King Ahab. You have continued their
                       policies, and so I will bring you to ruin, and everyone will despise
                       you. People everywhere will treat you with contempt.

Cast   [This is] the word of the Lord.
All   **Thanks be to God.**

Cast: **Micah, The Lord.**

The Lord's command to rebuild the temple
Haggai 1.1–15

Narrator   During the second year that Darius was emperor of Persia, on
                       the first day of the sixth month, the Lord spoke through the
                       prophet Haggai. The message was for the governor of Judah,
                       Zerubbabel son of Shealtiel, and for the High Priest, Joshua son
                       of Jehozadak.

                       The Lord Almighty said to Haggai:

The Lord   These people say that this is not the right time to rebuild the
                       Temple.

Narrator   The Lord then gave this message to the people through the prophet
                       Haggai:

Haggai   My people, why should you be living in well-built houses while my
                       Temple lies in ruins? Don't you see what is happening to you? You
                       have sown much corn, but have harvested very little. You have food
                       to eat, but not enough to make you full. You have wine to drink, but
                       not enough to get drunk on! You have clothing, but not enough to
                       keep you warm. And the working man cannot earn enough to live
                       on. Can't you see why this has happened? Now go up into the hills,
                       get timber, and rebuild the Temple; then I will be pleased and will
                       be worshipped as I should be.

                       You hoped for large harvests, but they turned out to be small. And
                       when you brought the harvest home, I blew it away. Why did I
                       do that? Because my Temple lies in ruins while every one of you
                       is busy working on his own house. That is why there is no rain

and nothing can grow. I have brought drought on the land—on its hills, cornfields, vineyards, and olive orchards4—on every crop the ground produces, on men and animals, on everything you try to grow.

Narrator   Then Zerubbabel and Joshua and all the people who had returned from the exile in Babylonia, did what the Lord their God told them to do. They were afraid and obeyed the prophet Haggai, the Lord's messenger. Then Haggai gave the Lord's message to the people:

Haggai and
The Lord   I will be with you—that is my promise.

Narrator   The Lord inspired everyone to work on the Temple: Zerubbabel, the governor of Judah; Joshua, the High Priest, and all the people who had returned from the exile. They began working on the Temple of the Lord Almighty, their God, on the twenty-fourth day of the sixth month of the second year that Darius was emperor.

Cast   [This is] the word of the Lord.
All   **Thanks be to God.**

Cast: **Narrator, The Lord, Haggai** (can be the same as The Lord).

The Lord calls for tithes
Malachi 3.6–12

The Lord   I am the Lord, and I do not change. And so you, the descendants of Jacob, are not yet completely lost. You, like your ancestors before you, have turned away from my laws and have not kept them. Turn back to me, and I will turn to you. But you ask:

Person(s)   What must we do to turn back to you?

The Lord   I ask you, is it right for a person to cheat God? Of course not, yet you are cheating me. You ask:

Person(s)   How?

The Lord   In the matter of tithes and offerings. (PAUSE) A curse is on all of you because the whole nation is cheating me.

Bring the full amount of your tithes to the Temple, so that there will be plenty of food there. Put me to the test and you will see that I will open the windows of heaven and pour out on you in abundance all kinds of good things. I will not let insects destroy your crops, and your grapevines will be loaded with grapes. Then the people of all nations will call you happy, because your land will be a good place to live in.

Cast   [This is] the word of the Lord.
All   **Thanks be to God.**

Cast: **The Lord, Person(s).**

Jesus tells the parable of the workers in the vineyard
Matthew 20.1–16

Jesus The Kingdom of heaven is like this. Once there was a man who went out early in the morning to hire some men to work in his vineyard. He agreed to pay them the regular wage, a silver coin a day, and sent them to work in his vineyard. He went out again to the market place at nine o'clock and saw some men standing there doing nothing [so he told them]:

Owner You also go and work in the vineyard, and I will pay you a fair wage.

Jesus So they went. (PAUSE) Then at twelve o'clock and again at three o'clock he did the same thing. It was nearly five o'clock when he went to the market place and saw some other men still standing there. [He asked them:]

Owner Why are you wasting the whole day here doing nothing?

[Jesus They answered:]

Man 3 No one hired us.

Owner Well, then, you also go and work in the vineyard.

Jesus When evening came, the owner told his foreman:

Owner Call the workers and pay them their wages, starting with those who were hired last and ending with those who were hired first.

Jesus The men who had begun to work at five o'clock were paid a silver coin each. So when the men who were the first to be hired came to be paid, they thought they would get more; but they too were given a silver coin each. They took their money and started grumbling against the employer. [They said:]

Man 1
(grumbling) These men who were hired last worked only one hour.

Man 2 While we put up with a whole day's work in the hot sun.

Man 1 Yet you paid them the same as you paid us!

Owner Listen, friend, I have not cheated you. After all, you agreed to do
(to Man 1) a day's work for one silver coin. Now take your pay and go home. I want to give this man who was hired last as much as I have given you. Don't I have the right to do as I wish with my own money? Or are you jealous because I am generous? (PAUSE)

Jesus (looking So those who are last will be first, and those who are first will be
round) last.

Cast [This is] the word of the Lord.   OR   This is the Gospel of Christ / *This is the Gospel of the Lord.*
All   **Thanks be to God.**   **Praise to Christ our Lord** / *Praise to you, Lord Jesus Christ.*

Cast: **Jesus** (as Narrator), **Owner, Man 3, Man 1, Man 2** (can be the same as Man 1).

The house of prayer
Matthew 21.12–16 [17]

Narrator Jesus went into the Temple and drove out all those who were buying and selling there. He overturned the tables of the money-changers and the stools of those who sold pigeons [and said to them]:

Jesus It is written in the Scriptures that God said, 'My Temple will be called a house of prayer.' But you are making it a hideout for thieves!

Narrator The blind and the crippled came to him in the Temple, and he healed them. The chief priests and the teachers of the Law became angry when they saw the wonderful things he was doing and the children shouting in the Temple:

Children Praise to David's Son!

Narrator So they asked Jesus:

Chief priest
(to Jesus) Do you hear what they are saying?

Jesus Indeed I do. Haven't you ever read this scripture? 'You have trained children and babies to offer perfect praise.'

[Narrator Jesus left them and went out of the city to Bethany, where he spent the night.]

Cast [This is] the word of the Lord. OR This is the Gospel of Christ / *This is the Gospel of the Lord.*
All **Thanks be to God.**   **Praise to Christ our Lord** / *Praise to you, Lord Jesus Christ.*

Cast: **Narrator, Jesus, Children** (at least two), **Chief priest.**

Jesus goes to the Temple
Mark 11.15–19, 27–33

Narrator When they arrived in Jerusalem, Jesus went to the Temple and began to drive out all those who were buying and selling. He overturned the tables of the money-changers and the stools of those who sold pigeons, and he would not let anyone carry anything through the temple courtyards. He then taught the people:

Jesus It is written in the Scriptures that God said, 'My Temple will be called a house of prayer for the people of all nations.' But you have turned it into a hideout for thieves!

Narrator The chief priests and the teachers of the Law heard of this, so they began looking for some way to kill Jesus. They were afraid of him, because the whole crowd was amazed at his teaching.

When evening came, Jesus and his disciples left the city. (PAUSE)

Next morning they arrived once again in Jerusalem. As Jesus was walking in the Temple, the chief priests, the teachers of the Law, and the elders came to him and asked him:

Lawyer 1	What right have you to do these things?
Lawyer 2	Who gave you this right?
Jesus	I will ask you just one question, and if you give me an answer, I will tell you what right I have to do these things. Tell me, where did John's right to baptize come from: was it from God or from man?
Narrator	They started to argue among themselves:
Lawyer 1	What shall we say?
Lawyer 2	If we answer, 'From God,' he will say, 'Why, then, did you not believe John?'
Lawyer 1	But if we say, 'From man . . .'
Narrator	They were afraid of the people, because everyone was convinced that John had been a prophet. So their answer to Jesus was:
Lawyer 1	We don't know.
Jesus (firmly)	Neither will I tell you, then, by what right I do these things.

Cast [This is] the word of the Lord. OR This is the Gospel of Christ / *This is the Gospel of the Lord.*
All   **Thanks be to God.**   **Praise to Christ our Lord** / *Praise to you, Lord Jesus Christ.*

Cast: **Narrator, Jesus, Lawyer 1, Lawyer 2.**

The widow's offering
Mark 12.41–44

| Narrator | As Jesus sat near the Temple treasury, he watched the people as they dropped in their money. Many rich men dropped in a lot of money; then a poor widow came along and dropped in two little copper coins, worth about a penny. He called his disciples together. |
| Jesus | I tell you that this poor widow put more in the offering box than all the others. For the others put in what they had to spare of their riches; but she, poor as she is, put in all she had—she gave all she had to live on. |

Cast [This is] the word of the Lord. OR This is the Gospel of Christ / *This is the Gospel of the Lord.*
All   **Thanks be to God.**   **Praise to Christ our Lord** / *Praise to you, Lord Jesus Christ.*

Cast: **Narrator, Jesus.**

The believers share their possessions
Acts 4.32–37

| Voice 1 | The group of believers was one in mind and heart. |
| Voice 2 | No one said that any of his belongings was his own, but they all shared with one another everything they had. |

223

Voice 1	With great power the apostles gave witness to the resurrection of the Lord Jesus, and God poured rich blessings on them all.
Voice 2	There was no one in the group who was in need. Those who owned fields or houses would sell them, bring the money received from the sale, and hand it over to the apostles; and the money was distributed to each one according to his need.
Voice 1	And so it was that Joseph, a Levite born in Cyprus, whom the apostles called Barnabas—which means 'One who Encourages'—sold a field he owned, brought the money, and handed it over to the apostles.
Cast	[This is] the word of the Lord.
All	**Thanks be to God.**

Cast: **Voice 1, Voice 2.**

Saul preaches in Damascus
Acts 9.19–25

Narrator	Saul stayed for a few days with the believers in Damascus. He went straight to the synagogues and began to preach that Jesus was the Son of God. All who heard him were amazed:
Hearer 1	Isn't he the one who in Jerusalem was killing those who worship that man Jesus?
Hearer 2	And didn't he come here for the very purpose of arresting those people and taking them back to the chief priests?
Narrator	But Saul's preaching became even more powerful, and his proofs that Jesus was the Messiah were so convincing that the Jews who lived in Damascus could not answer him. (PAUSE)
	After many days had gone by, the Jews met together and made plans to kill Saul, but he was told of their plan. Day and night they watched the city gates in order to kill him. But one night Saul's followers took him and let him down through an opening in the wall, lowering him in a basket.
Cast	[This is] the word of the Lord.
All	**Thanks be to God.**

Cast: **Narrator, Hearer 1, Hearer 2.**

Divisions in the Church
1 Corinthians 1.10–17

Paul	By the authority of our Lord Jesus Christ I appeal to all of you, my brothers, to agree in what you say, so that there will be no divisions among you. Be completely united, with only one thought and one purpose. For some people from Chloe's family have told me quite plainly, my brothers, that there are quarrels among you. Let me put it this way—each one of you says something different:

Person 1	I follow Paul.
Person 2	I follow Apollos.
Person 3	I follow Peter. (PAUSE)
Person 4 (emphatically)	I follow Christ.
Paul	Christ has been divided into groups! Was it Paul who died on the cross for you? Were you baptized as Paul's disciples? I thank God that I did not baptize any of you except Crispus and Gaius. No one can say, then, that you were baptized as my disciples.
(as an afterthought)	Oh yes, I also baptized Stephanas and his family; but I can't remember whether I baptized anyone else.
	Christ did not send me to baptize. He sent me to tell the Good News, and to tell it without using the language of human wisdom, in order to make sure that Christ's death on the cross is not robbed of its power.
Cast	[This is] the word of the Lord.
All	**Thanks be to God.**

Cast: **Paul, Person 1, Person 2, Person 3** (can be the same as Person 1), **Person 4** (can be the same as Person 2).

Christian giving
From 2 Corinthians 8.7–15; 9.6–15

Reader 1	You are so rich in all you have: in faith, speech, and knowledge, in your eagerness to help and in your love for us. And so we want you to be generous also in this service of love.
Reader 2	I am not laying down any rules. But by showing how eager others are to help, I am trying to find out how real your own love is.
Reader 3	You know the grace of our Lord Jesus Christ; rich as he was, he made himself poor for your sake, in order to make you rich by means of his poverty.
Reader 1	If you are eager to give, God will accept your gift on the basis of what you have to give, not on what you haven't.
Reader 2	I am not trying to relieve others by putting a burden on you; but since you have plenty at this time, it is only fair that you should help those who are in need. Then, when you are in need and they have plenty, they will help you. In this way both are treated equally. As the scripture says:
Reader 3	The one who gathered much did not have too much, and the one who gathered little did not have too little.
Reader 2	Remember that the person who sows few seeds will have a small crop; the one who sows many seeds will have a large crop.

Reader 1	Each one should give, then, as he has decided, not with regret or out of a sense of duty; for God loves the one who gives gladly.
Reader 2	And God is able to give you more than you need, so that you will always have all you need for yourselves and more than enough for every good cause. As the scripture says:
Reader 3	He gives generously to the needy; his kindness lasts for ever.
Readers 1–3	Let us give thanks to God for his priceless gift!
Cast	[This is] the word of the Lord.
All	**Thanks be to God.**

Cast: **Reader 1, Reader 2, Reader 3.**

God's power and the church
Ephesians 1.19–23; 3.20–21

Voice 1	The power working in us is the same as the mighty strength which he used when he raised Christ from death and seated him at his right side in the heavenly world.
Voice 2	Christ rules there above all heavenly rulers, authorities, powers, and lords; he has a title superior to all titles of authority in this world and in the next.
Voice 3	God put all things under Christ's feet and gave him to the church as supreme Lord over all things.
Voice 1	The church is Christ's body, the completion of him who himself completes all things everywhere.
Voice 2	To him who by means of his power working in us is able to do so much more than we can ever ask for, or even think of:
Voice 3	To God be the glory in the church and in Christ Jesus for all time, for ever and ever!
Voices 1–3	Amen.
Cast	[This is] the word of the Lord
All	**Thanks be to God.**

Cast: **Voice 1, Voice 2, Voice 3.**

God's chosen people
Colossians 3.12–17 [3.18–4.1]

| **Voice 1** | As God's chosen people, holy and dearly loved, clothe yourselves with compassion, kindness, humility, gentleness and patience. |
| **Voice 2** | Bear with each other and forgive whatever grievances you may have against one another— |

Voice 1	Forgive as the Lord forgave you.
Voice 2	And over all these virtues put on love, which binds them all together in perfect unity.
Voice 1	Let the peace of Christ rule in your hearts, since as members of one body you were called to peace.
Voices 1 and **2** (slowly)	And be thankful. (PAUSE)
Voice 1	Let the word of Christ dwell in you richly as you teach and admonish one another with all wisdom, and as you sing psalms, hymns and spiritual songs with gratitude in your hearts to God.
Voice 2	And whatever you do, whether in word or deed, do it all in the name of the Lord Jesus, giving thanks to God the Father through him.
[Voice 3	Wives, submit to your husbands, as is fitting in the Lord.
Voice 1	Husbands, love your wives and do not be harsh with them.
Voice 2	Children, obey your parents in everything, for this pleases the Lord.
Voice 3	Fathers, do not embitter your children, or they will become discouraged.
Voice 1	Slaves, obey your earthly masters in everything; and do it, not only when their eye is on you and to win their favour, but with sincerity of heart and reverence for the Lord.
Voice 2	Whatever you do, work at it with all your heart, as working for the Lord, not for men, since you know that you will receive an inheritance from the Lord as a reward. It is the Lord Christ you are serving.
Voice 1	Anyone who does wrong will be repaid for this wrong, and there is no favouritism.
Voice 3	Masters, provide your slaves with what is right and fair, because you know that you also have a Master in heaven.]
Cast	[This is] the word of the Lord.
All	**Thanks be to God.**

Cast: **Voice 1, Voice 2, [Voice 3** (preferably female)].

Leaders in the Church
1 Timothy 3.1–13

Voice 1	This is a true saying:
Voice 3	If a man is eager to be a church leader, he desires an excellent work.
Voice 1	A church leader must be without fault.
Voice 2	He must have only one wife, be sober, self-controlled, and orderly.

Voice 1	He must welcome strangers in his home.
Voice 2	He must be able to teach.
Voice 1	He must not be a drunkard or a violent man, but gentle and peaceful.
Voice 2	He must not love money.
Voice 1	He must be able to manage his own family well and make his children obey him with all respect.
Voice 3	For if a man does not know how to manage his own family, how can he take care of the church of God?
Voice 1	He must be mature in the faith, so that he will not swell up with pride and be condemned, as the Devil was.
Voice 2	He should be a man who is respected by the people outside the church, so that he will not be disgraced and fall into the Devil's trap.
Voice 1	Church helpers must also have a good character and be sincere.
Voice 2	They must not drink too much wine or be greedy for money.
Voice 1	They should hold to the revealed truth of the faith with a clear conscience.
Voice 2	They should be tested first, and then, if they pass the test, they are to serve.
Voice 3	Their wives also must be of good character and must not gossip; they must be sober and honest in everything.
Voice 1	A church helper must have only one wife, and be able to manage his children and family well.
Voice 2	Those helpers who do their work well win for themselves a good standing and are able to speak boldly about their faith in Christ Jesus.
Cast	[This is] the word of the Lord.
All	**Thanks be to God.**

Cast: **Voice 1, Voice 2, Voice 3.**

Thanksgiving and prayer
Philemon 3–7, 25

Voices 1–3	Grace to you and peace from God our Father and the Lord Jesus Christ.
Voice 1	I always thank my God as I remember you in my prayers, because I hear about your faith in the Lord Jesus and your love for all the saints.
Voice 2	I pray that you may be active in sharing your faith, so that you will have a full understanding of every good thing we have in Christ.

Voice 3	Your love has given me great joy and encouragement, because you, brother, have refreshed the hearts of the saints.
Voices 1–3	May the grace of the Lord Jesus Christ be with your spirit.
Cast	[This is] the word of the Lord.
All	**Thanks be to God.**

Cast: **Voice 1, Voice 2, Voice 3.**

Let us come near to God
From Hebrews 10.19–39

Voice 1	We have, then, my brothers, complete freedom to go into the Most Holy Place by means of the death of Jesus. He opened for us a new way, a living way, through the curtain—that is, through his own body.
Voice 2	We have a great priest in charge of the house of God. So let us come near to God with a sincere heart and a sure faith, with hearts that have been purified from a guilty conscience and with bodies washed with clean water.
Voice 1	Let us hold on firmly to the hope we profess, because we can trust God to keep his promise.
Voice 2	Let us be concerned for one another, to help one another to show love and to do good.
Voice 1	Let us not give up the habit of meeting together, as some are doing. Instead, let us encourage one another all the more, since you see that the Day of the Lord is coming nearer.
	[For there is no longer any sacrifice that will take away sins if we purposely go on sinning after the truth has been made known to us.
Voice 2	Instead, all that is left is to wait in fear for the coming Judgement and the fierce fire which will destroy those who oppose God! For we know who said:
Voice 3	I will take revenge, I will repay.
Voice 2	And who also said:
Voice 3	The Lord will judge his people.
Voice 1	It is a terrifying thing to fall into the hands of the living God!]
Voice 2	Remember how it was with you in the past. In those days, after God's light had shone on you, you suffered many things, yet were not defeated by the struggle. Do not lose your courage, then, because it brings with it a great reward. You need to be patient, in order to do the will of God and receive what he promises. For, as the scripture says:
Voice 3	Just a little while longer,

229

and he who is coming will come;
he will not delay.
My righteous people, however, will believe and live;
but if any of them turns back,
I will not be pleased with him.

Voice 1   We are not people who turn back and are lost. Instead, we have faith and are saved.

Cast   [This is] the word of the Lord.
All   **Thanks be to God.**

Cast: **Voice 1, Voice 2, Voice 3.**

How to please God
From Hebrews 13.1–21

Voice 1   Keep on loving one another as Christians.

Voice 2   Remember to welcome strangers in your homes. There were some who did that and welcomed angels without knowing it.

Voice 3   Remember those who are in prison, as though you were in prison with them.

Voice 1   Remember those who are suffering, as though you were suffering as they are.

Voice 2   Marriage is to be honoured by all, and husbands and wives must be faithful to each other. God will judge those who are immoral and those who commit adultery.

Voice 3   Keep your lives free from the love of money, and be satisfied with what you have. For God has said:

God   I will never leave you; I will never abandon you.

Voice 2   Let us be bold, then, and say:

Voices 1 and **2**   The Lord is my helper,
I will not be afraid.
What can anyone do to me?

Voice 1   Remember your former leaders, who spoke God's message to you. Think back on how they lived and died, and imitate their faith. Jesus Christ is the same yesterday, today, and for ever.

Voice 2   There is no permanent city for us here on earth; we are looking for the city which is to come. Let us, then, always offer praise to God as our sacrifice through Jesus, which is the offering presented by lips that confess him as Lord.

Voice 3   Do not forget to do good and to help one another, because these are the sacrifices that please God.

Voice 1   Obey your leaders and follow their orders. They watch over your souls without resting, since they must give God an account of their service. If you obey them, they will do their work gladly; if not, they will do it with sadness, and that would be of no help to you.

Voice 2	May the God of peace provide you with every good thing you need in order to do his will, and may he, through Jesus Christ, do in us what pleases him.
Voice 3	And to Christ be the glory for ever and ever!
Voices 1 and **2**	Amen.
Cast **All**	[This is] the word of the Lord. **Thanks be to God.**

Cast: **Voice 1, Voice 2, Voice 3, God** (can be the same as Voice 1).

The living stone and the holy nation
1 Peter 2.1–10

Peter	Rid yourselves, then, of all evil; no more lying or hypocrisy or jealousy or insulting language. Be like new-born babies, always thirsty for the pure spiritual milk, so that by drinking it you may grow up and be saved. As the scripture says:
Psalmist	You have found out for yourselves how kind the Lord is.
Peter	Come to the Lord, the living stone rejected by man as worthless but chosen by God as valuable. Come as living stones, and let yourselves be used in building the spiritual temple, where you will serve as holy priests to offer spiritual and acceptable sacrifices to God through Jesus Christ. For the scripture says:
Isaiah	I chose a valuable stone, which I am placing as the cornerstone in Zion; and whoever believes in him will never be disappointed.
Peter	This stone is of great value for you that believe; but for those who do not believe:
Psalmist	The stone which the builders rejected as worthless turned out to be the most important of all.
Peter	And another scripture says:
Isaiah	This is the stone that will make people stumble, the rock that will make them fall.
Peter	They stumbled because they did not believe in the word; such was God's will for them. But you are the chosen race, the King's priests, the holy nation, God's own people, chosen to proclaim the wonderful acts of God, who called you out of darkness into his own marvellous light. At one time you were not God's people, but now you are his people; at one time you did not know God's mercy, but now you have received his mercy.
Cast **All**	[This is] the word of the Lord. **Thanks be to God.**

Cast: **Peter, Psalmist, Isaiah.**

The message to Ephesus
Revelation 2.1–7

Voice 1   To the angel of the church in Ephesus write:

Voice 2   This is the message from the one who holds the seven stars in his right hand and who walks among the seven gold lamp-stands:

Voice 3   I know what you have done; I know how hard you have worked and how patient you have been. I know that you cannot tolerate evil men and that you have tested those who say they are apostles but are not, and have found out that they are liars. You are patient, you have suffered for my sake, and you have not given up. But this is what I have against you: you do not love me now as you did at first. Think how far you have fallen! Turn from your sins and do what you did at first! If you don't turn from your sins, I will come to you and take your lamp-stand from its place. But this is what you have in your favour: you hate what the Nicolaitans do, as much as I do.

Voice 1   If you have ears, then, listen to what the Spirit says to the churches!

Voice 3   To those who win the victory I will give the right to eat the fruit of the tree of life that grows in the Garden of God.

Cast   [This is] the word of the Lord.
All   **Thanks be to God.**

Cast: **Voice 1, Voice 2, Voice 3.**

INDEX OF
BIBLICAL REFERENCES